Pan Breakthrough Books

Pan Breakthrough Books open the door to successful self-education. The series provides essential knowledge using the most modern self-study techniques.

Expert authors have produced clear explanatory texts on business subjects to meet the particular needs of people at work and of those studying for relevant examinations.

A highly effective learning pattern, enabling readers to measure progress step-by-step, has been devised for Breakthrough Books by the National Extension College, Britain's leading specialists in home study.

Peter Clark is principal lecturer in business studies at Kilburn Polytechnic, London. He is a former lecturer in the teaching of statistics at Garnett College (a teacher training college) in London and is a past adviser to the ILEA on business education. He has worked in further education for a considerable time, teaching on a variety of courses at different levels, and has also spent several years working in business.

Pan Breakthrough Books

Other books in the series

The Business of Communicating:
    Improving Communication Skills
Keep Account:
    A Guide to Profitable Bookkeeping
Making Numbers Work:
    An Introduction to Business Numeracy
Management: A Fresh Approach
Practical Business Law
Using Statistics in Business 2
What Do You Mean 'Communication'?
    An Introduction to Communication in Business

Pan Breakthrough Books

Using Statistics in Business 1

Peter Clark

A Pan Original
Pan Books, London and Sydney

First published 1982 by Pan Books Ltd,
Cavaye Place, London SW10 9PG

© Peter Clark 1982

ISBN 0 330 26540 7

Printed and bound in Great Britain by
Richard Clay (The Chaucer Press) Ltd, Bungay, Suffolk

If you wish to study the subject-matter of this book in more
depth, write to the National Extension College, 18 Brooklands
Avenue, Cambridge CB2 2HN, for a free copy of the
Breakthrough Business Courses leaflet. This gives details of
the extra exercises and professional postal tuition which are
available.

Acknowledgements

To my wife and small son, who were very tolerant about me being locked away in the study for hours on end writing.

To Eileen, who typed the initial manuscript very competently despite often being given very little time.

To Michael Skudder, for his comments on the book and to all the various other people who read through it and tried the exercises. To Richard Freeman of the National Extension College, whose advice on the presentation of the material in the book was invaluable. The final responsibility for the book is, however, mine, and the responsibility for anything in it which may be incorrect or misleading must be laid at my door.

Contents

Introduction   9

Part 1: An introduction to business statistics   13

Scenario 1: Setting the scene   15
1   What is business statistics?   20

Part 2: Collecting statistical data   37

Scenario 2: Rising costs in the canteen   39
2   Finding out for ourselves   42
3   How to collect data   63
Scenario 3: A new product   87
4   Letting a few represent many   89
5   Methods of selecting from available data   111

Part 3: Making sense of the data collected   147

Scenario 4: The number of babies born   149
6   How far can we rely on the data collected?   152
7   Using approximations   179
Scenario 5: Late for work   209
8   Amalgamating data   211
9   Representing data by graphs   247
Scenario 6: A dispute about wages   286
10   On the average   288
11   When an average on its own is not enough   318
Scenario 7: The effects of inflation   343
12   Bringing out the changes clearly   345
Scenario 8: Machine breakdowns   379
13   The effects of chance   382

Appendix: Where to find statistical data   413
The contents of *Using Statistics in Business 2*   427
Index   428

Introduction

This book, along with its companion volume *Using Statistics in Business 2*, has been written as an introduction to statistics for those people who are preparing themselves for a career in business. It has also been written for those people already in business who want to refresh their memory of statistics or to begin studying – and using – statistics for the first time.

It is especially suitable for people studying for a Business Education Council (BEC) award at national level, since it covers much of the statistics element of the Numeracy and Accounting core module and the Applied Statistics option module. However, it can also be used profitably by students of statistics at RSA Stage II and LCCI Intermediate levels; as well as by students of various professional bodies – in particular, the Institute of Marketing, the Institute of Personnel Management, the Institute of Chartered Accountants, the Institute of Cost and Management Accountants, the Institute of Chartered Secretaries and the Association of Certified Accountants.

Volume *1*, the present volume, introduces you to the 'discipline' of business statistics and describes how statistical data is collected, validated, sorted and simplified. It tells you how to get hold of accurate and reliable statistical data, economically, and how to reduce it to a manageable level. The last chapter (Chapter 13) shows how chance plays a part in determining exactly what data is collected and acts as an introduction to the methods of drawing conclusions from statistical data, which start volume *2*. An appendix, 'Where to find statistical data', lists sources of various statistical data which may be used instead of collecting it yourself.

Volume *2* uses the ideas developed in Volume *1* to show how you can draw conclusions from statistical data, and warns you about some of the errors that can occur when doing so. It covers the presentation of statistical data and outlines some of the pitfalls that may be encountered when using such data. The last chapter (Chapter 8) shows you how to make a case based on statistical evidence and draws upon the ideas and methods discussed in both volumes.

At the end of this volume (on page 427) I have included a brief outline of the contents of Volume 2 to give you an idea of the topics covered in it. I hope you will be encouraged to read it when you have finished the present volume.

No algebra is used in either volume; all you will need is a knowledge of arithmetic.

How to use this book

Throughout this book you will find self-assessment questions which you are encouraged to answer before reading on. There are three types of question:

Self-check. Usually short questions requiring quick answers. They either help to prepare you for the text which follows, or they provide a means for you to test for yourself whether you have understood a particular principle or technique. Answers almost invariably follow directly after the questions.

Review. These are similar to self-checks in their purpose, but are usually placed at the end of a chapter, or at the end of a section, and are intended to review your understanding of several principles or techniques.

Activity. Again, these are designed to test your understanding of the text, but they usually ask you to use some information which you will not find in the text. To answer these questions you have to use your own experience, discover some fresh facts for yourself, or try out an experiment away from the book.

It is obviously best for you to try to answer all questions before reading on but, whether you think you've got the answer right or wrong, read the answers before moving on to the next topic. If you have somehow made a mistake, the answer will usually tell you where you went wrong. You can, of course, 'cheat' and read the whole book from beginning to end without attempting to answer the questions at all. But you probably don't need me to tell you that you will only be cheating yourself if you do.

Graphic examples, and answers to the self-check questions in the text, have been drawn by a professional artist. Your answers need not be so elaborate. The three-dimensional effect of the illustrations in the text is for visual impact only.

A note on the 'scenarios'

The book contains a number of 'scenarios', all of which are based on one fictional company, Gourmet Foods Limited. Each scenario acts as an introduction to a topic, or several topics, by providing a realistic situation which illustrates why and how statistical techniques should be used in business. Each scenario provides information which the chapters immediately following it make use of, so don't be tempted to skip them. They are designed to broaden your understanding of statistics and to show you how statistical techniques can be applied, not just in a food manufacturing business but in a very wide range of business or public organizations.

The first scenario, which follows on page 15, introduces Gourmet Foods Ltd to you. The other scenarios deal with particular incidents or problems which the company experiences; they appear on pages 39, 87, 149, 209, 286, 343 and 379.

Part 1
An introduction
to business statistics

Scenario 1
Setting the scene

This scenario introduces you to Gourmet Foods Ltd. (See page 11 for an explanation about the scenarios.)

The company was started in 1896 by Roderick Bradley, who at that time was an importer of caviare and similar luxury foods. He decided to branch out into supplying up-market canned foods, such as game soup and pheasant in aspic, so he opened a small plant in Essex for that purpose.

As business grew, the company expanded. It remained in Essex, but moved to larger premises on several occasions. The growth was due mainly to market penetration rather than any great expansion in the market itself. The food products remained exclusive. The Second World War, however, drastically affected the availability and market for such foods. During the war the company's resources were switched largely to the production of basic foodstuffs.

After the war the then chairman, Roderick's son Geoffrey, decided that, though the company would try to regain its market in specialist foods, it would broaden the range offered. So, when a food company with premises only a short distance away from the Gourmet Foods plant ran into grave financial difficulties, Geoffrey decided to take it over. It specialized in potted meats, crab and shrimp paste and the like, and these products made an ideal addition to those offered by Gourmet Foods. This company's plant was rather small and dealt mainly with jars and pots of food.

At about the same time, Freda Bradley, Geoffrey's wife, had an idea for a new product. She was a major shareholder in the company and had, in fact, brought much needed capital into the business when she married; capital that had, indeed, helped in the above take-over. Any ideas she had were thus treated fairly seriously. This one was for a range of up-market baby foods, which she suggested should be called Baby Gourmet. This was to include such delicacies as venison broth, creamed asparagus tips and so on. She felt that these would appeal to mothers who wanted their children to have 'only the best'.

So some of the production capacity at the newly acquired plant was turned over to making jars of Baby Gourmet food. Though the company had great expertise in obtaining the raw foodstuffs, it lacked experience of marketing in this exact area. However, the brand rapidly became a great success. Its launch happened to coincide with the beginning of the postwar prosperity boom and the turn towards convenience foods. Eventually, virtually all the resources of the small plant were devoted to this one product.

Geoffrey Bradley retired and a new chairman was appointed. This was Austin Fletcher, his son-in-law, as Geoffrey had only daughters of his own. The company was very traditional but, occasionally, there were sudden shake-ups. Austin caused one of them, shortly after he was appointed, by reorganizing the company and changing its structure. One of his actions was to create 'brand managers' in the marketing department, including a brand manager for Baby Gourmet. He got that idea from a visit to America. The current management structure of the company is shown in figure 1.

After this initial shake-up, however, things settled down to pretty much as usual at Gourmet Foods. Everyone felt the company was in a reasonably secure position. Customer loyalty seemed high and the competition in their particular market not especially fierce.

However, very little of the profit was being ploughed back into the business. Plant and machinery were beginning to wear out. The marketing department was not very dynamic either.

Numbers play a large part in the operation of any firm, and Gourmet Foods is no exception. In the first place, all matters of finance involve amounts of money and these are expressed in figures. Other numbers of interest include

- production figures
- sales figures
- the number of working days lost through illness or stoppages
- the number of miles travelled by sales representatives
- the number of jars of baby food found to be below standard by quality inspection
- the number of kilogrammes of asparagus purchased in a given week
- the price paid per each of these kilogrammes, and so on.

If you work in a business, perhaps you deal with some of these figures yourself, in which case you can see at first hand how important they are. If you are not an employee then perhaps you

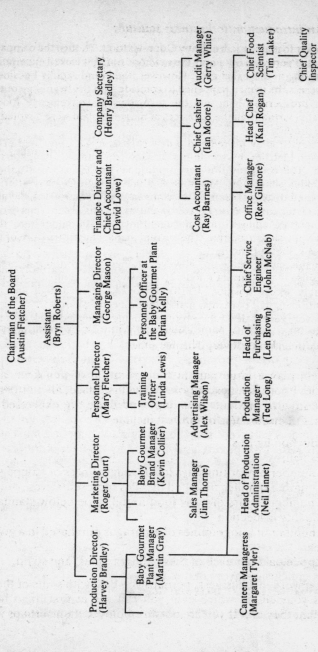

Figure 1. The management structure in Gourmet Foods Ltd

are an employer! No doubt you are then even more aware of how vital it is to have a good knowledge of the kind of numbers listed above. If you are a full-time student, you should have no difficulty in thinking of some important figures: what mark did you get for the last piece of work you handed in?

Numbers do not, however, just fall into your lap; someone has to collect them. The price of the asparagus would, for example, have been recorded by a purchasing clerk, and the number of days lost by a wages clerk.

But collecting the figures is generally only part of the process. A jumble of numbers is of little use to anyone. They must also be processed in some way to make them intelligible. This may involve sorting them out into logical groups. For instance, the poor-quality jars of food may be categorized according to flavour or the date, and even time, of production. Sometimes further processing may be required. It is, for example, unlikely that upper management would want to know how much each individual employee earned. They might, however, be interested in the total or average. Where decisions are to be made, based on the information collected, some relatively complex processing may be needed. This could happen, for example, when management tries to compare the present performance of the Baby Gourmet plant with that of similar ones, or with its own past performance. Finally there is the necessity to convey information, derived from the figures collected, to other people. For example, in general, the higher the level of management, the less detailed are the figures required. But the information supplied must still faithfully reflect the picture as conveyed by the figures collected. So the board would want brief, accurate and reliable summaries of the situation in the firm, with any relevant changes shown. This needs skill in methods of presentation.

There is then obviously a need for techniques which will enable people in business to

- find out the facts
- make sense of them
- draw conclusions from them, and
- inform others of the facts and the conclusions.

Such techniques make up the subject of business statistics.

In Chapter 1 (which forms the whole of Part 1 of this book) the subject of business statistics is defined and distinguished from other subjects, such as accounting and data processing, which also deal with information in business and those, such as mathematics, which also deal with numbers.

Later chapters, contained in Parts 2 and 3 of this volume and Parts 1 and 2 of Volume *2*, cover each of the four aspects of statistics listed above, while Part 2 of Volume *2* also shows how all four aspects can come together in the solution of a business problem.

1 | What is business statistics?

What is, or are, statistics and what is special about business statistics?

The answer to the first question is complicated by the fact that we use the word 'statistics' in three different, but connected, ways. They are all basically concerned with data. Nowadays the word 'data' is used indiscriminately in either a singular or a plural sense, though strictly the singular is 'datum'. By data we mean those facts and figures relating to whatever it is we are talking about or studying – the flight of birds across a particular marsh, the profitability of a business, examination results, scientific experiments, or the behaviour of microbes.

The word 'statistics' is commonly used to mean

(a) a set of data, e.g. the figures on population growth, births and deaths, the so-called vital statistics;
(b) the science of collecting and processing data to produce information, such as the change in the population from year to year;
(c) figures which in some way represent, summarize or otherwise relate to a set of data, e.g. the birth rate (number of babies born per thousand of the population).

The word cannot be singular when used in sense (a), is always singular when used in sense (b) and is almost always singular when used in sense (c), i.e. we refer to 'a statistic'.

Definition (b) needs some amplification. What kind of processing? Basically, the kind that produces the statistic in sense (c). For example, one type of processing, called 'descriptive statistics', is concerned solely with turning the data collected into understandable and usable form and with presenting this in a suitable way. Some simple statistic may also be calculated, e.g. an average. Another type, called 'inferential statistics', takes us beyond the figures themselves. This mainly means prediction, e.g. Will the same or very similar results occur again? Will the present trend continue into the future? Which would be the most profitable course? Or, can we extend the result to include all possible cases?

We can find examples of these from Gourmet Foods Ltd. When the sales department produces figures showing sales of the various flavours of baby food over the preceding months, it is dealing in descriptive statistics. Of course, the actual figures produced are statistics in sense **(a)**. When it projects such sales into the future then it is dealing in inferential statistics.

Self-check

In what sense do you think the word 'statistics' is being used in the title to this book?

It is being used in the sense of **(b)** above. This book is, then, about the 'science of collecting and processing data to produce information'. Of course, within the text, the word 'statistics' will also be met in each of its other two interpretations.

Self-check

In which sense is the word statistics being used in each of the paragraphs below?

1 'The government today released statistics showing that the money supply is at last coming under control.'
2 'In quality control, an important statistic is the percentage of defective items in a batch.'
3 'It seems to me that statistics is just "guesswork" dressed up to look like a science.'

ANSWERS

1 The government released data, so that 'statistics' is being used in sense **(a)**.
2 The word 'statistic' is singular, and refers to a figure which summarized the quality of a batch, so the term is being used in sense **(c)**.

3 The validity of statistics as a science is being questioned, so
the term is being used in sense **(b)**.

It is often incorrectly stated that statistics deals only with numerical data. It doesn't; it can, however, only deal with data that can
be *turned into* numbers. For example, suppose we want to sound
out attitudes on some public issue. It is obvious that people's
attitudes are not numbers. But if we classify them into, say, 'very
hostile', 'somewhat hostile', 'neutral', 'friendly' and 'very friendly', what we can do then is count the number of people
expressing each class of attitude. Of course, in a great many
cases statistics does deal directly with figures, but we must not
forget those cases when it doesn't.

What is the difference between statistics and mathematics?
Well, mathematics deals with figures which obey rules. That is,
given a set of circumstances, mathematics will tell you exactly
how to obtain some given figure(s), e.g. with an interest rate of
sixteen per cent per annum, how long it will be before your
savings double. Statistics, on the other hand, rarely makes any
claims to certainty. Of course, it uses mathematics a great deal,
but only as a tool to obtain figures to operate on statistically. For
example, the calculation of the birth rate is purely a mathematical exercise given the figures for the number of births and the
population. But getting those figures in the first place, estimating
their accuracy and then interpreting the birth rate are all statistical operations.

What about the difference between statistics and data processing? Here the distinction is not quite so straightforward. Data
processing is, basically, the science of *how* you actually carry out
the processing required by, amongst other disciplines, statistics.
Statistics tells you *what* processing should be performed. The
same is true of accounting. It has long been the misconception
that accounting only involves writing figures down in columns in
books. This is the data processing aspect of accounting, which
itself is concerned with just what to write down and why.

For example, collecting the statistics, from clock cards, on
how many hours each employee worked in some given week in
the Baby Gourmet plant is a statistical problem. Organizing the
wage sheets, informing the wages clerks how to prepare wage

slips from these slips, coordinating the activities of the wages clerks and so on are, on the other hand, data processing tasks.

Let's look at an example of how these various disciplines work together. On the books of Gourmet Foods Ltd, the machines at the Baby Gourmet plant will appear as assets. But, over the years, they become worth less and less; that is, their value depreciates. Accounting will tell how this depreciation appears in the books. Mathematics will say what calculations should be performed. Data processing will indicate the best methods of carrying these out in conjunction with all the other operations involved in totalling the company's assets. Statistics comes in when the question of what percentage depreciation is appropriate. In order to answer this, some idea is required of how long such machinery might last and what kind of resale value it could have. This information has to be obtained by examining real data.

Self-check

For each task below, state whether it properly belongs to (a) statistics (b) mathematics, (c) data processing or (d) accounting.

1 Calculating how much interest is due after one year on a given loan at some stated rate.
2 Displaying the interest payments made and the outstanding amount owing on a loan to inform the borrower.
3 Showing a clerk how to use an electronic calculator to work out the interest due on a loan.
4 Finding out the interest rates charged by various hire purchase companies.

ANSWERS

1 (b) This is a mathematical problem as it is concerned with the calculations to be carried out in order to obtain the value of the interest on the loan.
2 (d) The display of information about money matters is the province of accounting.

3 (c) *How* to actually carry out the calculations in practice is a data processing consideration.

4 (a) Finding out the figures is a statistical operation.

We started off asking what was business statistics. We have considered what is meant by statistics. What happens when we add the term 'business'? It serves to inform us that the sort of data being dealt with is that encountered in the running of a business. The next section goes into this in more detail, but we can discuss it briefly here. Consider the company in the scenario, Gourmet Foods Ltd. To operate this successfully, a knowledge of the market is required: how large it is, how it will react to various products, how likely it is to change, and so forth. These are matters for market research, which makes use of statistical methods. The quality of the product has to be controlled. This involves statistics. Financial control over the business enterprise has to be exercised. This entails some statistical work too. The list could go on.

One other question needs to be answered. What is the difference between statistics and other business techniques like, for example, budgetary control (keeping business expenses within budget)? In budgetary control figures have to be collected and analysed and, just as in statistics, the results often are not exact! In fact, the techniques used in budgetary control are often statistical in nature but, as seen earlier, statistics can be used in many different fields. So, though it can be used as a tool in business techniques (like budgetary control), it cannot be considered in the same light as them since it is much more general in nature.

Thus statistics is never employed as an end in itself in business or in any other field. The results of a statistical inquiry are always to be used as a basis for action in some way: Do we try to expand sales? Introduce a new product? Modify an existing product? Reject a production batch? Inject new capital into the business? And so on. The intelligent use of the techniques described in this book can assist business greatly. But they should never be used carelessly, or as an end in themselves, otherwise they can be counter-productive.

Self-check

Underline the correct option below.

Sales forecasting is

a a statistical technique for forecasting sales;
b a business technique for forecasting sales which makes use of statistical methods;
c a mathematical technique for calculating future sales;
d an accounting technique for taking into consideration future sales.

ANSWER

b is the correct response. If you chose **a** you were confusing the purely business technique of sales forecasting with the statistical method it uses. If you chose **c** you were forgetting that forecasting is *not* exact: we cannot *calculate* future sales. Response **d** confuses the purpose of accounting, which deals with statements of what has occurred, with a business technique dealing with prediction.

How statistics can help business

In any organization, including Gourmet Foods, even the everyday operations depend on obtaining good statistical information. For example, knowledge of stock levels is required so that new supplies can be ordered when necessary, and data from clock cards is needed to make up wages.

Accurate statistics are also the lifeblood of management. Effective control of an organization's performance is based on them. Here detailed information is not wanted, but rather a few figures which capture the essentials. For instance, though the total wage bill and average wage will be of interest, the pay of individual employees will not be, in general.

Self-check

Think of the organization in which you work or study. List as many as you reasonably can of the different types of

|| statistics from inside that organization that are required for it to operate effectively.

Statistics which originate within the organization can be called 'internal statistics'. A few such statistics that may be associated with the five* major activities of organizations, including Gourmet Foods, are given below:

administration
- staffing levels
- maintenance costs
- number of mailings

finance
- wage rates
- bad debts
- cash in hand

marketing
- sales figures
- advertising expenditure
- representatives' mileage

production
- machine reliability
- stock levels
- productivity

purchasing
- raw material prices
- overdue deliveries
- consumption of stationery

Figure 2 illustrates the part played by statistical information in controlling some aspects of the production process in a company such as Gourmet Foods Ltd; specifically in

- *progress control* (controls production programmes and schedules in order to meet planned output figures);
- *quality control* (controls the standard of the product);
- *stock control* (controls stock of raw materials/components to ensure continuous supplies).

* Not all five will apply to every organization, of course.

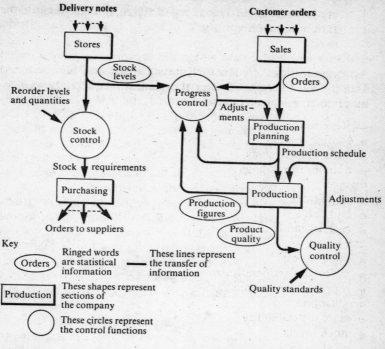

Figure 2. Some control aspects of the production function

Other controls which are generally applied here, but which are not shown in the diagram, are

- *machine utilization control* (controls machine loadings to make the best use of production capacity);
- *cost control* (controls material, labour and other costs to ensure budgeted production costs are met).

These require statistical information too.

Further examples of the importance of statistical information in control could be found in any of the other areas listed.

Self-check

Do you think that the only statistics that a company needs

are internal ones? What kind of statistics might the organization in which you work, or study, require from outside itself?

An organization often needs statistics from outside sources. These may be called 'external statistics'. For example, any business should keep itself informed about the economic climate. It can do so by consulting government sources for the values of certain 'economic indicators' which show how production, unemployment, investment and so on are faring. Gourmet Foods Ltd would also be interested in statistics on the numbers of births, in connection with its Baby Gourmet range. This information is also published by the government.

The government is not the only source of such statistics, however. For instance, many trade associations, such as the British Radio Equipment Manufacturers Association, publish statistics of their own; in this case, figures for deliveries of television receivers. The United Nations, and other international bodies, also issue statistics which are of value to exporters. Sources of external statistics are described in detail in the Appendix.

Occasionally, an organization requires some external statistics which do not appear in any published source. For example, a company launching a new product may want evidence of likely public reaction to it. This type of information is gathered by 'market research', which deals with the impact of advertising and distribution, the habits and attitudes of purchasers, as well as other similar aspects of marketing. A company either carries out its own market research or, if it is a small one, employs an agency. This research often takes the form of a survey conducted by a team of investigators in which, for example, public reaction to a planned new product is tested. This is discussed further in Chapters 2 and 3.

Figure 3 gives a diagrammatical summary of the statistical information requirements of a typical organization.

Self-check

1 Use figure 2 to make a short list of the most important data that is required for

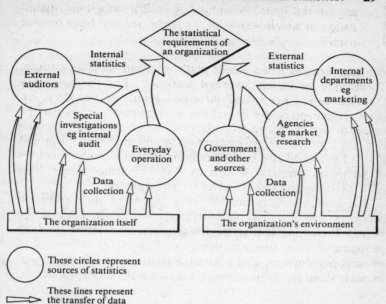

Figure 3. An organization's statistical information requirements

    a progress control;
    b quality control;
    c stock control.
    In each case, say which data you think is statistical in nature.
  2 What specific *special* external statistical data is needed by a company which manufactures jeans aimed at the teenage market if it is to sell its product efficiently?

ANSWERS

1 a Stock levels, orders, production figures, and the production schedule. All but the last are statistical in nature.
b Product quality and quality standards. Only the first of these is statistical in nature.

c Stock levels and reorder levels and quantities. Only the first is statistical in nature.

2 The company would need to know the spread of sizes amongst teenagers. Over the last few generations children have tended to be larger. It would be very inefficient to produce jeans which fitted only a few of the teenagers. It would also need to know how many teenagers there were so as to estimate the potential market.

It is not sufficient merely to collect statistical information, however. As we saw at the beginning of this chapter, statistics also means the set of techniques used to process such data. Its sheer volume may be confusing, in which case other figures could be derived from it, such as averages. Whether this is done or not, data in isolation is seldom sufficient. It is often compared with

- what was expected, as in quality control;
- past data, as with sales figures;
- data from other sources, as when comparing performance;
- what would have been liked, as in economic statistics;

and so on. Conclusions would be drawn from such exercises which could be acted on with some confidence if the data was reliable and the techniques correct. This topic is dealt with in Chapters 3 and 4 of Volume 2.

Finally, statistical methods of presenting data and results are also of value to business. Nearly all of a manager's time is spent in communicating. Good presentation of information reduces this load considerably. It also lessens the chances of errors occurring through misinterpreting the information. For example, if a market survey has been carried out into the purchasing habits of baby foods, it is useless to present managers with the answers from each individual questioned. This would be a waste of their time and most probably only confuse them. The data needs to be collated, summarized and presented in tabular or graphical form. This aspect of statistics is covered in Chapter 6 of Volume 2.

Self-check

Why is it generally insufficient merely to collect statistical data?

After having collected statistical data, what you usually have is a jumble of figures. These must first be sorted out into some pattern and possibly even 'boiled down' to a few representative figures, such as an average. Often these are then compared with other statistics collected earlier or from elsewhere and some decision made on the basis of the result obtained. In any case, if statistical information needs to be communicated to others it must be presented properly.

Misusing statistics

It is worth including just a brief word here about the misuse of statistics (in all the three senses). Throughout this book you will be warned of mistakes and errors that can occur when using the techniques described. There is even a chapter (Chapter 7 of Volume 2) devoted entirely to this topic. These warnings are intended as a guide to where to tread warily: they are not intended to frighten you off taking any steps at all.

Statistical methods are perhaps more open to abuse and misuse than many other methods. The very thing that gives statistics its strength, i.e. its ability to deal with uncertainty, is also the source of its difficulties. There is a common feeling among non-statisticians that statistics can be twisted to prove almost anything. Any truth in this belief derives from the fact that there is usually conflicting evidence in any statistical inquiry. Abuse generally lies in the balance of selection and in the presentation of this evidence, to sway the conclusions reached.

In fact, the analogy between a statistical and a police inquiry is an illuminating one. In each, pieces of evidence are collected and an attempt made to form a complete picture. Some evidence is rather circumstantial, some more direct, some may point in one direction, some in another. But at the end of the day a decision has got to be made. Criminal proceedings in the UK even have a similar basis to a branch of statistics concerned with testing out hypotheses. The maxim 'innocent until proved guilty' is like what statisticians call the 'null hypothesis'. They are both the starting points for the review of evidence. While the prosecution has to establish guilt beyond all reasonable doubt, so the statistician attempts to show that the null hypothesis is improbable.

Statistical evidence must, then, be treated like evidence in a court of law. 'Miscarriages of statistics' can occur, just as can those of justice, and, like them, very seldom come to light. But when one does, we should not throw away statistics any more than we throw away the law under similar circumstances. The fact that statistics makes use of the exact science of mathematics is thus of no more significance than that criminology makes use of the 'exact' forensic sciences.

Let's look at an example. Suppose a car manufacturer wants to state the petrol consumption of a particular model in an advertisement. A test car achieves 57 mpg on a run on the company's test track. Trials on the roads in London show 32 mpg, while on a run from London to Edinburgh an average of 47 mpg is obtained. What does the manufacturer put in the advert? An unscrupulous one, of course, puts 57 mpg.

Self-check

In what ways in this figure misleading?

Apart from the fact that it does not reflect performance under typical driving conditions, it represents one car and, probably, one driver. Who is to say that the figures thus obtained are fully representative of normal production models and ordinary drivers? Indeed, the car is probably specially assembled and the driver an expert, in which case the figures are definitely untypical. To get proper figures the average consumption of a number of normal production models driven by ordinary drivers under typical road conditions should be obtained.

Review

1 Choose an organization with which you are familiar – your employer if you have one, or a college that you

attend. Consider its statistical needs and make a list of those areas of activity where (a) it makes use of statistics and (b) it could make use of statistics. You will probably need to do some research to find out these answers. Your list need not, of course, be absolutely exhaustive, but you should make an effort to discover at least major examples. Indicate which of the statistics in your answer are internal and which external.

2 A paint manufacturer has produced a paint which is designed to cover a greater area than other paints, using the same amount of paint. The manufacturer wants to produce an advertisement which shows some evidence for this. Outline the steps through which the manufacturer will need to proceed to obtain and show these results and justify them. What temptations do you think the manufacturer faces in conducting the statistical exercise?

(Note: do not go into any great detail here, just an outline of the steps is asked for, and you can briefly describe some of the major possible abuses.)

ANSWERS

1 While an answer based on your firm is not, of course, possible, one will be given based on a college: some of you may be studying in one.

(a) A college is run for the students. A good deal of information has to be collected on them in order to enable it to operate effectively. This includes

- past examination successes,
- age,
- nationality, etc.,

collected before they join the college, and

- attendance,
- marks in tests and internal examinations,
- results of external examinations,

while they are at the college. Taking the students to be internal to the college, all of the above are internal statistics, with the exception of the results of the external examinations.

In addition, a college, like a business, has to run an office, order materials, equipment and so on. It will thus need to collect financial data on income and expenditure. These will for the most part be internal statistics. Prices of materials and equipment would, however, be external statistics. The income for a college comes largely from the local authority, so you can regard data on what money it is going to make available to the college as external statistics also. The college acts as an agent for the authority in collecting student's fees. It would have to collect good (internal) statistics on these for accounting purposes.

(b) A college could often do more in the line of collecting external statistics on its market. There are figures available from the local authority on the numbers of pupils in the top forms of the local schools. There will be potential college students amongst them. There are national figures on the 'take up' rate in further education: that is, the proportion of school leavers who enter some kind of further education. More difficult to obtain would be the figures for the likely day-release students. These would depend on the recruitment pattern of local industry and of the willingness of the local firms to give day release.

This is not a comprehensive list of all the statistics used by a college. It should give you some idea of how statistics are used in colleges, however. Don't worry if your answer wasn't as detailed as this one, this answer was intended also as an example of data collection for you to learn from.

2 The manufacturer will have to go through the following steps.

(a) Finding out the facts. This would involve actually painting various types of surface with the paint and other good paints. If it was to be done correctly, different painting techniques should also be used and compared for quality. The results would be recorded.

(b) Making sense of the facts. This would involve sorting out the data so that it was clear what happened. The type of surface, type of paint, method of application, quality of result and so on would all need to be carefully related to the covering capability. Here it is descriptive statistics.

(c) Drawing conclusions. Using the statistics obtained in **(a)**, the performances of the various paints need to be compared under the different conditions. This is inferential statistics.

(d) Informing others. The last stage involves preparing the data and the conclusions to put in the advertisement.

It is at the last stage that temptation may arise. If the work at stage **(c)** had been carried out correctly, then there would be sound conclusions reached. But they may be mixed in their support of what the manufacturer wants to claim. For example, the new paint might give consistently better coverage only where the quality of the finish is suspect. The manufacturer might then wish to publish only those figures, but leave out the fact that the finish is then inferior.

Part 2
Collecting statistical
data

Scenario 2
Rising costs in the canteen

As you read through this scenario (which illustrates the main methods of data collection) make a mental note of occasions on which data is being gathered in any way whatsoever.

Gourmet Foods Ltd provides several amenities for its employees at the Baby Gourmet plant. One of the most valued of these is subsidized meals. Shortly before the manageress, Margaret Tyler, joined the company, rising costs had led management to put up prices in the canteen. After only a few months as manageress, she realized that this move had been inadequate: a budget deficit in the current financial year seemed certain. Margaret decided to take action to avoid it. She did not want to recommend another increase in prices, as resentment over the last one had only just died down. So she examined the alternatives.

The previous manageress had already made a great many improvements in efficiency. Margaret did not see what more could be done in this direction without lowering the standard of service, something she was prepared to do only as a last resort. So she turned to one area where savings might be made: the food itself. Her training had covered the use of textured vegetable protein (TVP) as a meat substitute in dishes such as pies and stews. This reduced costs but not the portion sizes or nutritional content. It seemed a good idea to Margaret to try this at the Baby Gourmet canteen.

Not wanting any discontent among the workforce at the plant, however, she decided to obtain the views of the employees before going any further with her plan.

So one lunchtime, Margaret approached several people queuing in the canteen. She talked to them about the situation, explaining that they would either have to pay more for their meals or have the meat dishes extended with TVP where possible. She then asked them which alternative they would prefer and why, given the actual figures for the percentage of TVP and the price rise. Replies from the women favoured using a meat substitute while the men's answers were mixed. As a result, Margaret decided that it would be a good idea to offer meals containing

TVP for a trial period. This would give those who were against the idea a chance to taste one and, she hoped, change their minds.

Margaret arranged for various dishes having a proportion of meat substitute to be on the menu for a time. She also launched a campaign to persuade everyone eating in the canteen to try some of these. At the end of the period, those who had done so were requested to fill in a short form. This contained a brief statement of the budget situation and the proposed alternatives of either increasing prices or using TVP as a meat extender. Relevant figures were given. It then asked, 'Would you object to having TVP as a permanent ingredient in all suitable meat dishes if it helped to keep prices down?'

About sixty per cent of those who ate in the canteen returned the form. The results showed that most were in favour of using TVP. Additional evidence on reactions was collected by checking the wastage rate on the TVP dishes. This produced a most interesting result. There was actually less leftover food than normal. Taking everything into consideration, Margaret decided to go ahead with the plan to use TVP as a meat extender.

In the scenario Margaret's problem is to determine what would be the reaction if she were to put TVP in the meat dishes. She is in the same position as anyone providing goods or services and who wants to make a change in them. It would be poor business practice simply to undertake the change without first making an attempt to find out how customers would respond.

In order to discover this, evidence needs to be obtained from the customers themselves. It can be seen, by referring to the last chapter, that such an operation is a statistical one. In particular, data needs to be collected. Because the scenario contains all the ingredients of a typical marketing problem, it illustrates the techniques available for collecting data in such cases.

There are, of course, many reasons, other than marketing ones, why an organization might want to collect statistical data. We saw several in the last unit. For example, in quality control, data on the quality of a product must be obtained, and in stock control, stock levels must be determined. In fact, the scenario contains instances of all types of data collection methods, including those used in these two cases. So it illustrates data collection techniques in general.

Furthermore, Margaret needs to make sure that the data she collects is accurate, reliable and representative, i.e. that it does not contain any errors, that it reflects a true and lasting situation and that it takes account of the various strands of opinion. Any techniques used should take these considerations into account. This, again, is typical of any data collection exercise.

So in the next two chapters we will be looking at why an organization needs to collect data, from both within and outside itself, and what the different ways of doing this are. In addition we will be discussing the advantages and disadvantages of each of these methods and when each one should be used. You ought then to be familiar with the principal methods of collecting data and be able to examine examples of the collection of statistical data critically and carry out small data collection exercises yourself.

2 | Finding out for ourselves

Why collect information?

Very often the information we need is not readily available, either because it is not on record at all or because it is scattered about in various documents. In such cases we must gather it ourselves. This point is illustrated in the scenario. Margaret Tyler wanted 'customers'' views on the use of TVP in canteen meals and had to find these out for herself.

Although Margaret's attempt at data collection was amateur, it nevertheless serves as a good example of the sort of investigation that might well occur in business. This could be because some major change is being planned, such as a move to a different location. Management ought then to be concerned with employee response. Furthermore, Margaret's actions reflect, on a small scale, the kind of steps that statisticians themselves might go through, for example before the launch of a new product.

We have also seen, in Chapter 1, how any organization needs to collect data for its everyday operation. It was pointed out, too, that management requires statistics derived from this to make decisions and exercise control. However, in the present unit we will be more concerned with less routine situations, such as that described in the scenario.

What information should be collected?

Before starting to collect data, we must have some clear idea of what it is we want to know. This is, in itself, governed by the purpose of the investigation, which should thus be made perfectly plain. Information should not be gathered indiscriminately in the hope that something useful may emerge.

Self-check

What do you think Margaret's purpose was in collecting data about people's preferences in the scenario?

ANSWER

Margaret wanted to be sure that the introduction of TVP into the canteen meals would not receive too bad a response from the workforce. She also, no doubt, required evidence to put to management to show that there was a majority in favour of the use of TVP should any of the workers actually complain to, say, the union.

If we collect some data and then find that a vital piece of information is missing it can prove expensive. This is because we may then be forced to abandon the whole project, or an important part of it. Alternatively, we might have to collect more data. We must thus take care that we obtain all the information required for our particular purpose in the first instance.

Self-check

Tom and Jean lived in rented accommodation in Grimethorpe and wanted to buy a house or flat in nearby Luxley. They calculated the maximum they could afford to pay, and set off one Sunday to look in the windows of estate agents there. Even the cheapest property they saw advertised was about £1000 more than they had available. They returned home depressed and decided they would have to look at a cheaper area.

Comment on their decision.

ANSWER

Tom and Jean made the mistake of collecting the wrong data for their purpose. The prices of the houses in the estate agents' windows represented

(a) the prices being *asked*, not those paid;
(b) the prices only of those houses that were on the market at that time;

(c) the prices of those houses that were advertised through estate agents.

The decision they made on the basis of this wrong data (i.e. to look elsewhere) was thus an incorrect one. They should have tried making an offer on one of the cheaper properties or have looked in the local Luxley newspaper to see if there was anything in their price range there.

Ways of collecting information

Where everyday operations are involved, the actual data collection methods used will depend on the organization, although there are some general principles. The two main ones are:

- collect the right data, neither more nor less than is needed at the time or in the future;
- build in sufficient checks to ensure that errors, or deliberate malpractices, do not go undetected.

In other, less routine, situations, such as that described in the scenario, there are various standard techniques which may be employed. The one(s) chosen in any particular case will depend on various considerations discussed later. The scenario itself contains examples of these.

The principal ways of collecting data are as follows:

Interviewing Where the sources of information are people, a series of questions may be put to each of them in an interview and that information obtained verbally.

Self-check

When in the scenario did Margaret conduct an interview?

Margaret did this when she talked to customers in the queue to get their views.

Questionnaires Sometimes interviewing is impractical, as, for instance, when large numbers of people are involved. In such cases the questions may be set out on forms, called questionnaires. These are then filled in by those from whom the information is required.

> ## Self-check
>
> When in the scenario did Margaret use the questionnaire technique?

Margaret used this method to obtain the preferences of customers who had tried a TVP meal, rather than talk to them all.

Observation When first-hand information about some event is required, it must be observed.

> ## Self-check
>
> Though Margaret did not use this method in the scenario, she could have done. When was this?

Margaret could have watched people eat their TVP meals and obtained their reactions in this way. (Instead, she relied on indirect evidence, the amount of left-over food, as it was probably a reliable indicator of these and easier to check.)

Inspection Where the sources of information are objects, these must be inspected and the relevant information noted. This may be size, weight, colour or any other factor.

> ## Self-check
>
> Where did inspection take place in the scenario?

Checking the amount of food left over from the TVP meals is an example of inspection.

Abstraction Where the sources of information are documents, these must be consulted and the relevant information abstracted from them.

Self-check

Although this technique is not referred to directly in the scenario, there is one indirect reference to it, i.e. there is a time when Margaret must have had to consult some records. Can you spot where this is?

Margaret must have used this method when examining the records of previous wastage rates for comparison with those for the TVP meals.

These techniques are discussed in more detail in the next chapter.

Self-check

What would be the appropriate data collection method for obtaining the following information?

1 Employees' views on a planned change in location of their work.
2 The proportion of car drivers who don't stop at a particular halt sign.
3 The amount of column space devoted to advertising in a specific newspaper over a given period of time.
4 The wishes of the membership of a large society regarding a proposed change to its rules.
5 The number of words typed by a particular secretary on a given day.
6 The number of goals scored in first division football matches last season.

ANSWERS

1 It would be best here to interview the employees. This would allow management to explain about the move and to judge the employees' emotional reaction to it. Furthermore, it would be less impersonal than a questionnaire. If however the firm was too large to make interviewing everyone practicable, a letter from the management explaining their action and attaching a questionnaire would be an alternative. The interview is to be preferred for the reasons given above, if at all possible.

2 Observation is the only feasible way of obtaining this. If you chose the interview or a questionnaire, remember that few people will admit to doing wrong. If you chose abstraction – from police or court records – remember that these only show how many drivers were prosecuted for this: there would be many more that were either let off or, more likely, not even caught.

3 The only possible way of obtaining this is by inspection. If you chose abstraction, you are confusing getting information from a written source with the physical appearance of that source.

4 A questionnaire would be the only feasible way of getting this information. If you chose an interview, think of the time and effort this would take to get what is, after all, a reasonably straightforward reply – though the change itself may be far from straightforward.

5 This is a tricky one. It might appear at first sight that inspection of her output would be the answer. But what about the sheets of paper she has torn up and thrown away? Perhaps too, she used an eraser or correcting fluid to remove several words. The only real way would be to observe her at work. Unfortunately, this is likely to slow her up considerably and to increase her error rate. Short of secretly filming her, there is no really satisfactory answer to this problem. Actually, we would probably only be interested in her correct output in practice.

6 As the events have already happened, there is no alternative to abstraction here. Note that if the results had not been recorded anywhere, it would not be practically possible to find out what they were.

Recording the information collected

It is vitally important that, before attempting to collect data, we should plan how it is to be recorded. We might otherwise end up with an incomprehensible jumble. We shall see in the next chapter how data from interviews and questionnaires is recorded. Here we shall deal with information gathered by observation, inspection and abstraction.

To start with, we have a choice of collecting the data first and, possibly, classifying it afterwards, or constructing some classes beforehand into which each item is placed as obtained. For instance, if gathering details on the number of pages in various books, we could record them exactly, or classify them straight away. 1–50, 51–100, 101–150. . .700 and over, is a possible scheme.

Self-check

Suppose you were carrying out an investigation into what features people wanted in their car, e.g. what top speed, colour, seating. What do you think would be the advantages and disadvantages of waiting until the data had been collected before classifying it?

The advantages of waiting until the data has been collected are:

* it may become apparent later that the unclassified data is required after all, and it won't otherwise be available. For example, preferences for the car's seating capacity would be needed exactly at the lower end – say 1 to 6 – but a class of 7 and over may have been used for the upper end: if, then, a company wished to manufacture a very large car, it may want exact details of the higher value which it would not have;
* the classes themselves may prove difficult to use (though a pilot project could help here). For example, think how difficult it would be to have a classification system for body styling.

The disadvantages are:

* it may be extremely difficult or confusing to use all the possibilities where there are a great many of them. For example, think about all the colours that cars are available in;
* we are forced to use classes anyway in a great many cases. For example, the capacity of the car boot could be specified to any degree of accuracy (to the nearest cubic millimetre if desired!), but we obviously have to draw the line somewhere, and this creates our classes for us (this point is taken up again in Chapter 8).

When using preconstructed classes, a system of 'tally marks' can be employed. It can also be used if simply counting off, as when finding the number of customers going into a particular shop in some given period. Each time an 'event' occurs that is to be recorded, whether it is a book with between 51 and 100 pages or a customer entering a shop and so on, a mark is made. The following sequence shows how the record of the total number of customers who have entered the shop would change over time, i.e. each line represents the same record at different times.

After	1 customer,	the record looks like this	/
,,	2 customers,	,, ,, ,, ,, ,,	//
,,	3	,, ,, ,, ,, ,, ,,	///
,,	4	,, ,, ,, ,, ,, ,,	////
,,	5	,, ,, ,, ,, ,, ,,	ﬀﬀ
,,	6	,, ,, ,, ,, ,, ,,	ﬀﬀ /
,,	7	,, ,, ,, ,, ,, ,,	ﬀﬀ //
,,	8	,, ,, ,, ,, ,, ,,	ﬀﬀ ///
,,	9	,, ,, ,, ,, ,, ,,	ﬀﬀ ////
,,	10	,, ,, ,, ,, ,, ,,	ﬀﬀ ﬀﬀ
,,	15	,, ,, ,, ,, ,, ,,	ﬀﬀ ﬀﬀ ﬀﬀ
,,	20	,, ,, ,, ,, ,, ,,	ﬀﬀ ﬀﬀ ﬀﬀ ﬀﬀ

A form would be required, which listed the preconstructed classes where appropriate, and which allowed space in which to put the tally marks.

If actual values are to be collected this system obviously cannot be used. Instead, space has to be left for these to be recorded on the form. There are three simple rules that should be kept in all cases:

- allow sufficient clear space for each entry and for the total number of entries;
- lay out the form logically and clearly;
- when recording the data, write legibly and do not use abbreviations unless they are clearly defined, or in common use.

Overleaf is a form used by a farmer recording the milk yield of each cow in a small herd over a week.

Sprotts Farm, Weasdale				**Daily milk yield record**		
Week beginning Sunday _____						

Cow	Milk yield (litres)						
	Su	M	Tu	W	Th	F	Sa
Totals							

Self-check

A supermarket wants to know what type of customer uses its late night shopping facilities, men, women, families and so on. Observers are to be stationed at the checkouts to collect the relevant data. Design a form suitable for recording it.

You should have preclassified the customers. There would be very little time for the observer to write down descriptions. The count for each type of customer would be made using tally marks. Your form should be similar to the one shown below. Note that there is an extra category, 'others', to cover the odd cases.

_____Supermarket	Date _____Time period from _____	
	To _____	
Customer type	*Tally count*	*Totals*
Lone male		
Lone female		
Lone male with children		
Lone female with children		
Couple – no children		
Family – with children		
Other (please specify)		

Review

1 A recruitment agency keeps data on the personal qualities, qualifications, etc., of job applicants. Say how each of the data collection techniques listed in the text would be used, if at all, in gathering that data.

2 A food manufacturer tests a new range of products by sending out representatives into the streets and giving people there a taste of them. The purpose is to find out whether people think the product range as a whole is a good idea, i.e. if they would buy it, and what they think of the various flavours. The price is to be ignored at present. The company also wants a breakdown of the responses by sex and age, which the interviewer has to estimate. Design a form for the representative to fill in assuming that the information listed above is all that is to be collected. Call the different flavours A, B, C and D.

ANSWERS

1 The agency would use several different techniques. Job hunters may well be asked to fill in a questionnaire which gives all their personal details, age, past experience and so on. Often this is just a screening process; that is, the unsuitable ones are not considered further. Those selected then proceed to an interview. Data collected here can include details of exactly what was done in previous employment and other similar expansions on the data in the questionnaire. But it plays a more important part: the interviewer can assess the personal qualities of the applicant. In fact this brings in observation as a data collection technique. Abstraction would also be used to obtain data such as references, confirmation of qualifications and so on. The only data collection technique that would not be used is inspection.

If you did not include observation as one of the techniques that would be used, this may be because you included assessment of personal characteristics under the heading of 'interview'. This is understandable. You should not have called it 'inspection', however. Apart from certain medical connections, this is properly reserved for 'things'.

2 There are many different ways a correct answer could be given here. However, the basic information should be collected as shown in the form opposite.

Note: the form is to be completed by the interviewer so it does not have to give detailed instructions on how to fill it in. For example, it can be assumed that the interviewer will know that ticks (or crosses or whatever) have to be put in the boxes. If you have put in detailed instructions this is not really a mistake, though. Nor is it a mistake if you put M/F for the male and female record, and said that whichever is inapplicable should be deleted. If you put a list of ages, though, and expected the interviewer to delete all but one, then this would increase work and waste time. Always try to save the work that needs to be done in filling in a form. The same goes for the answers to the other questions.

You should not have just left a space for age. Remember that the interviewer is to fill this in from an estimate and it

Details of taster		Tasters reactions		
Sex M ☐	*To range*	Would buy never ☐		
F ☐		sometimes ☐		
		frequently ☐		
Age under ☐ 16	*To flavours*			

Flavour	Reaction				
	strongly dislikes	dislikes	undecided	likes	strongly likes
A					
B					
C					
D					

Age: under 16 ☐, 16–19 ☐, 20–29 ☐, 30–44 ☐, 45–64 ☐, over 65 ☐

Interviewer _____
Date _____

cannot be a very accurate one. Nor should you have left one for tasters' reactions. Remember it is better to make sure that the categories are consistent. If categorizing is left till the forms are collected, it is more likely to cause an error here, as replies will have to be interpreted. Giving the categories on the form makes it clear what is wanted. It also, of course, makes less work for the interviewer.

Obstacles to obtaining reliable information

There are several obstacles that may, however, prevent the collection of reliable information. Perhaps the most obvious is not having access to it. This may be due to a variety of reasons.

Self-check

Do you think that it would be very easy, for example, to find out how many staff there were in MI5 (military intelligence)?

No, it would not. Such data is very sensitive and would not be disclosed to the public. So one obstacle, then, is secrecy.

Self-check

Can we ever know what the exact population of the United Kingdom is?

Despite the fact that the Registrars General keep a record of all births and deaths, the figures change so quickly that it would be impossible to keep abreast of them. So up-to-date information is sometimes unavailable because it changes too rapidly.

When historical data is required, it may simply not exist and be impossible to gather after the event.

Self-check

What would be required to answer the question, How many people were there in the British Isles in 55 BC? Can this data then be obtained?

To answer this question, a record of that figure would be needed. Since no population records were kept at that time, the data can never be collected.

So data may not be collectable at all because

● considerations of secrecy will not allow it
● it changes faster than it can be collected
● it is not accessible in any way whatsoever.

Self-check

Can you think of an example where it would be prohibitively expensive to obtain the data?

Cost is generally a factor where there is a great deal of data that could be collected. For example, it would cost more than the data was worth to find out what every person in the country thought about a new brand of soap. So another obstacle is cost.

The first three obstacles are insurmountable. That of cost may, however, sometimes be overcome by collecting only a portion of the possible data. For example, in a market research survey on men's shaving habits, a relatively small number of males can be questioned provided they are reasonably representative of the whole group. Again, an auditor will not check every figure in a mass of transactions, but only a few typical ones. Data collected in this way is called a 'sample'. A survey conducted on a sample is called a 'sample survey'.

Such a solution can only be adopted where the data collected can be made to reflect the total picture, as in the above examples. However, it is quite surprising how many situations satisfy this requirement. The crucial factor is the selection process. Samples are discussed in detail later on in the book. In the scenario, Margaret ought to have made certain that the people she questioned in the queue were broadly representative of the customers as a whole.

One further important obstacle to collecting the complete set of data is that it may involve the destruction of the source of that data. For example, testing the quality of light bulbs in some batch may involve determining how long they stay alight before failing.

Self-check

To collect the *complete* data would mean testing each bulb made. What is wrong with that? Can you suggest how the problem may be got round?

It is obvious that if all of them were tested in this way none would ever reach the market. The solution here, too, is to select just a *representative* sample of them.

The same technique might also be used where the amount of data is infinite. Indeed, this is the only course of action available to us when we meet this obstacle, since we could not possibly collect it all. For instance, if we wanted to obtain figures for noise levels in a factory, any figure we recorded would only apply to one instant of time. A set of such figures would be only a few of the (infinite) total number possible.

So *all* the data may not be collectable because

● it would cost too much

- it would totally destroy the source of the data and
- there may be an infinite amount of data.

Instead, a sample is taken.

Another obstacle is people's reluctance to provide certain types of information. For example, most men are less likely to admit to reading children's comics than, say, the *Economist*. The situation is considerably better where there is a legal obligation to provide accurate and truthful information as far as possible. But details supplied on tax forms are still prone to 'error' and some people even refused to answer sensitive questions on the 1981 Census of Population.

This problem can sometimes be overcome by putting the question in a certain way. For example, suppose we wish to discover how much a man spends on cigarettes a week. The straight question will almost certainly produce a substantial underestimate as it is usually more than he wants to admit, even to himself. If, instead, we ask him how many a day he smokes, then find out which brand, a short calculation will give us the required data. This figure may still be too low, but it should be nearer the truth than the other. Such a strategy does not work in all cases, of course.

So *reliable* data may not be collectable because the source itself cannot be relied on.

Self-check

What would be the major obstacles to obtaining the following information?

1 The number of trees on Forestry Commission land at any one time.
2 The proportion of dog owners who don't have licences for them.
3 The number and tonnage of non-peaceful nuclear devices possessed by some nation.
4 The number of acres under wheat in the British Isles in 1799.

ANSWER

1 There are two problems here. One is the sheer cost of counting every tree. The other is in fact that there are always trees being chopped down and new ones planted, so the situation would change before a figure could be found.

2 We are likely to get told an untruth if we just go around asking people if they have a licence for their dog. On the other hand it is difficult to think of any other way of getting this information. Possibly, a list of all dog licence owners could be obtained and this checked with people in a given area.

In any case, of course, not all dog owners could be found, so we would have to make do with a sample. It is not likely that any such sample would be representative. Those without dog licences would be more likely to deny even having a dog than those with them.

3 Here we would undoubtedly run across a problem with secrecy.

4 The difficulty here is that there are no accurate records of this figure for that date.

Employing someone else to collect the information

In most cases it is not practicable for those who want the information to collect it themselves. They have to employ agents to do this for them. For example, a national market survey will involve a team of investigators spread over the country. They may well not even work for the organization which initiated the survey, but for an independent market research agency. Again, one of the major reasons clerks are needed is to gather the information necessary to run an organization.

This presents a further obstacle to obtaining reliable information. Unless such agents are well trained in the techniques involved, frequent errors may occur. There must also be a system of checks to ensure that they carry out their jobs as required. This is not just because of the possibility of malpractice, but because of misunderstandings, laxity and other occurrences as well.

For example, in market research, investigators must be instructed not to help people with answers to their questions, nor to change the wording of these, as they could thus inadvertently change the meaning. Frustration and boredom could easily lead them to do this. Controls must also exist to prevent them returning fictitious results, most probably out of a desire to fulfil their quota after a bad day.

One particular problem which arises here is that of interpretation. It is not easy to specify rules for data collection which can always be consistently applied by all agents. Yet this must be attempted, otherwise the results will be of little value. The difficulty of devising a classification scheme for recording information gathered is a case in point.

Suppose, for instance, we want to find out the proportion of cars of various different colours.

Self-check

We saw earlier how this may cause a problem with classification. What is it? How could it be overcome when using agents?

There are so many possibilities that it would be impractical to use them all. Some set of categories is needed into which each one can be placed as met. There should not be so many of these that it leads to confusion, but neither should there be so few that the results are worthless. A colour chart would be appropriate, which might differentiate, say, between light brown and dark brown but not between beige and fawn.

Self-check

An internal auditor may be regarded as the agent of management in the collection of financial and allied data. Why is it desirable that he should not report to the chief accountant?

The internal auditor is likely to be inhibited in criticizing the operations of the chief accountant's section if he is a member of it. He should be a disinterested party, in terms of who his superiors are, who decides his salary and so on. He should report direct to the managing director or, if there is one, to the management services manager.

Getting it right

In this chapter we have only looked at some of the more obvious problems which might occur when collecting data. The following chapter will look into the more detailed difficulties encountered when using the specific methods listed earlier. There are also other ways in which unreliable data could be obtained, but over which we have more control. These are called 'errors', and they will be covered in a later chapter, too.

The key to good data collection is planning. Obstacles and errors should be anticipated as far as possible and steps taken to eliminate or reduce them. However, when dealing with non-routine situations, problems are always likely to occur. Rather than have this happen during the data collection proper, it is better to have a trial run and attempt to iron out any which are met before going on. Where the main investigation is a survey, the preliminary exercise is called a 'pilot survey'.

Review

1 There is a vending machine in the corridor near an office that provides staff with their coffee, tea, etc. The management feel that too much time is wasted by certain staff going to the machine and drinking. How would you go about gathering data to use in making a decision as to whether or not this was so? Give reasons for your choice.

2 A food manufacturer is worried that the sales of one of its, up till then, most popular lines have fallen sharply. It wants to know why. How could it go about finding why people have stopped buying? What obstacles, if any, do you see to getting this information?

3 A survey is being made of the amount and kind of traffic, e.g. cars, lorries, that uses the main street of a small country village. This is in response to complaints by locals that it is too busy and that heavy lorries sometimes have to mount the pavement to get through. Two observ-

ers are employed to check the number and type of vehicles passing, one for each direction.

a Design a classification scheme for vehicles which could be used in this investigation.

b What problems do you think could arise in obtaining reliable data?

ANSWERS

1 Firstly, the machine itself may well give a record of the number of drinks bought in any day. That is, the data can be gathered by inspection. Though this is a useful starting point, it does not give any indication of which staff are buying drinks. If the number of drinks per member of staff is small, there is no point in going any further.

If it is large, then another technique will have to be employed. It would not be a very good idea to send out a questionnaire. It may well upset the staff and would probably not get the required data anyway. Staff would be suspicious of the motives behind it, and would tend to grossly understate the amount of drink consumed. It would scarcely be politic to ask them outright how much time they spent drinking either, even if they knew, which is unlikely. An interview would be possible, but the objections raised about the questionnaire are still largely valid for this technique too. The benefit of the interview would be that the interviewer would be able to observe the staff's reactions, and possibly reduce adverse reaction marginally. Abstraction is not possible here since there are no records of who buys a drink and when. This leaves only observation.

The difficulty here is that it would look suspicious for someone to hang about the vending machine writing in a notebook. The matter does not seem important enough for concealed cameras or the like. A simpler solution would be to move the vending machine on some pretext or other to somewhere it is more convenient to observe. Indeed, this move may actually solve the problem. Before going to the trouble of observing the use of the vending machine in its new position, the data on the total drinks sold should again be examined over a period to see if any change occurs.

2 It would probably conduct a survey, using interviewers. The major difficulty would be getting to those people who would know the answer: those who used to buy the product but have now stopped. On the assumption that these people will not have stopped buying food altogether, a good idea would be to stage the interviews outside a supermarket in an area in which sales have fallen a lot. Of course, it would be necessary to first ask whether the person did, or does, buy the product at all. Then, if that person is one of those who stopped buying, they could be asked why.

The usual controls would need to be operated with the interviewers. In this case, though, it would be unwise to give them a number of interviews to aim at, and to pay them by results. This might tempt them to invent data if they didn't happen to find many customers who stopped buying the product.

In practice, too, the representatives who visit the small shops might pick up some data: small shopkeepers often talk to their customers and discover things that supermarket managers and staff do not.

You might not have picked up the point about the interviewers not being payed by results; this is not an obvious one. If you just said the equivalent of the use of small shopkeepers, then you were relying too much on hearsay. This information is valuable as a pointer, but we need backing up by a proper statistical investigation.

3 a The purpose of the investigation is to find out about heavy good vehicles. The classification system should take this into account. The other point to bear in mind is that the observers should be able to quickly determine which class any vehicle is in and to record it. A suitable classification scheme might be, then, as follows:

'car', 'van/truck', 'lorry (two axles)', 'lorry (three axles)', 'lorry (more than three axles)'*, 'motorcycle', 'other'.

You cannot be expected to have exactly the same classes. You might, in addition, have pedal cycles. It would not be

*Including those on any trailer.

wrong if you had. They would be covered by 'other' in the above. The same applies to such things as caravans.

If you have not broken up the lorries into any smaller groups at all, then this ignores the point in the question that it is *heavy* lorries that are doing the damage. If you have a great many more classes than above, then remember that the observers have to make a very quick decision as to what type of vehicle it is and the more choices, the more time it takes to decide.

b The use of the classes would be one problem. Hopefully, a good choice of these would help to cut down the difficulty. Time might well prove the crucial factor. When there is heavy traffic it might be difficult for the observers to record every vehicle. If it takes too much effort, they might well take a small breather.

If you have any other points, you may well be right. Just check carefully to make sure they are relevant. You should have included the point about missing some vehicles, though.

3 | How to collect data

Choosing the right method

The main methods of collecting data were outlined in the previous chapter and some indication was given of the circumstances under which each could be used. Any particular case would, of course, have to be examined carefully for its own individual requirements. The following sections look at these methods in more detail and give further criteria for selecting the correct one in the light of such requirements.

Observation: looking at events

Self-check

Imagine that you have been given the task of observing workers in a factory to see if they take the proper safety precautions. What advantages do you think this would have over the other possible methods of collecting that data? What do you think would be the disadvantages?

A more general list of advantages and disadvantages of observation is given below. The answer to the above questions can be inferred from this.

The main advantages of *direct* observation are:

- actual events can be viewed, as opposed to getting second-hand reports which may be inaccurate, e.g. whether a worker takes the proper safety precautions or not (he may say he does);
- data can be collected over reasonably long periods of time;
- work is not interrupted.

The principal disadvantages are:

- there is often a high cost in terms of time and effort;
- considerable skill is often required;
- it is never certain that what is observed is really representative of what happens normally, especially if people know they are being watched, e.g. the safety precautions again;
- it is not always feasible to observe what is of interest, e.g. how often people bath;
- the past cannot be directly observed, e.g. were proper safety precautions taken in the past?

Observation may, however, be indirect, via films or closed circuit TV.

|| *Self-check*

Can you see what advantages and disadvantages this would have?

It has the following additional advantages:

- it allows repeated viewing, which reduces the chance of something significant being missed and, therefore, does not require such skilled observers;
- it is easier to keep the people being watched in ignorance of the fact.

It also has one disadvantage:

- the camera may miss something important.

In the scenario, Margaret Tyler did not use the technique of observation as she believed she could obtain evidence, from the amount of left-over food, of how her customers reacted to the TVP meals. Observing them would have been time consuming and may, in any case, have upset them. The situation scarcely merited the use of film or closed circuit TV.

Some cases in which observation can be used are:

- works study, where workers are observed performing their duties so that such things as work rate can be examined;
- traffic censuses;

- discovering what people do in some specific situation, e.g. when passing a particular advertising poster;
- determining queuing patterns.

> ### Self-check
>
> A county council is examining the work done by secretaries in its offices and wants to know what proportion of their time is spent typing as opposed to filing, taking dictation and so on. A proposal has been put forward to have each one observed every day for a month to obtain this information. If you were asked to advise on this what would be your general reaction?

ANSWER

The scheme is not a very good one. Think how you would feel if you were the typist being watched! She is likely to perform considerably differently from normal under such conditions. Furthermore, a month is a very long time for such an operation, and it would be very expensive. On the other hand, if there is reason to suppose that the secretaries spend a good deal of their time doing nothing, asking them to report on their work is likely to yield distorted figures. The best answer, if it was in some way possible, would be to use *indirect* observation. Otherwise self-reporting, with built-in checks, should be used. For example, time spent taking dictation could be recorded by the person giving the dictation as well as by the secretary and a check made to see if the two agreed.

> ### Activity
>
> Design a form for recording the country of manufacture of cars to be observed. Go into a busy road and actually record the nationality of every car that passes. How far do you think you can say that your results represent the situation in the local area as a whole, in the county and in the country? What was the proportion of British-made cars in your sample? What foreign country did best? Did you encounter any difficulties?

Inspection: looking at objects

Self-check

By considering quality control of incoming glass jars at the Baby Gourmet plant, say what you think the advantages and disadvantages of inspection are over the other data collection methods.

The answer can be obtained from the more general list given below. The chief advantages of inspection are:

- very often it is the only way of obtaining the required information, e.g. the mileage covered by cars in a fleet (on the 'clocks');
- the information is obtained first-hand and is, therefore, more reliable, e.g. incoming goods are inspected despite suppliers' own quality checks;
- past events can be inferred this way, e.g. automatic counters used for traffic counts can be inspected after the event.

One disadvantage is:

- the cost could be high (but it is often worth it, e.g. quality control, and if it isn't, perhaps the data is not really needed!).

Margaret used this technique in preference to observation, as explained earlier. She believed it indicated what her customers thought of the TVP meal. But did it? The fact that the wastage rate was less than usual casts doubt upon this. It may have merely reflected a desire to do a thorough job of testing it! It is a common finding, called the Hawthorne effect, that people who have extra attention paid to them behave in a manner different to normal. They may, for example, make greater efforts in some direction. This must always be watched for.

Inspection can be performed in many instances, including:

- quality control;
- stock control;
- determining agricultural yields (tonnage per acre);
- measuring physical characteristics, e.g. birth weight.

Self-check

The owner of a large timber plantation wants to find out how many trees he has in it. How could he do so? How could the cost be kept to a reasonable level?

ANSWER

The only possible method of collecting this data is by inspection. However, to count every tree would be very expensive. We saw, in the last chapter, how cost could be reduced by taking only a sample. This could be done here. One plan would be to measure out an area of, say, 3000 square metres. The number of trees in this area would be counted. An estimate of the total number of trees in the plantation could then be found, by making the assumption that the density of trees throughout the plantation was uniform, as it generally is in a plantation.

Activity

Prepare a form for an investigation into the prices of paperback books as against the number of pages in them for different publishers. Then go to your local bookshop and actually collect that data. Is any one publisher cheaper per page than any other? Are book prices per page consistent even for one publisher? Did you run up against any snags?

Abstraction: looking at documents

Self-check

You have been asked to find out how many part-time students there were at your local technical college in 1973. What do you think would be the advantages and disadvantages of abstraction as a method of collecting this data over the other possible methods?

Again you should be able to get the answer from the more general list given below. The principal advantages of abstracting information from documents are:

- the cost is relatively low since someone else has already done the major portion of the data collection task;
- it may be the only way to obtain certain historical data.

The main disadvantages are:

- the data may be unreliable, for any of the reasons given in the previous chapter;
- the data may be out of date;
- there may be limitations on the data that are not obvious, e.g. figures may be for firms of size fifty staff and upwards only (though if so it should say so);
- the data may have been collected for a different purpose and might, therefore, be inappropriate, e.g. figures for the home sales of British cars could include imports of British models manufactured abroad and so not be suitable for calculating the share of the home market held by British made cars.

If the figures for the wastage rates in the Baby Gourmet canteen had not been kept, Margaret would have had to gather them again if she wanted to compare them with those for the TVP meals. Good records are always advisable.

Abstracting information from documents is by far the most common method of collecting data in organizations. Their everyday operation depends on it. Examples are:

- creating delivery notes and packing slips from order forms;
- completing wage sheets from clock cards;
- transferring figures from one book to another in accounting;
- producing sales figures.

Other cases where this technique may be used include:

- consulting past records;
- using published data.

Self-check

Someone wanted to find out the record for the highest ascent made by a balloonist and went to the *Guinness Book of Records*. Was this a good decision?

It would very much depend on why he wanted the data. If only a rough idea of that height was needed, this would be all right. It would not be advisable, however, if a correct and definitely up-to-date figure was wanted, as it takes some time for the book to be produced and the record may have been broken while this was being done.

Activity

Look at the weather report in your daily paper every day for a week. (If you don't take one go to the library and ask to see the back copies for the previous week, borrow ones from a friend or get hold of them in some other way.) Find out what the temperature was in London each day. At what time was the temperature taken? What does one of these figures tell you about the temperature in London at the time you read the paper? What other data would you need to say whether or not it was warmer than usual in the capital at those times?

Review

1 There is a free car park near a shopping precinct in a town. The local chamber of commerce wants to find out how many cars use it at various times of the day and also how often, and at which times, it gets full up. How would you advise them to go about doing this? Would your answer be any different if it was the kind of car park where you take a ticket at the entry barrier and pay on the way out?

2 You have been asked by your office 'tea club' to find out the prices of coffee and tea in five different supermarkets in the area, in connection with an attempt to cut costs. Describe in some detail how you would go about doing this. State also how you would record the data and give an illustration.

3 Jill and Keith are thinking of buying a small village shop. Before committing themselves, however, they want to make certain that the profits are good enough. How can

they find this out? What problems do you think they could encounter?

ANSWERS

1 If it is an ordinary car park, it would need a team of observers to record the cars going into and coming out of it. This would allow figures for the number of cars in the car park to be calculated, provided it was known at the beginning of the period how many cars were in it then. This data should not be difficult to get as, presumably, this would be a time when the park was virtually empty. The total capacity of the park should be known, so it would be a simple matter to find out when it was full. This might be difficult if there is no attendant, and there probably wouldn't be as it is free. Cars would still go in and come out, only they would be the same ones as they wouldn't have been able to park!

If the park was a pay-as-you-leave one, the same data could possibly be obtained from an analysis of the tickets handed in. These have the time of entry on but the time of exit would also have to be recorded if they didn't have this as well, or obtained in some other way.

You should have got the point about observation, even if it was expressed differently. The abstraction of the data from the ticket where available, you should also have spotted. But did you see the problem with the ticket of not necessarily being able to get the number of cars in the car park from this? This is not such an obvious point, so you may not have.

2 The first point to note is that if an attempt to cut costs is being made, it is only the cheaper brands of tea or coffee that are of interest. On the other hand it would not be wise to record only the very cheapest, as these may be terrible. The exercise has in fact two separate aspects. One is to find the cheapest brands, the second is to find the cheapest sources of those brands. One possible scheme would be to record the prices of the three cheapest brands of tea and of coffee at each super-market. This, of course, would necessitate a visit to each of the supermarkets to *inspect* the prices of the goods. These should be recorded on a form.

As the cheapest brands would not be known beforehand,

the form of recording the data should leave these blank. There should also be spaces for the prices as well as the name of the supermarket. One possible layout is shown below.

Brand of tea	Supermarket and price				
	A	B	C	D	E
A's own brand ($\frac{1}{4}$lb)	32p				
Brand of coffee					

Note that there are only eleven lines for tea and eleven for coffee. It is unlikely that the brands selected in each supermarket are totally different, so this should be enough. The idea of the layout is to save having to write down each brand more than once and so to make comparison easier.

There is one complication that must be dealt with. The prices are only comparable if they are for the same weight so this must be noted in all cases. Since the club is likely to bulk buy, the largest weights would be chosen in general. Even tea does not always come in quarters. One other point to watch is that the goods may be on special offer. If they are, the prices are not really representative of those over a longer period. There should be some way of showing any price that is not a normal one.

You are unlikely to have designed a form with the same layout. You should have one which covers the same basic points, though. It should also enable comparisons to be made easily.

3 There is only one good way of finding out the profits and that is to abstract the data from the records. To ask the owner and to take his word for it is rather risky. Observation would be impractical and profits are not something that can be inspected.

But there is no guarantee that the records are correct. Even without blatant falsification, they could be very misleading.

Interviewing: talking to people

Self-check

Suppose you are a manufacturer who wants to launch a new product but who is not certain what customer response wll be. You decide to find out what people think of the idea of your new product. What do you think would be the advantages and disadvantages of using interviews to obtain this information?

A more general list of advantages and disadvantages of interviews is given below, but your answers should be covered by it. The main advantages of interviews are:

• only about one in twenty people refuse to be interviewed in surveys, which is far lower than the proportion who fail to return questionnaires;

- the interviewers can assist the people being interviewed (the 'respondents') to understand the questions (though they must take care not to influence the answers);
- difficulty with one question does not result in the loss of answers to all of them as it may do with questionnaires (which people tend not to give back in such cases);
- the respondent does not know what other questions are coming when he answers one, and so these cannot influence his reply;
- spontaneous answers can be obtained;
- face-to-face contact can tell the interviewer a lot about respondents, e.g. whether they are reluctant to answer the question.

The chief disadvantages are:

- when used in surveys, they are very expensive because interviewers with the right personal qualities (e.g. tactful, methodical, unbiased) have to be recruited, trained and paid;
- the interviewers, despite their training, may influence respondents' answers;
- it might prove difficult to find a convenient time for interviewing certain people, e.g. those on night work;
- the face-to-face situation may itself affect replies, especially when the interviewer is of the opposite sex to the respondent, e.g. men may exaggerate their masculine qualities to a woman interviewer;
- there is little time for considered replies or looking up information.

In most interviews an 'interview schedule' is kept to strictly. This is just like a questionnaire. It tells the interviewers what questions to ask. They then have to fill in the answers they receive. The construction of interview schedules is discussed later in this chapter.

Interviews may also be conducted over the telephone.

Self-check

Can you think what advantages and disadvantages this may have over ordinary interviews?

The principal advantages of telephone interviews over face-to-face ones are:

- they are cheaper;
- they save time, e.g. on travelling.

The main disadvantages are:

- not everyone has a telephone;
- they have to be fairly brief;
- there is not the same degree of personal contact;
- it is easy for people to put the phone down at any point.

The fact that not everyone has a telephone can be a serious drawback if a cross-section of the public is required, since possession of one tends to depend on social class. Distorted results would then be obtained. This point is taken up again in the next chapter. Because virtually all businesses are on the telephone, this method can safely be used with business market research, however.

Margaret used the interview technique when asking some people queuing in the canteen what they thought of having TVP in the meat meals. She undoubtedly did so because she wanted to judge their reactions as well as get an answer to her question. She also wished to make sure they understood the question. For this, she had to have personal contact.

Interviews are used to obtain information such as:

- beliefs, opinions, attitudes, e.g. in public opinion polls;
- intentions, e.g. in polls on voting intentions;
- preferences, e.g. in market research surveys;
- habits, e.g. in market research surveys.

Self-check

You have to be very careful when using data on intentions. Can you see why? Think of Margaret in the scenario. She asked her customers how they would react if she were to put TVP in their meat. Would this mean that, if they said they wouldn't mind, she could safely go ahead and put it in?

The problem with intentions is that they tell us only what people *say* they will do, which is not necessarily what they will do in the event. When it comes to it, Margaret's customers might hate the TVP.

Self-check

A market research firm has been asked to find out what proportion of GPs in the UK have a telephone answering service. They select a number of doctors from whom to obtain the sample data. What data collection technique do you say they should use?

Since all GPs have a telephone, it would be possible to phone them up to find out if they had a telephone answering service. This would have the added advantage that if the phone was answered by such a service, the question would also be answered. A questionnaire could be used, but the disadvantages outlined in the next section may well be unacceptable here.

Activity

Select some 'victims', preferably family or friends, and interview them to find out whether, if there were to be another referendum on staying in the EEC, they would vote for Britain to stay in or get out. What was the percentage in favour of staying in? Were there many don't-knows? Did you run up against any difficulties?

Questionnaires: writing to people

Self-check

Imagine that you want to find out how many firms in your area have job vacancies. You decide to send out a questionnaire to them to get this data. Could you think of what advantages and disadvantages this would have over other possible data collection methods?

You should find the answer to this question covered by the following list, which is in fact more general.

The main advantages of using questionnaires are:

- low cost;
- they can be distributed widely and to a great many people;
- the respondents can complete them in their own time;
- there is no possibility of interviewer bias;
- they allow time for considered opinions, consultation of records, etc.

The principal disadvantages are:

- the proportion of forms returned (the response rate) can be very low, less than one in five sometimes;
- there is no control over how long it takes people to reply;
- the answers may not be those of the respondent alone;
- there is no spontaneity;
- knowledge of what questions are to come later may influence answers to earlier ones, e.g. if a later question is thought impertinent by the respondent, or if its purpose is one with which he deeply disagrees;
- if a respondent has difficulty with a question, he may not return the form;
- misunderstanding of the questions cannot be corrected;
- only rather straightforward questions can be set;
- they are difficult to design;
- they can be irksome to complete.

A poor response rate is a much greater disadvantage than might at first sight appear.

Self-check

Can you see why? Think of the kind of people who would and wouldn't reply to a questionnaire asking them how profitable their small business was.

The major problem here is that those replies which are returned are unlikely to be representative of the whole group to whom questionnaires were sent and so give misleading data. For example, if a questionnaire is sent to firms asking for information reflecting on their performance, those not doing very well may be less likely to respond than ones which are flourishing.

This particular problem is seldom met where there is a legal obligation to reply. In other cases, following up the initial contact can increase the response rate significantly. Where a telephone call is possible this is the cheapest and most convenient way to do it. This would apply, for example, in a survey of business.

Margaret used a questionnaire, albeit a simple one, to collect views from as many of those who tried the TVP meals as she could. She did this because she could not spare the time to talk to them all. Sixty per cent of those who normally ate in the canteen returned her form. However, this did not mean that only sixty per cent had tried a TVP meal, since some of those who had may not have bothered to complete a questionnaire. There are thus a few doubts about the results of this exercise (as in most cases whatever the method, in fact).

Questionnaires are used, for example, in:

- surveys of business;
- government censuses;
- members of a club, society, etc.;
- ballots.

Self-check

A micro-computer manufacturer sends round a questionnaire to further education colleges asking what computing facilities they have. There is a space on the form where they can write 'none' if they have none. It is fairly obvious from the form that the purpose of it is to get information that will help the firm to find out where the market lies. What type of college is likely to reply and what type is not likely to? How could the manufacturer get a better *initial* response rate?

Basically, colleges with someone there interested in computers would tend to be the ones who replied. Often this would be to get further information on the product for teaching purposes, rather than out of any serious desire to buy. Those colleges with no computer facilities and no one interested in them would tend not to reply. An increased initial response rate could be obtained by offering an inducement, such as a chance to win one of the microcomputers (if the information and the attendant publicity is worth it to the firm).

Questionnaire design: the art of asking questions

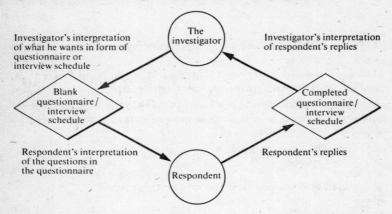

Figure 4. Information flow for data collection by questionnaire or interview

The design of questions for both interview schedules and questionnaires requires careful thought. Figure 4 illustrates some of the points where communication may break down in the data collection process when using either.

To avoid this, questions must be designed to obtain the exact information required as directly as possible. So, 'If cigarettes were cheaper would you smoke more?' is a poor question.

Self-check

Can you see what is wrong with it?

Hypothetical questions of this type can yield information *only* on what the respondent thinks would happen, not what actually would happen. Quite obviously such information could only be collected after the event.

Questions should, as far as possible, be incapable of misinterpretation by the respondent. So, 'What is your favourite drink?' can give you false data.

|| *Self-check*
||
|| What's wrong here?

This may be taken to mean either alcoholic ones or all drinks including water.

Questions should be short, simple and to the point. 'Have you ever been involved in an accident while driving a vehicle not belonging to you in which a third party was injured who subsequently received compensation on an insurance policy held by you?' would put anybody off.

|| *Self-check*
||
|| Can you suggest how it could be improved?

It would be better split into separate questions and rephrased.

It should be within the competence of the respondent to understand and answer the questions. So, 'Is the microchip a threat to employment?' may cause problems.

|| *Self-check*
||
|| Can you see why?

As phrased, this implies a godlike awareness on the part of the respondent. It ought at least to begin with something like 'Do you believe. . .' Even then it presumes a knowledge of what the microchip is. Despite extensive media coverage, not everyone has this.

Questions should not involve the respondent in any calculations (which he may get wrong). So, 'What is your weekly wage?' should not be asked where people are paid monthly.

> *Self-check*
>
> Why?

If the correspondent is paid monthly he would have to multiply his monthly salary by twelve and divide by fifty-two to get the right answer. He will probably just divide by four.

Questions should be precise. 'Do you spend a lot of money each week on cigarettes?' would receive very unreliable responses.

> *Self-check*
>
> What's the problem here do you think?

What is 'a lot'?

Questions should not lead respondents. 'Do you agree that the government should act to save lives by making it an offence not to wear a seat belt when driving?' is a leading question.

> *Self-check*
>
> What answer does this suggest?

This suggests a 'yes' answer.

Questions should not use emotive language. 'Do you think it right that the government should interfere with a driver's freedom not to wear a seat belt if he or she so wishes?' could well unduly influence the respondent.

> *Self-check*
>
> Can you offer a better version of the same question?

'Interfering with freedom' is emotive and unnecessary. 'Should there be a law that all car drivers wear seat belts?' is quite sufficient.

Questions should not be offensive. 'Do people complain that

your breath smells?' might well be considered at least an impolite
question by many.

The questionnaire, or interview schedule, should itself be:

- as short as possible while consistent with its objectives;
- well laid out, with adequate space for answers where
  necessary;
- structured so that the questions have some logical order. This
  can sometimes help the respondent to recall a past event by
  taking him through ones that lead up to it.

Wherever possible a choice of answers should be given on the
form. The one selected can then be ringed, ticked, underlined or
otherwise indicated. These should be as simple as can be devised
while adequately representing what is intended. This problem
was discussed earlier in terms of classifying data collected and
you should consult the relevant sections for details. Here we will
look at some examples in relation to questions on question-
naires/interview schedules.

Suppose we ask Scotsmen, 'Do you wear a kilt?' If the answer
were left to the respondent we could get a number of different
replies, such as, 'Only on Burns Night.' These could prove hard
to categorize (something that must be done before a statistical
analysis can sensibly be made).

If the choice of answers is 'yes' or 'no', 'no' could mean 'not all
the time', while 'yes' could mean 'occasionally'. A 'rating scale'
might be used, allowing more choices. Five is a number commonly used. With this question we could have, for instance,
'never', 'occasionally', 'sometimes', 'often', 'always'.

Take another question, 'Do you prefer face powder A or B?'
Allowing the answers 'A' or 'B' or 'neither' does not tell us the
extent of the difference.

Self-check

How could we get round this difficulty?

We could ask the respondent to choose from 'A strongly', 'A
slightly', 'no preference', 'B slightly', 'B strongly'.

We could also ask her to give each powder a mark out of ten. Where a comparison of more than two items is required, respondents can be asked to place these in order preference.

Numeric answers do not have to be classified (though they may be) as statistical operations can be performed on them directly. Consider the question, How many cigarettes do you smoke a day on average? The answers could be recorded as given (and grouped later if required). However, it is unlikely that we are going to get answers like 'Thirteen' or 'Twenty-one'. The respondents themselves will 'round' their replies to at least the nearest five. It would actually be better in this case to offer them the choice of say 0–5, 5–10, 10–20, 20–30, 30–40, 40–50, 50 and over. This would ensure that everyone was using the same classification system for their answers.

Self-check

1 Look at the questionnaire below. What do you think are its faults? Rewrite it to correct these.

   Questionnaire on opinions on a new political party

   If there were to be a brand new political party, say the Middle-of-the-Road Party, which Roy Perfect and his cohorts – together with other deserters from the Labour Party – have publicized, would you vote for them if they joined in with the Liberals or didn't?

   yes/no   Delete whichever alternative you don't think is the right one.

2 Design a short questionnaire in order to find out whether people believe that smoking should be banned in various types of specified public place – e.g. cinemas, buses, trains, cafes; make up your own list. Include in the questions one on whether or not they smoke and if so how much.

   If possible, get several of your family and friends to fill in the questionnaire. What was the result? Did you encounter any problems? Were the views of smokers and non-smokers different?

ANSWERS

1 There is a great deal wrong with the questionnaire. Basically the question is far too complicated. The instructions on how to complete it are very bad too. The description of Roy Perfect's 'cohorts' and of 'deserters' is emotive and should be deleted. There are actually at least two questions here so they have to be stated separately. You should have a questionnaire that looks something like this:

Questionnaire on voting intentions for a new political party
Suppose that a new 'Middle-of-the-Road' Party is formed with policies as outlined by Roy Perfect and others.

Q1 Would you vote for a candidate of such a party if   Please tick
there were an alliance between it and the Liberal
Party?   *yes* ☐ *no* ☐

Q2 Would you vote for such a candidate if   Please tick
there were no such alliance?   *yes* ☐ *no* ☐

2 A suitable questionnaire would be as follows.
Q1 Do you think smoking should be totally banned in
(a) cinemas?
(b) cafés?   *yes/no**
(c) all parts of buses?   *yes/no**
(d) all coaches in trains?   *yes/no**
                                                  yes/no*

Q2 Do you think smoking should be banned in any other public places?   *yes/no**
If so, which (please specify) _____

Q3 Do you smoke regularly (i.e. once or more each day)?   *yes/no**
If so, do you *mostly* smoke   *a pipe/cigars/cigarettes**

Q4. How many times do you have a smoke each day on average? (Please tick one answer)

less than once	
once or twice	
from three to five times	
from six to ten times	
from eleven to twenty times	
from twenty-one to forty times	
more than forty times	

* Please delete the inappropriate answer.

Note that 'regularly' has been defined exactly; that, except in one case, the respondents have been given a set of answers to choose from; and that the different types of smoker have been separated out.

Review

1 In January 1973, Haymarket Publishing brought out a weekly magazine, in conjunction with the British Computer Society, called *Computing*. This was supposedly to replace the monthly *Computer Bulletin* which had been published by the society until December 1972. Both were free to its members. A telephone survey of some of them at work showed, however, that while *Computing* was felt to be good (and indeed is still going strong) it was not thought to adequately take the place of the old *Bulletin*. A new series of this was, therefore, started again in September 1974, and it still continues to be published. Why do you think it was thought possible/desirable to conduct a telephone survey in this case?

2 The committee of the Fir Cone Collectors Society of Great Britain wanted to make several amendments to the rules which would allow 'children' aged ten to eighteen to join but not be eligible to serve on the committee. The secretary sent a questionnaire to all members, with the monthly newsletter, which set out details of these. They were asked to return, at their own expense, a form indicating their willingness or otherwise to accept these changes. About fifty per cent of them did. Roughly half of these rejected the idea while the rest were in favour. What would you advise the secretary to do now? What do you think were the major reasons why some members didn't reply.

3 Comment on the wording of the question in Margaret's questionnaire in the scenario.

ANSWERS

1 The British Computer Society is composed of computer professionals. It is unlikely that they would not be available on the telephone at work or at home. The society would also

have a good set of information on their members, including their current address and place of work in many cases. So it was possible to contact them by phone in this case.

It was thought desirable to do so because the response rate would be much higher than with a questionnaire and because the members' views could be obtained better this way. They could be taken up on certain points or asked to explain. In terms of the data gained, it was cheaper than a postal questionnaire too.

You may have missed the point about it being actually cheaper, but you should have got the idea that the members were on the phone and so could be contacted directly.

2 The committee have received about twenty-five per cent of the members' support. Assuming that there are no special rules the club has in such circumstances, it is worth while the committee going ahead with their plan nevertheless. The majority of those who did not reply would be 'don't cares'. They would be willing to take either step. Of course, there may be some who had views but who did not think they should spend their own money to tell the committee what these were. There does not seem any justification for assuming that such people would be mostly for, or mostly against, the proposal, however.

As the committee was elected by the members to run the club, and as no clear view either way was obtained from the questionnaire, it should do what it thinks fit. Since the proposal comes from it, this would be to make the amendments.

It is possible that you have said that there was no mandate for going ahead with the changes. In this you are right. Equally, though, there is no clear majority against doing so. In cases like this, those who do not reply need not be considered unless there is any reason to suppose that their views on the point in question show any similarities.

3 The question is not emotive; which it easily could have been under the circumstances. It is important to note that all the figures were given on the form so the workers were able to make a reasoned judgement. Given this, the question is a good statement of what must be decided, though the last phrase about keeping the prices down is probably unnecess-

ary. The notes would have made clear what the savings would be. One point of difficulty, though, is that 'suitable meat dishes' is a little vague. However, short of going into a cookery lesson, it is hard to see what else Margaret could say.

There is one major point about the whole questionnaire. The workers are asked to respond to *one* plan only. It would have been possible to have offered them a choice of percentages of TVP, with different consequent savings. The question would then have been much more complicated, of course. But it would have given a wider range of choice, and some of those who answered no to the given question may have said yes to a different mix.

You may have a somewhat different answer. If you have covered the same sort of points then this is all right. You probably won't have mentioned the last part about choice though. You could easily have said other things about the question. Check back with the text to make sure what you said is valid.

Scenario 3
A new product

In Chapter 2 the idea of collecting not all data, but only a representative sample, was introduced. As you read through this scenario, which illustrates how this technique may be used in business (in marketing research, in fact), make a mental note of where sample data is collected. You will see how the data collection methods outlined in Chapter 3 are employed. Chapters 4 and 5 outline the techniques that can be used for selecting exactly what data should be collected.

Gourmet Foods Ltd had been turning in consistent but rather uninspiring results for some time, while similar companies seemed to be expanding and increasing profits. Finally, at one board meeting, the chairman expressed his dissatisfaction with this state of affairs and said that something ought to be done to avoid stagnation. After some discussion, the board decided that, as well as mounting a special drive on current products, some new ones should be introduced.

Roger Court, the marketing director, was asked to look into the possibilities in this direction. He remembered an idea which Kevin Collier, the Baby Gourmet brand manager, had told him about several times. This had originated with customers and been passed on to Kevin by the sales representatives. It was to extend the Baby Gourmet range to cater for the older baby also. The new meals would not be so bland nor have such a smooth consistency as the existing ones. So Roger asked Kevin to prepare a proposal for such a new product.

A short time later, after having consulted colleagues in various departments, Kevin produced his report. In it he concluded that sales of the new product should be good, and cited the success of other companies in the same field. When Roger presented Kevin's report to the board they reacted very favourably to it. The directors gave the go-ahead for a detailed study to cover what foods should be included in the new range, as well as projected production and marketing costs, estimates of sales and so on.

The detailed costings were undertaken and proved satisfactory. The next stage of the exercise was 'concept testing'. It was assumed that the vast majority of potential customers would already be purchasing Baby Gourmet foods. So a number of retail outlets which stocked these were selected. In each of them, spot interviews were conducted over a period of time. Women who bought any Baby Gourmet jars were asked whether they would purchase Junior Gourmet foods later, if these were available at the projected price. This survey was carried out with the aid of a market research agency.

When results of this inquiry showed wide approval for the new product range, the Baby Gourmet chef was asked to prepare some samples for trials with babies. The main objective of these was to obtain the reactions of babies and their mothers to the meals themselves, regardless of brand or price. For this reason, the trial jars were labelled only with their contents. The same market research agency was involved in selecting those who took part in these 'blind tests' as carried out the survey.

Each mother involved in the trials was issued with enough Junior Gourmet foods of various types to last a month. In return, she was asked to fill in a questionnaire at the end of this time (explained to her beforehand). This asked a number of questions on each different type of meal. For example, she was asked to report on how much the baby liked or disliked it and on her feelings about its nutritional goodness. She was also asked to give each one an overall mark out of ten.

After the tests, the unpopular meals were discarded. There were still a number that had good overall scores and these were chosen to form the basis of the new range of products under the Junior Gourmet brand name. The board gave the go-ahead on this range and everyone involved began to work hard to make it a success.

In the scenario, the market research into the acceptability of the new product was carried out on samples; that is, not even all the available data was collected. Cost is obviously one reason why this may be done. But there are others, and these are discussed in the following chapter. Just how the samples are chosen is of vital importance. Remember that they should really be representative of the data as a whole.

This is the question that is looked at in the next two chapters. The scenario will be used to illustrate the answers, but other examples will be given in addition. When you have completed these units you should understand why sometimes sample data is used and be familiar with the major techniques available for obtaining samples. You should also be able to select an appropriate one from these in simple cases and to comment critically on those adopted for obtaining samples in other investigations.

4 | Letting a few represent many

Why we might not collect all the data available to us

As outlined above, sometimes we do not collect all the data that is available to us, but only a proportion of it. The data we do collect is called a 'sample', and the process of collecting it is called 'sampling'. When we collect all the data this is called a 'census'. Some reasons for sampling were given earlier, but we are going to look at them in more detail here.

Self-check

A car manufacturer wants to find out whether its customers are satisfied with their products. So they send out a questionnaire to a smallish sample of them. Why didn't they send one to them all?

It would have been ludicrously expensive to have done so. So expense is one reason for taking samples.

Self-check

One of an auditor's jobs is to make sure that items of data (e.g. receipts) are correctly processed. When auditing a company's accounts, rather than looking at all receipts, an auditor will generally follow through just a few of them. Why is this?

The main difficulty is that he just simply would not have the time to look at them all. So lack of time is another reason for taking samples. Of course, since time is money, the problem is to a certain extent also one of money.

Self-check

The owner of a timber plantation organized a team of twenty-five people to count all the trees in it and got 27,402. Do you think that this was exactly right?

It is highly unlikely. Almost certainly some trees were counted twice and one or more miscounts occurred. Provided that the density of trees was fairly constant, it would have been very nearly as accurate to have counted the number of trees in, say, 1000 square metres and multiplied up to get the total in the whole plantation. For example, if there were 280 trees in the 1000-square-metre sample, and if the plantation was 100,000 square metres in area (i.e. 100 times 1000 square metres), a good estimate of the total number of trees would be $100 \times 280 = 28,000$. Another reason for taking samples, then, is that collecting all the data could, because of the complexity of the operation, be virtually as inaccurate as if a sample were taken.

Self-check

Suppose we wanted to measure the blood pressure of a group of executives. How many readings would it be possible to take *in theory* from each of them, supposing a reading could be taken as quickly as required?

The answer is as large a number as we care to name. If we could take a reading in zero time we could take an infinite number of them. In practice, of course, it would not be possible to take more than a few of these readings. That is, we would be forced to take a sample. Yet another reason for taking a sample is, then, that the amount of data may be infinite.

As a matter of interest, we could take a continuous reading of blood pressure, using some device that drew it on a graph. The point still holds, however, since if we wanted *figures* for it, we could still only choose some of the *infinite* number of points on the graph.

Self-check

A firm makes poles for vaulting. It wants to test them to find out what their breaking point is. What can't all of them be tested?

If they were, the firm would never produce any poles for sale! So yet another reason why sampling may be used is because getting the data might actually destroy its source.

There are several reasons then, why we may take samples rather than collect even all the *available* data.

- the cost of collecting it all may be prohibitive, e.g. no market research could be afforded which surveyed the whole population;
- the time scale may be such that the results would not be ready in reasonable time if all the data was used, e.g. in an audit not every single figure can be checked;
- sample data might actually prove more accurate; being less of it, there is less chance of error, e.g. a large group of people cooperating to collect data could introduce errors;
- it may be impossible even in theory to examine all the data, e.g. when it is infinite, such as a person's blood pressure over time;
- obtaining the data may damage the source, e.g. in destructive testing, such as with vaulting poles to find their breaking point.

Self-check

What were the examples of sampling in the scenario? In each case, why were samples taken rather than the whole of the available data being collected?

There were two examples of sampling in the scenario. The first was when the concept testing was carried out. A sample of the views of those buying Baby Gourmet food was taken. The second was when a number of babies were chosen to be fed with 'sample' Junior Gourmet food. Note that this use of the word 'sample' is not quite the same as that in statistics, though it is connected. You should not, then, have included the production of Junior Gourmet food samples in your list of examples of sampling.

In both cases the reasons for not collecting all the data that was available were:

(a) it would have been too expensive (you should have this one if not the other two);
(b) the whole exercise would have been so cumbersome that many errors would have crept in anyway;
(c) the job could never have been finished in time.

Choosing from the available data

Activity

Get your local telephone directory out. (If you haven't got one you should find one in a telephone booth or post office.) Suppose we want to find out about the length of subscribers' surnames. Pick twenty private subscribers from it, in any way you like. Count the number of letters in the subscriber's surname in each case and write down the results.

You have not counted the number of letters in the surnames of every private subscriber in the directory. So you have actually taken a sample; you have not collected all the data that was available to you.

Self-check

What data was available to you?

Well, you could have counted the number of letters in the surname of any of the private subscribers listed in the directory. These, then, together make up the data available to you. Such data is called the 'population'. That is, the population consists of all the data that could be included in the sample; here, all the private subscribers' surnames.

Note that a population does not need to refer to people. It

might, for instance, be some data concerned with all cars with UK registration, all entries in a set of accounting books and so on. In practice, it is often the sources of information themselves which are said to be the population. So, in the example above, this would be all cars with UK number plates and all entries in the books. The same applies to samples: we apply the term to those sources which are chosen. This is merely a convenience and it must always be remembered that, strictly speaking, it is the data we are sampling and not its sources.

Self-check

From what populations were the samples in the scenario taken?

A sample of babies (and their mothers) was used to test the new junior food. The population in this case was all babies in the UK in the appropriate age range and their mothers. But, prior to this, the choice of people for the concept testing also involved sampling. The population here was everyone buying a jar of Baby Gourmet food during the period of the survey.

Sampling, is, however, only justified if the results obtained are reasonable; that is, if we can draw valid inferences about the population as a whole from the sample taken. Obviously, this can only be so if it adequately represents that population, at least as far as our purposes are concerned. Whether or not this is the case depends crucially on the methods used to select it.

Self-check

In the activity you performed earlier, on the telephone directory, how did you pick out the subscribers whose surnames you used? Do you think the data you obtained was representative of the directory as a whole?

Whether or not it was representative would depend on how you selected the sample.

Self-check

If you had just taken the first twenty private subscribers in the directory do you think this would have given a typical set of data?

In my local directory, fifteen out of the first twenty private subscribers are called 'Aarons'. Obviously taking these would give a very distorted picture. The problem here is that we are giving the names in the first position in the directory an unfair advantage. But, of course, this would be true of any successive set of names. What we really want to do is to dot the names chosen about the whole directory in a 'higgledy-piggledy' way, i.e. such that there is no obvious pattern in their distribution about the directory. The names would then be said to be taken 'at random' from the directory, and the sample so obtained is called a 'random sample'.

Self-check

Suppose we were to base our opinion of what types of car people drove by observing traffic on a busy motorway on a weekday. Would we get a true picture? If not how could we improve it?

We would not get a true picture. We would exclude 'Sunday drivers' and probably many second cars driven by wives, for example. To improve this we would have to observe traffic at a number of different places at random and at a spread of random times.

An equal chance for all

Let's look a little more closely at what random means. We'll use ERNIE (Electronic Random Number Indicator Equipment) as an example. ERNIE is the machine that picks the winning premium bond numbers.

| *Self-check*

| Given any two premium bond numbers, what can we say about each one's chances of winning a prize?

We can say that they should be equal. No one bond should have a better chance of winning a prize than any other.

| *Self-check*

| And what can we say about the pattern of winning numbers?

It should be a random one. So, for example, ERNIE shouldn't consistently produce more winners from among the later issues of bonds than the earlier ones, as it is rumoured is the case.

The fact that the bonds have all got equal chances of winning will, of itself, produce random patterns of winners. These two conditions are thus, in effect, equivalent. This can be seen from a simple experiment.

| *Activity*

| Take a sheet of paper and cut it into fifty equal-sized rectangular shapes. Number them from 1 to 50 and fold them up so that the number written on each is concealed. Put them all into a small box and shake them up, then pick out just one of them. Copy down its number, refold it and put it back in the box. Repeat the process ten times, shaking the box each time.

This activity imitates the operation of ERNIE. In this case, though, there are only fifty bond holders and only one winner each time. What results have you got? There should be no pattern in the winning numbers. If there is, it is by sheer chance. Do it again and you shouldn't get one a second time. When the author tried it he obtained the following winners: 9, 49, 48, 28, 1, 28, 20, 21, 47, 29.

|| *Self-check*

Self-check

Do you see something interesting in this set of numbers?

There are two 28s. Because the slips were returned to the box each time, it was possible for a number to come up more than once. This is what happens with ERNIE. Just because a bond wins one prize, it doesn't prevent it from winning another.

Now how does all this tie up with random sampling? Well, saying that the items of data in a sample should be taken at random from the population is equivalent to saying that all the data in the population should have an equal chance of being included in the sample.

If each member of the population were allocated a number, this could be written on the equivalent of a raffle ticket. The draw could be made from a revolving drum and the 'winning' ticket would be included in the sample. Note that it is the mixing up of the tickets when the drum is turned that makes the draw random. This operation will be repeated a number of times equal to the required size of the sample. A sample selected in such a way is called a 'simple random sample'.

Self-check

In your activity, the slips were replaced after each draw. What would happen with the above random sample if the same thing was to be done?

Some of the data could be included more than once in the sample. This is not generally desirable. We wouldn't, for example, interview someone twice, or even count their views twice, in a survey! We could get round this by not putting the slip back in the box after a draw. This is then called 'sampling without replacement', as opposed to 'sampling with replacement', which is when they are put back.

Self-check

For each case below, say whether the sample is a simple random one or not. Give the reasons for your decision.

1 A survey interviewer goes to a busy supermarket on its late night closing and interviews the first twenty women she meets about their views on supermarkets being open for a late night.

2 A school head-teacher, who is a strict disciplinarian, wants to find out what the views of the other teachers in his school are on corporal punishment. He sends round a note asking anyone who wishes to let him have their opinion to do so within twenty-four hours.

3 In a dispute at a factory, the management agree to meet with the shop stewards to discuss the problem. But they also ask for five other men from the shop floor to be present and for these to be chosen on a random basis. The names of all shop floor workers are written down on pieces of paper, identical in appearance, which are then folded over once and put into a hat. They are then all shaken up together and a shop steward pulls out five of them.

ANSWERS

1 This is certainly not a simple random sample. In the first place, to ask late night shoppers their views on late night shopping would result in a very biased picture. But, in addition, it isn't even a random sample of these shoppers, with the first twenty met being interviewed. A small group of them could even be friends, with similar views, out shopping together.

2 Volunteers never form a random sample, since, by definition, they are not representative of the population in that they have come forward while the others have not. In this case it is even worse. The head is a strict disciplinarian, so teachers with contrary views would be inhibited from putting them forward. Furthermore, the time limit of twenty-four hours will ensure that many teachers, those absent, for example, do not reply anyway.

3 Here there is a true simple random sample, since the selection is performed exactly according to rules that define one. Each shop floor worker has an equal chance of being picked.

It is important to note that having a random sample does not *guarantee* that it will be highly representative of the population as a whole. This is illustrated most easily by means of an example. Suppose we decide to check how adequate the maintenance on a fleet of 200 hire cars is by inspecting a random sample of twenty of them.

Self-check

If there are three that have not been serviced properly, how many of them do you think might be included in the sample?

By sheer chance it would be possible for none, one, two or even all three of these to be included in the sample. If all three were, you would think the fleet was more badly maintained than it really was, but if none were, you would think it was better.

Activity

Collect three two-pence pieces having the same date and seventeen more having a different date to this (but not necessarily to each other). These coins represent cars in a fleet (a small one to save you expense!). The three coins having the chosen date are cars which have not been serviced properly. Put all the coins in a bag and shake them up. Take out four at random. This represents a twenty-per-cent random sample of the cars. How many of the poorly maintained ones are in it? Repeat the experiment several times to see what different samples occur.

What results did you get? Did any one of your samples contain all three poorly serviced cars? If you didn't know exactly how many poorly maintained cars there were, what would you have thought about the maintenance standards of your fleet of twenty cars from the results of your samples?

Self-check

Which do you think more likely: that your sample contains all three poorly serviced cars or just one of them?

It is more likely that it would contain just one of them. To see this, look at the very simple situation outlined below (which would, of course, never occur in real life). Say there were only six cars in the fleet and that two of them were badly maintained. Let's call the cars A, B, C, D, E and F. Suppose A and B are poorly maintained.

Self-check

Write down the constitution of all the possible random samples of three cars.

The easiest way to do this is to write them out in alphabetical order. If we do this we get

ABC	ABD	ABE	ABF
ACD	ACE	ACF	
ADE	ADF		
AEF			
BCD	BCE	BCF	
BDE	BDF		
BEF			
CDE	CDF		
CEF			
DEF			

Note that ABC is the same sample as BCA, CBA, BAC, CAB or ACB. That is, the order in which the sample data is chosen is immaterial.

Self-check

Is there any reason why any one of these samples should have a different chance of occurring than any other?

None whatsoever. Since each car has the same chance of being chosen, we could change round all the letters and it should make no difference to the actual results. This, incidentally, shows that in simple random sampling, each possible sample has the same chance of occurring.

Self-check

How many of these samples have
a both badly maintained cars in them?
b only one of them in?

The top four are the only samples with both A and B in them, but there are six with only A in and six with only B in. If you said that there were ten in each case, you were including the ones with both in again! So if each possible sample is equally likely to occur, and there are more of them with only one of the badly maintained cars in than there are with both of them in, the former must have a greater chance of occurring than the latter. This explains the answer to the self-check on page 98.

To some extent, the problem of the non-representative sample can be avoided by taking bigger samples. This point will be taken up in Volume 2. Furthermore, you will be shown how allowances can be made for the fact that a sample may not be fully representative of the data as a whole. For the time being, however, you should remember that there may be this problem.

Self-check

A greengrocer has stored some apples in a box. He opens it up and takes out two apples completely at random. They are both bad. Does it necessarily mean that all or even most of the apples in the box are rotten?

No it doesn't. Since only two were chosen, it might well be that these are two of the very few rotten ones in the whole lot. Had he taken more out and found that these too were rotten, it would, of course, have made the situation more likely to be that there were a number of bad apples in the box.

Review

1 The proportion of people in the UK who were dissatisfied with the cars they drove was estimated from a sample. From what population would this have been drawn? Why weren't all of its members contacted?

2 The temperature in a particular room housing a computer had to be kept within strict limits otherwise errors occurred in the functioning of the computer. An automatic control system was used for this purpose. It was important to know if at any time the temperature had gone outside this range.

A check was kept on the automatic system by taking the temperature in the room daily at noon. From what population was this taken? Was it adequate? Why weren't all temperatures in the population taken?

3 An interviewer for a sample survey on the purchasing habits of young mothers goes to a baby clinic when it opens. She interviews the first mother to come *out* of the clinic. When she has finished, she approaches the next one to come out and so on, until ten of them have been interviewed. Does this constitute a random sample of young mothers who attend the clinic? If not, why?

ANSWERS

1 The population here is all drivers of cars in the UK. The reasons that not all of them were contacted were that it would be grossly expensive, even if it could be done, and that it would take far too long to find them all, even if the funds to do so were made available. It is also likely that, with so large a volume of data, too many mistakes would be made. You may have simply.said that it was the expense. Naturally this is the overriding reason, but it should be realized that, even if there was no problem in that area, not all the available data would need to be collected anyway.

2 Here the population was all the temperatures at every possible time of the day. Since there were an infinite number of such possible times, it would have been totally impossible to have taken the temperature at all of them. However, the one sample daily at noon was scarcely sufficient. The control system could have gone wrong at any time. Say at one minute past noon! Indeed, it would not have been possible to take the temperature often enough to protect the computer unless there was someone full time on the job. This was an obvious

case for automation. A warning bell could have gone off should the control have failed.

You should have got the idea about the infinite population. If you said it was a matter of cost, you forgot it would be impossible to collect all the data in this case.

3 No it does not. The essence of a random sample is that each member of the population is equally likely to be picked for it. Here, the mothers who get to the clinic first are the ones chosen. They are likely to be mothers who differ substantially from the others who come later. Those who come later may have part-time jobs, for example. Mothers with part-time jobs may have purchasing habits quite different from those without part-time jobs.

Knowing what data exists

Self-check

If every item of data in the population is to have an equal chance of being included in the sample, this presupposes certain things. Can you say what the most important of these are?

It does, of course, presuppose that all the data is accessible. This was discussed in Chapter 2. Also, since each item of data must be allocated a number, we need to know about them. This implies that we could either specify all the sources or, if there were too many, at least give a rule for finding every one of them. That is, we could produce what is termed a 'sampling frame'. Suppose, for example, that the management of a steelworks wanted to find out if customers were satisfied with the quality of the steel delivered to them. If this was to be done by selecting a random sample of customers, a list of these would be required from which to choose. This would be the sampling frame.

Self-check

Suggest a possible source for a sampling frame for a survey of medical doctors. How suitable would it be?

The General Medical Council keep a register of doctors eligible to practise. You have heard of being 'struck off the register', no doubt. The register would be a very good source for a sampling frame if you wanted to compile information on medical doctors. However, it should be remembered that they would not all be general practitioners or even practising doctors at all (e.g. they could have retired).

One case when it is always impossible to produce a list of this type is where the population is infinite. For example, if we wanted to sample the blood pressure of a hospital patient over a 24-hour period, we could not list all possible times at which measurements might be taken. But here we could simply say that any random set of times in the given period would be suitable, i.e. we could state a rule. Thus we have a sampling frame and could still take a random sample. There are, however, several obstacles which could actually prevent the taking of such a sample.

Self-check

Where in the scenario on page 87 would it have been possible to produce a sampling frame and where not? Where possible, would it have been practically feasible?

Sometimes the population is so large that the preparation of a sampling frame is not financially feasible. For example, in the scenario, there was no frame for the babies who tested the new product. In theory one could have been compiled from the registrations of birth. In practice, however, this would have been impossible. The government, with the resources at its disposal, can often keep information on large populations. For instance, it has details of all cars registered in Britain. Local government keeps a register of electors and this is frequently used in sample surveys.

Another common obstacle is the sheer difficulty of listing some of the populations. Perhaps the relevant data is simply not available or the population may change too rapidly. Again, in the scenario, there was no frame for those buying a jar of Baby Gourmet food. Confidentiality of the information on births given to the registrar would also make it impossible to compile a frame for babies to test the new product, even if resources were available to attempt it.

Where no sampling frame exists, random samples cannot be taken. Other techniques are, however, available and these are discussed in the next chapter.

Even if a sampling frame does exist it may prove difficult to use. Problems will occur if it is not complete or if it contains some member of the population more than once. When the latter happens the chances of that one being included in the sample are stronger than if it appeared only once. The frame may also contain unwanted members. The problem then arises of what to do if one of these is selected in the sample. This is discussed later in this chapter. Changes to the sampling frame to remove these difficulties are not always easy to make where there is a large population.

Self-check

Suppose that we want to contact a random sample of suppliers of different products and that we have a list of suppliers for each. To obtain the sampling frame we combine these separate lists. What difficulties do you think we may encounter?

The sampling frame constructed by merging lists of manufacturers of different classes of product may contain some repetition where, for example, a manufacturer makes more than one of the products. It is also possible that some lists may be out of date, so that some manufacturers that should be included are left out while others which have ceased trading are left in. Great care should, therefore, be exercised when using sampling frames, especially when they are taken from other sources.

Self-check

The electoral register is very often used as a sampling frame at some stage of a sample survey. List some of the drawbacks you think it would have if you wanted to use it for a random sample of families.

One of its biggest drawbacks is that it lists each individual elector. If a random sample is taken straight from it, the larger families, having more entries in the register, have a greater chance of being selected. Also, children are not listed on it, so it doesn't give us any information about how many there are in the family, if any. This may be one of the things we are interested in. There is another possible problem in the presence of lodgers and so on, who also appear on the register. These, too, could throw out the selection procedure.

A simpler method

Selecting a simple random sample can be wearisome, as each single item of data in it must be selected at random. It is for this reason that a rather simpler method is generally used when there is a suitable sampling frame. To introduce it, let's look at an example.

Suppose we want to take a sample of the voting intentions in a particular ward in a city. A sampling frame exists which is absolutely exact, in that it contains the names of everyone entitled to vote. We decide to take a five-per-cent sample.

Self-check

What kind of a sample do you think we would get if we chose every twentieth name on the list? Would it be representative?

First, we can see that this would give us a five-per-cent sample, as required. Second, there is no reason to suppose that it would be unduly unrepresentative of the voters as a whole. For this to be the case, there must be something special about every twentieth person on the register, or at least about many of them. It is difficult to see what this could be. In this respect it is very much like a simple random sample.

Self-check

But, as explained so far at any rate, it is very unlike one in one way. What is this, can you see?

If we start at the beginning, then each person's chances of being included in the sample are far from the same. In fact, each twentieth person is certain to be picked, while all the others are certain not to be.

Self-check

Can you see a way of getting round this?

We can make each person's chances of being included the same if we start the process *at random*. Of course, once the start has been chosen, it becomes certain which persons are going to be selected. Indeed, it is this that makes the method easy to operate. But this does not matter: it is what the chances are before the whole selection process begins that is important.

Self-check

How many names on the register should be eligible to be the first in this sample?

Since we are going to select every twentieth one, it would be sensible to choose one of the first twenty to start from. We could do this by the equivalent of putting the numbers 1–20 in a hat, mixing them up and pulling one out. (In practice, we would use tables of such 'random numbers' that statisticians have provided for this purpose.)

This method of selecting a (random) sample is called 'systematic' or 'equal interval' sampling. Figure 5 illustrates the connection between simple random sampling and systematic sampling.

Self-check

Can you see how systematic sampling could be used in quality testing, of ballpoint pens, for example.

Well, suppose a producer of ballpoint pens wants to examine one per cent of the output for defects. The random number tables are consulted each day to obtain a starting point in the

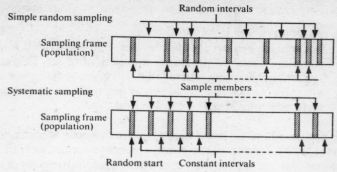

Figure 5. Simple random and systematic sampling

range 1–100. (A different start should be used each time.) Every 100th pen from then on is examined. So if, for instance, the 67th pen off the production line is the first selected, the next will be the 167th, then the 267th and so on. This process will yield a one-per-cent sample as required.

Self-check

Can you see what kind of problems could arise with systematic sampling if the sampling frame were ordered in a particular way? Suppose, for example, that the sampling frame is of streets and house numbers in a new town laid out geometrically, such that every twentieth house is a corner one on each side of the road.

While systematic sampling doesn't guarantee a true random sample, it can give a close approximation if the frame itself is in roughly random order. Problems arise though when there is some regularly recurring pattern in the frame, as in the above one. If a five-per-cent sample is wanted here, and every twentieth house is selected, then there will be either no corner houses in the sample or a great many of them. Either way, the sample will not be a representative one.

Self-check

An interviewer is required to contact five-per-cent of the households in a street of 600 houses. She is provided with a sampling frame of the house numbers in order. Design a systematic sampling scheme that will give as representative a sample as possible. NB: this is not quite as straightforward as it appears.

The problem here is that if every twentieth house is contacted, and the frame consists of the house numbers in order, only those houses down one side of the street will be visited (the odds or the evens, depending on where the start was made). It may well be that the detached houses are all down one side of the road, or some other peculiarity. The sample would not then be representative. The solution is to contact every twentieth house on each side. So two random starts are made, one from an odd random house number between 1 and 39, and the other from an even one between 2 and 40.

Review

1 A college canteen has been losing customers and is threatened with closure in the expenditure cuts taking place. A sample of students' reasons for not using it so much is to be taken. The plan is to get the class registers, shuffle them up and pick twenty out of the sixty. Then interview ten students from each class. Is this a simple random sample? If not, why not? Is it likely to yield a very representative sample? What sampling frame is being used here?

2 Systematic samples of households are to be taken from each of a number of streets in a town. Why is it important that starts should be made at a random house number? Why couldn't they always start at number 1, say?

3 An auditor wants to verify a sample of balances on an accounts receivable file (i.e. the amounts of money owed to the firm). Why would he probably not use a random sample? Could he have done so had he wanted?

4 A lake has been specially stocked with fish for angling.

The owners want to find out how big the fish are. Could they get a simple random sample of them? If not, why not?

ANSWERS

1 The sample here is *not* a simple random one. If you said it was, you missed the fact that not all the classes would have an equal number of students in them. This means that a student in a big class will have less of a chance of being approached than one in a small class. All *classes* will have an equal chance of being chosen, of course, but not the students in them.

   The sample is not likely to be very representative either. With whole classes being excluded, there could easily be no secretarial students, or no craft students, say. As they are likely to differ from other students, this would mean the sample would be unrepresentative. Note that this is *not* just a case of the possibility of such a sample occurring by chance, as described in the text. The fact that whole classes are excluded means that either there are ten secretarial students or none, if there is only one class of them, This could never be the case with simple random sampling. There is a very good sampling frame here indeed. The set of registers would contain the names of all the students at the college (though it might just be possible that the same student is on more than one register!).

2 To answer this question you had to think what could be special about the first house in a street, and possibly about every tenth or twenty-fifth one from then on, or whatever. In the terraced house areas of many parts of Britain the first house in the road could well be a shop. In any case it will be a corner house and, as such, a 'cut above the others' in desirability. The danger in always starting at 1, then, is that too many corner houses would be included and, probably, too many shops.

3 The job of an auditor is basically to prove the company's accounts. But he should also make it his business to check on possible sources of error, fraud, theft, etc. To this end he should investigate thoroughly any 'suspicious' figure. On the accounts receivable file, there may be some amounts which are in excess of what is thought appropriate. If a simple random sample is taken, it is possible that one or more such

figures might escape scrutiny. What usually happens is that all balances over a certain amount are validated, together with a random sample of the rest.

If you said that he couldn't have taken a simple random sample, think of the sampling frame. Here it is the actual figures themselves. All the data is there: it is a matter of choosing what to look at, and follow up. So it would be relatively easy to take a random sample.

4 They could certainly get a simple random sample of the fish in theory. But how would they go about it? It would involve identifying the different fish in some way, e.g. by tags, and then finding exactly the ones picked! Simply to fish for them would not guarantee you would get these, in any reasonable time at least. If you said that it could be done, plan how you would actually go about doing it. Blocking off a section of the lake and gradually forcing the fish out to the edge would not give a random sample. Ask any fisherman and he will tell you that the fish in different sections of a lake are themselves different.

5 | Methods of selecting from available data

Why we need different methods of selecting the data

Self-check

A company manufacturing drugs decides to undertake a survey of doctors' attitudes to prescribing expensive drugs. It is going to use the medical register as a sampling frame. Can you suggest what the difficulties would be in using this to obtain a simple random sample of doctors' opinions?

The answer to this question is contained within the more general list of reasons why a simple random sample may not be used, given below.

The *simple* random sample provides the theoretical basis for sampling. In practice, however, it is not used all that often. The major reasons for this are:

- in surveys the cost would be too high: the sample may, for instance, be widely scattered geographically;
- sometimes some members of the sample are difficult to access; for example, in a survey a person chosen may be ill, out of the country or otherwise unavailable;
- with large populations and samples it is an extremely tedious process, though computers can help here;
- it does on occasion, as mentioned earlier, lead to a distorted sample – a simple random sample of the British electorate could, in theory, contain all Londoners, for example;
- it is seldom that a good enough sampling frame is available.

There are various sampling methods which have been designed to overcome these problems. We can divide them into two basic types:

(a) *Random sampling*, which depends on having some form of sampling frame. Each member of the population has a known and equal chance of being included in the sample.

   Here we can predict the type of sample we are likely to end up with and make allowances for any distortions introduced. How this is done will be covered in Volume 2.

(b) *Non-random sampling*, where the chance of any particular member of the population being included in the sample is not known with any accuracy. Indeed, the members themselves may not be known in any detail so that no sampling frame exists.

   Here we cannot say with any great degree of accuracy what type of sample we are likely to end up with, though a common-sense analysis can give us a good idea.

   These methods are necessitated by the difficulties that can be met with when trying to obtain a random sample, as outlined earlier.

Simple random and systematic sampling are, of course, examples of (a). But there are other types in this category that can be used in cases when these two cannot easily be employed. This is discussed below, while the non-random methods are discussed later.

An improvement on simple random sampling

We saw in the last chapter how simple random sampling, and for that matter systematic sampling, can produce samples which are unrepresentative. This problem is worst when the population from which the sample is to be drawn contains various groups of different types of data. Let's take an example to make this clear. Suppose a car manufacturer wants to sample customer satisfaction with its products. If it has several products and it takes a simple random sample of owners of all makes, it could get a sample with one or more of the makes over- or under-represented. If it only made one model, the problem would not arise: it is the diversity that causes it.

Self-check

Can you think of a way of ensuring that the sample of the various models of cars, above, contains the correct proportion of each model, i.e. the same as that in use? Suppose, for example, that the company made two models, A and B, and that there were twice as many As as Bs.

The most straightforward way of doing this is to 'share out' the sample among the various models in the same proportion as they are in use. (Actually, these proportions would have to be estimated from the sales figures.) In this case, twice as many As as Bs. So if a sample of 600 car owners was required, there should be 400 for model A and 200 for model B. Provided that some suitable sampling frame existed, a random sample of the owners of each type of car could be taken separately.

To summarize, then, when the population from which a random sample is to be taken contains groups of different types of data, the danger of getting a non-representative sample may be unacceptably high. To avoid this, the population is first divided up into groups or 'strata', which, as far as possible, contain data only of one type. Samples are then taken from each of these. This method is termed 'stratified random sampling'. It is illustrated in figure 6 overleaf. If, in addition, the proportions of each strata in the sample are the same as those in the population, we speak of 'proportional stratified random sampling'. This was the case in the above. The other types of stratified sampling will not be discussed here.

One further point is that stratified sampling can be used without necessarily having to select items from the strata by a simple random process. Systematic sampling could be, and very often is, used to select from the strata. If, for example, the car maker above had a list of all car owners for each model, a systematic sample would be the simplest way of selecting from each list to form the sample. We will also see later how stratified sampling can be used in conjunction with non-random sampling methods.

As a simple example of where stratified random sampling may be used, suppose an inquiry into the sales of certain cosmetics is

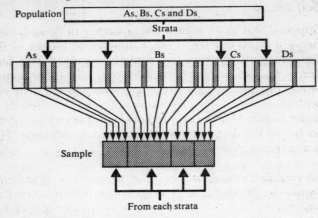

Figure 6. Stratified random sampling

being conducted. It is likely that different types of retail outlet will be treated differently. Sales in multiples, large, medium and small independents are likely to differ considerably and to get the full picture the proper representation of each of these is required. This would need some form of stratified sampling, with the different types of outlet as strata.

Getting a more representative sample is not the only reason for using stratified sampling, however.

Self-check

The electoral register applies only to the local voting area, the ward or whatever. Suppose we want a random sample covering a larger area than this? We would then have to combine several registers to get the sampling frame (a tiresome job) or use some other method. Can you suggest what this other method might be?

One way would be to treat the different wards as strata. This would have the advantage of also ensuring that each ward was properly represented in the sample.

Self-check

Suppose that in an area where a survey of households is being undertaken there are a number of blocks of flats dotted about. The data that could be obtained from families in the flats is thought to differ from that other families would provide. Special sampling techniques are to be used with them, which involves using different interviewers. In order to give them a feasible workload, the number of flats to be visited needs to be determined in advance. How could this be done?

Again a stratified sample would solve the problem. The households would be divided into those in houses and those in flats, and these would form the strata. A definite number of each type could then be chosen. This would give a sample which was more representative of the area as a whole than a simple random one.

Self-check

A company has a list of its customers in each region of the country. It wants to sample their views on a new product. Why do you think it would use stratified sampling?

Although getting a representative sample and avoiding having to merge the lists could be part of the reason, it would do so mainly because it would be administratively convenient, the sales force would be arranged in regions and sales areas.

So, to summarize, there are three other major reasons for using stratified sampling, namely

- to save having to merge existing sampling frames, e.g. the electoral registers, so that a sample can be taken from a wider area than that covered by just one;
- to allow for different sampling techniques to be used with different sections of the population, e.g. in the sample census of 1966, hotels and similar establishments were not treated in the same way as private households;
- to produce administratively convenient units, e.g. the strata could correspond to the national regions.

It should be noted that we can stratify according to several different factors simultaneously. So, for instance, if we are interested in whether or not a person is married *and* in what sex he/she is, we could use four strata.

Self-check

Can you see what they are?

Well, they are: (a) married and male; (b) married and female; (c) single and male; and (d) single and female. These strata are then used as normally.

Self-check

Does stratified sampling require there to be more information in the sampling frame than does simple random or systematic sampling?

Stratified sampling does, of course, require that more information is available than for the simple random sample. A reasonable estimate of the numbers in each stratum is needed. Furthermore, the stratum to which each member of the population belongs must be known *before* the sample is chosen. An electoral register, for example, does not even give the sex of those on it (though it can, of course, be inferred from the names). Thus this would not be suitable on its own for stratification into anything other than geographical areas.

Self-check

Where in the scenario do you think it might have been advantageous to employ stratified random sampling had an appropriate sampling frame been available? What features of the population could have been used to stratify on?

In the scenario, it would probably have been advantageous to have obtained views on the proposed new product from a sample of mothers stratified according to socio-economic group and age at least. It is quite possible that customer reaction would differ in relation to these two factors (and probably others). However, lack of a suitable sampling frame ruled this out. The equivalent of such a sample could have been obtained using one of the non-random sampling methods described later. This point is returned to then.

> ## Self-check
>
> The headmaster of a boys' school decides to interview a five-per-cent sample of the pupils to find out their views on a proposed change in the way it is run. Suggest how he should select this sample.

There will be boys of several different ages in the school and their views will no doubt differ from age to age. If they are streamed, then the same can probably be said of pupils in the different classes in any year. To get a good cross-section of views, the head should stratify the school pupils according to the class they are in. Since the school has an excellent sampling frame in the registers, a systematic sample from each class could then be taken.

> ## Self-check
>
> A large mixed-sex social club has 200 lady members, 160 of whom are married, and 400 gentlemen ones, 200 of whom are married. The committee want to test the members' views on a proposed merger with another club. If a five-per-cent sample is taken, stratified according to both sex and marital status, what will be the constitution of the sample?

There are 600 members, so there will be $\frac{5 \times 600}{100} = 30$ in the sample.

$\frac{5 \times 160}{100} = 8$ are married women; $\frac{5 \times 40}{100} = 2$ are single women; $\frac{5 \times 200}{100} = 10$ are married men; $\frac{5 \times 200}{100} = 10$ are single men – by taking five per cent from each of the strata in the population.

Cutting down the searching

One of the difficulties with random sampling of any kind is, as was mentioned in the previous chapter, getting hold of the data. Once an item has been selected for the sample, that data really ought to be gathered. But this can often be difficult or costly.

Self-check

Suppose we want to undertake a survey of people's opinions on health foods, and we decide to contact households. What would we have to do to try to ensure that we get the data from those households selected in a random sample where nobody is in when we visit them?

We would have to keep going back to the houses where we had not been able to get a reply. This might take a very long time and be very wasteful of resources.

One way round such problems is to postpone selecting the items for the sample until the data is collected and to allow the collector of the data to choose which items are sampled according to what is available.

Self-check

Can you see how this would work in the case of the health food survey above?

The interviewer would be allowed to ignore any houses where no answer was received and to substitute others to make up the total. Generally, the substitutes should match those items missed as closely as possible. Usually, the interviewer is not given a list of particular houses that must be visited.

This technique is called 'quota sampling', because the collector of the data is given a certain amount of data to collect – the quota. Its most well-known use is in surveys, where, for example, interviewers stop people in the street. But it can also be employed in applications such as quality control and auditing. For instance, an auditor may select a certain number of items for checking from a set of books.

Self-check

There is one obvious problem that can arise. What is it, do you think?

It is that the data collector will obtain a very unrepresentative sample if left a completely free choice of which data to collect. For example, since a survey interviewer is generally a paid helper, it will almost always be the data that is encountered first and is most easily found that will be collected. For this reason it is not usual to give complete licence for selection. Quota sampling is most often used in conjunction with some form of stratification. Thus the interviewer will be given a table, such as that below, indicating the numbers in each stratum to be interviewed.

SAMPLING QUOTAS

Age	Sex	
	Male quota	Female quota
under 18	2	1
18–30	4	3
30–45	8	6
45–65	4	3
over 65	2	2

Self-check

Where in the scenario might quota sampling have been used? Why do you think it wasn't? If it had been, and socio-economic group and age were used for stratifying, what problems do you think would have been encountered?

In the scenario, a time when quota sampling could have been

used was in the interviews of people buying Baby Gourmet food. It was not actually used then because *everyone* purchasing such food was included in the sample, so as to make best use of the interviewers' time. It is unlikely that there would be a great many buyers at any one time, so it would be pointless not interviewing everyone.

If socio-economic group and age had been used to stratify the sample, the main difficulty would have been in determining where people fitted in *before* they were interviewed. Since these factors affect who is approached in stratified quota sampling, they must be determined beforehand, for some of the sample at least (i.e. for those near the end when some quotas have been almost met). With age, a further problem that could arise is that, to play safe, the interviewer will choose those who look as though they are in the middle of the age range. Taking the above figures, for example, those of age 24, 38, 55 and 75, or thereabouts, would tend to be selected. This means that those on the borderline, i.e. aged 18, 30, 45 and 65, are under-represented.

The major problems that can arise with quota sampling, then, are that

- the strata are sometimes difficult to distinguish, e.g. social class is not easy to determine from appearance alone;
- 'extremes' tend to be under-represented, e.g. to be 'safe', an interviewer will choose people aged about the middle of the given age ranges, rather than near the limits;
- the sample cannot, by its very nature, be really free from bias, e.g. the interviewer will affect the selection (this can be controlled to a certain extent, but never completely);
- there could be difficulty in meeting the quota, e.g. in the scenario, not enough people would be buying Baby Gourmet foods to warrant ignoring any of them, as this would just be wasting the interviewer's time, so no quota is set.

However, because of its simplicity and low cost, this method is very popular. It is also true to say that, in practice, the results it yields are generally good enough for the purpose. The use of random sampling techniques would not usually produce results of significantly greater worth because of almost inevitable problems, e.g. non-response.

Self-check

A Member of Parliament has expressed disagreement with the leaders of his own party on an important issue. The local newspaper in his constituency wants to conduct a poll to see if opinion is for or against this stand. How would it probably go about doing it?

A random sample, using the electoral register, would be a statistically good way of going about it, but this is almost certainly not what would happen. The paper would not wish to spend too much time or money on the project. What would probably happen is that the paper would conduct the survey using a quota sampling method. It should attempt to stratify the sample at least according to age and social class, but it might well not.

Cutting the costs

Another problem that was identified in the previous unit concerned the physical distribution of the members of a random sample.

Self-check

A mail order catalogue company wants to interview a small sample of its agents to gain an insight into their problems. It has a very good sampling frame in its list of agents. The firm does not, however, use a random sampling method. Why not, do you think?

A simple random sample would take no account of the geographical location of the agents. So there may be one in the Outer Hebrides, three in Greater London, one in Redruth and so on. This would mean a large cost in time and fares for the interviewers. A random sample stratified according to geographical area would be an improvement. But even this would be wasteful of resources. The areas represented by each stratum need to be reasonably small or the initial problem remains. But if they are that small, it would be more economical for the interviewer to visit every agent in the district.

This principle forms the basis of a technique called 'cluster sampling'. In this, *all* the members of a few particular sub-groups of the population (called 'clusters') are included in the sample. These clusters may represent geographical areas, but they may also represent business units, storage units and so on. They need not be of equal size. Unlike strata, which should contain members which are very similar to each other, clusters should be as representative of the population as a whole as they can be.

> *Self-check*
>
> Why is this, do you think?

It is because the idea is to have only relatively few clusters, to cut down the expense. If any one of these was seriously unrepresentative, it would make the whole sample so.

The clusters used in the sample are themselves selected from the group of clusters which together make up the population. This is illustrated in figure 7. This process of selection is itself one of sampling. That is, the clusters in the sample can be regarded as a sample of the clusters in the population. They are generally chosen at random, though stratification can be used.

> *Self-check*
>
> Suggest how the clusters of mail order catalogue agents, in the self-check on page 121, could be selected.

There it would probably be a matter of dividing up the country into small geographical areas. But it is unlikely that a simple random sample of these would be selected. Because clusters should be as representative as possible of the whole population, areas would be selected in which the social mix, age distribution and so on were like in the country as a whole. So it is not always a random sample of clusters that is selected.

> *Self-check*
>
> Where is cluster sampling used in the scenario? What form do the clusters take?

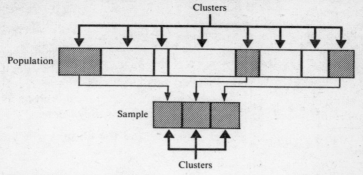

Figure 7. Cluster sampling

An illustration of cluster sampling can be found in the concept testing phase of the new Junior Gourmet products in the scenario. The clusters there were defined as the retail outlets that sold Baby Gourmet food. Gourmet Foods could not afford to send interviewers to each of these, so a few were chosen as representative of them all. In these, *all* those purchasing a jar of Baby Gourmet were interviewed.

|| *Self-check*

Using the scenario as an illustration, show what the disadvantages of cluster sampling are.

The major drawbacks of this method are that

- the exact sample size cannot always be controlled, e.g. as in the Junior Gourmet example, where all the Baby Gourmet customers are interviewed;
- occasionally, lack of time prevents complete sampling, e.g. if there were a sudden rush of customers buying Baby Gourmet foods;
- it is not always easy to find representative clusters, e.g. of the retail outlets for Baby Gourmet, none may be totally representative of the various types of customer that buy Baby Gourmet food.

Self-check

A company is making a check on the condition of some raw material stock which hasn't been touched for some time. A random selection of cases of this material are opened. All the packages inside each case are examined for signs of deterioration. Is this an example of cluster sampling? If so, what are the clusters?

It is an example of cluster sampling and the clusters are the boxes.

Review

1 The management of a supermarket chain decide to organize surprise visits to a ten-per-cent sample of their stores to conduct an extensive inquiry into their operation. They have a large number of high street mini-markets still in operation, slightly fewer supermarkets of 4000 to 12,000 sq ft and a number of large supermarkets over 12,000 sq ft. What type of sampling scheme do you suggest could be used and why?

2 A local newspaper conducted a survey into how satisfied commuters were with the service to London. Fifty of them were interviewed one Tuesday morning at the local station, five between six and seven a.m., fifteen between seven and eight a.m., twenty-five between eight and nine a.m. and five between nine and ten a.m. The interviewer was free to select the particular passengers. What type of sampling was this? On what basis do you think the figures for each period were chosen? What criticisms do you have of this strategy? What improvements would you make?

3 At the beginning of each day, the first ten jars of Baby Gourmet food produced by each machine in the plant are examined extremely carefully, just to check there are no serious problems. What type of sample is this? (Hint: think of the day's production being divided into tens.)

ANSWERS

1 The three types of store will almost certainly have their own distinct ways of operating. Any sample would need to have a number of each type in. The danger in a simple random sample, if that was what you chose, is that not one of the large supermarkets may be included. There, are after all, a lot fewer of them. A quota sample is really not applicable here. The stores aren't just stumbled on, nor do they pass by. You shouldn't have chosen that then. But what about a cluster sample? At first sight this seems a good idea. However, the clusters do not guarantee that the different types of stores will be properly represented. If you chose this you were taking the costs of the exercise into account, but not the representativeness of the sample.

The answer is to use a stratified sample. The types of store would form one of the strata. Geographical region and area could be another. This would enable an investigator to cut down on travel. Actually, clusters may well be used in addition, to select the stores from within these strata. This point is taken up in the next part of this chapter. But you would not have been expected to know this yet.

2 The first point to note is that there is some stratification involved. The different times form the strata. But how are the actual passengers selected? The interviewers were free to choose. This means that it is a quota sample. What we have, then, is a stratified quota sample.

If you said it was a random sample, remember the definition. Not all passengers stand the same chance of being included. For a start, any of them that are in a rush are unlikely to cooperate. If you chose a cluster sample, ask yourself if *all* the passengers in some group or groups were interviewed. The basis for choosing the figures for each period was the density of traffic during those times. But no instructions were given as to what type of passenger was to be interviewed, e.g. male or female. Some further stratification would be needed then, including age and sex, to improve the strategy.

3 This is quite a tricky one. If you took the hint and divided up the day's production into tens, you might have guessed that it is cluster sampling. Each group of ten can be regarded as a

cluster. It's also possible that you got it by a process of elimination. It is certainly not a random sample of the day's output. Any jars after the tenth have no chance whatsoever of being included. There are no strata involved, so it cannot be a stratified sample either.

However, there is some justification for your choosing a quota sample. The situation has many features in common with its use. Basically, the cluster sample answer is to be preferred since it is decided beforehand that it will be the *first* ten always.

Taking it in stages

It is rare for us to be able to use just one of the sampling techniques described so far in this and the previous chapter. We saw this already to some extent with cluster sampling. Basically, as we have seen, there are problems with random samples in many cases. The sampling methods dealt with in this chapter so far have been attempts to overcome these. But, often, these methods are the cause of problems of a different nature. In general we do not use random samples because it would cost too much. The problems encountered with them are ones connected with resources then. When we try to overcome these, we create problems of accuracy. That is, the samples we get tend to be unrepresentative. By using a mixture of methods, we hope to minimize the effects of each type of difficulty.

One general technique that attempts to do just this is called 'multi-stage sampling'. This technique divides up the sampling process into stages. In the first, or 'primary stage', 'primary sampling units' are chosen from the whole population, each containing a number of members. Of course, no member should belong to more than one unit and each one should belong to some unit. 'Secondary sampling units' may then be selected from the primary ones and so on until the 'final stage' is reached. This is illustrated in figure 8. At each stage, samples may be taken by an appropriate method, and different sampling frames can be used each time. In general, however, it is necessary to use some form of random sampling at all but the final stage, to avoid getting an unrepresentative sample. Where one or more of the stages involves sampling by geographical area, the term 'area sampling' is often applied.

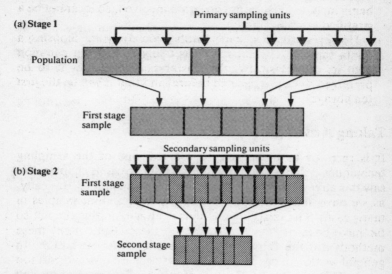

Figure 8. Multi-stage sampling

Suppose, for example, that we want to find out what is the probable result of a general election to be held soon. We could take a sample of people's voting intentions. But how would we choose that sample?

Self-check

Can you suggest how it could be done using multi-stage sampling? Can you see why it is so important that a different sampling frame can be used at each stage?

It could be done by dividing up the country into areas, the constituencies would be suitable ones. A stratified random sample could then be taken of these areas, using socio-economic mix and similar factors. The process could then be repeated at constituency level, by dividing each up into wards. A stratified random sample of wards could be selected from each constituency in the first level sample, using the same factors as at the first level. Finally, a quota sample of households in the selected wards could provide the voting intentions. These could be chosen from the electoral register. A systematic sample is possible here, but it would suffer from the problems outlined earlier of actually contacting the people in the households. Another possibility would be to use people in the street at the final stage, but they need not necessarily come from the ward in which the street lies, and so difficulties might arise. This could be done, though, if the stage before that stopped at just the general area.

If we had to have a sampling frame for the whole population, you can see what problems there would be. We would need to have a list of all the voters in the country. But such a list exists only divided up into the different voting districts. To combine all these would be a mammoth job. With multi-stage sampling, we use a list of the constituencies at the first level, a list of wards at the second and the electoral register at the final level.

Self-check

Where in the scenario do you think multi-stage sampling might have been used?

This technique might well have been used to select the mothers and babies to test the new product. Almost certainly they would have been chosen from a number of geographical areas. This is not because the babies would be any different, but because mothers' reactions might well vary, for instance from north to south. A possible sampling scheme for use in this case is as follows:

First stage – a stratified random sample of geographical areas.

Second stage – a stratified random sample of districts, towns or villages in each area selected.

Third (and final) stage – a stratified quota sample of mothers with babies of the right age from the shopping areas within the second stage units.

Self-check

What would you identify as being the principal sources of problems in the above scheme?

One problem with the above scheme is that those mothers contacted would almost certainly be non-working ones. There would also probably be a smaller proportion of them in the 'higher' socio-economic groups than in the population as a whole, but it is in these matters Gourmet Foods are most interested. An alternative approach would be to use postnatal clinics, but this doesn't really overcome these difficulties either. The obstacle here is really the lack of a suitable sampling frame for young mothers. A further source of difficulty would be those mothers who decline to cooperate. But there is very rarely anything that can be done about that particular problem.

The concept testing phase also made use of multi-stage sampling. The first and second stages would probably have been the same as with the product testing, as outlined above. At the final stage, of course, every purchaser of Baby Gourmet food was approached. As has already been mentioned, this phase of the investigation used cluster sampling.

As an example other than from a sample survey, let's look at the inspection of goods at a customs point. Suppose a fleet of lorries is crossing a border carrying a consignment of spring water and the customs officers decide to check it.

Self-check

Assuming that the customs men are not going to open every case, can you suggest how they might select which cases and bottles they examine?

One way of doing it would be to use multi-stage sampling. A possible scheme is:

First stage – a random sample of lorries.
Second stage – a random sample of cases.
Third stage – a cluster sample of bottles.

As a final and much more complex example, let's look at the Family Expenditure Survey. This is included just to show how complex the sampling methods can get. This survey is undertaken by the government to discover how families spend their money. In the primary sampling stage, the country is cross-stratified into 168 strata, according to geographic region, population density and mean rateable value. Each stratum contains a number of areas. One of these is selected at random from each stratum, giving a sample of 168 areas. Each area selected is used four times at quarterly intervals and is then replaced by another one from that stratum, i.e. a quarter are changed each time. The 168 areas in the sample at any one time are divided at random into three sets, each of which is used for one month only in that quarter.

In the secondary stage, four geographical sub-units are selected from each area in the sample, using systematic sampling. They are used one at a time in random order over the four months during which this area remains in the sample. The third stage involves the selection, by systematic sampling, of sixteen heads of households from each of the geographical sub-units. Thus, in any one month sixteen households from each of the fifty-six areas are used. That is, $16 \times 56 = 896$ households.

Self-check

A retail grocery cooperative in the Midlands has 500 small shops under its banner. These are scattered about the towns and villages in the area. The cooperative management want to interview a five per cent sample of the shop owners to find out what their financial position is. Suggest a suitable sampling scheme.

As there are shops in the country and the town areas, the first stage of the sampling process should be to stratify the population, i.e. the shops, by type of area, town or country. Each of these strata should be divided into geographical clusters. A stratified sample of *clusters* should then be obtained by some random method, say systematic sampling. Each shop in the selected clusters should then be visited. If your answer is somewhat different, check to see that you have included the following points. If you have, then it should be acceptable:

- there should be a stage that ensures that town and country shops are both properly represented.
- The final sample should not involve the interviewers in too much travel.

Other methods

There are an enormous number of different ways of sampling. The ones described in this and the previous chapter are the ones which are commonly used and which give reasonable results. They are an attempt to balance cost against statistical considerations. But in any given case there may well be a simpler method of selecting the sample which satisfies both these requirements. Here is an example to show what can be done.

Suppose an employment agency wants to follow up roughly ten per cent of clients that have been found work, to find out what they think of their new job. It decides to contact all those in that category whose birthday falls in March.

> *Self-check*
>
> Does this provide a random sample? Can you see what the problems are with this method?

Unless you believe in astrology, their birth date should have no bearing on whether or not the agency's clients are now satisfied with the jobs they were found. So those born in March should form a representative sample. It can't really be called a random one, though. What we can say is that, *as far as the information we are interested in is concerned*, it behaves like a random sample. Of course, there are drawbacks to this method, the principal ones being that

- the exact sample size cannot be controlled;
- it is not always easy to find a suitable independent feature, like birth date, to use.

Nevertheless, such 'attribute sampling' can prove very effective in many cases and it should not be neglected.

As a final example of how sampling can be simplified, let's look at a way of saving a great deal of time and expense where the circumstances are suitable. In cases where continual sampling is required, one simple way of reducing the amount of work may be to use the same sample over and over again. Obviously this can only be done in certain circumstances, such as might occur in, for example, market research. It wouldn't be much use in quality testing, however!

These constant samples are called 'panels'. They have been used in such applications as TV audience ratings, purchasing habits and in a long-term study of child development. Of course, the members have to be selected in the first place. This is done using the techniques described in this chapter. As well as saving time and money, accurate data on changing attitudes and opinions can be obtained. However, panels do also have some disadvantages.

Self-check

Can you see what the problems might be with this method? Think of a panel of wine tasters employed by a vineyard.

The most obvious problems are that:

- members may die, move away or simply cease to cooperate; this means replacements have to be selected and the constitution of the panel may change erratically;
- members may react differently just because they are on the panel; e.g. they may get used to the wine; periodic replacement of a proportion of them can help overcome this problem.

Self-check

1 Suppose the employment agency mentioned in the text had wanted to follow up about four per cent of clients for whom they had found jobs. Could they have done this by using as the sample those whose surnames began with M? If not, why not?

  2 Why would Gourmet Foods be unlikely to use a panel to test new baby foods products as they were developed?

ANSWERS

1 No they couldn't. To see why, just think of the type of people that would have a surname beginning with M, McTavish, Macdonald, and so on. Do you think the Scots would be entirely representative of Britishers as a whole?
2 Because the babies grow up, and it would be pointless testing baby food on a child who has moved on to 'grown-up' food.

An example of sampling and data collection

In this section, an example will be given which illustrates the sampling techniques of this and the previous chapter and also the data collection methods of Chapters 2 and 3.

JICTAR is the Joint Industry Committee for Television Advertising Research.* Its job is to find out what kind of people watch television, which programmes they watch and how often. The starting point is a large-scale survey which provides a profile of the population in the various ITV areas. This is called the 'establishment survey'. This yields data on the family size, socio-economic group, age group and so on of each household. It also establishes which households have a TV or TVs and which ITV channel(s) the sets can receive. Such surveys are carried out annually to check for any changes.

A multi-stage stratified random sample of over 18,000 households is used. In the first stage, the country is divided into geographical regions. Within each of these, strata are devised based on the density of the population in an area and whether or not it is covered by the transmitters from more than one ITV area (the so called 'overlap areas'). In each ITV area, a number of 'administrative districts' are selected within each stratum, this number being proportional to the relative populations of the strata in each ITV area. Postcode sectors are then selected within these administrative districts, those with greater populations

*The details of JICTAR's work appear by kind permission of that organization.

having a greater chance of selection. Finally, a random sample of households is selected for interview from the postcode sector using the postal address file as the source of the addresses.

About 4000 interviews are carried out in the London ITV area and 1000 in the less densely populated North-east Scotland ITV area.

The results of the establishment surveys are used, together with government data, to give potential audiences according to a number of different categories, for example children. The households interviewed may also be used as a master sample for the selection of a panel of viewers.

The panel is a multi-stage proportional stratified random sample selected from the above sampling frame. From each ITV area, households are selected for the sample so as to be representative of the known ITV households of that area, in terms of socio-economic class, number of children and so on.

In all, there are over 2500 households (7000 individuals) in the sample, about 350 in London and 100 in North-east Scotland. No panel has less than 100 households, as it has to be large enough to yield separate data on broad audience categories, such as housewives, children and so on. Occasionally members of the panel drop out. They are then replaced by similar households from the sampling frame. Data on viewing patterns is collected in two ways. A metering device on the TV set automatically records the exact times it was on and off and which station it was tuned to. In addition, each member of the household over four years old has an individual viewing diary which they complete.

Several features of this system are worth commenting on. The meter performs three functions. Not only does it provide a very accurate record of viewing times, it also considerably reduces the demands on the individuals reporting back. This greatly assists cooperation. Furthermore, it provides a check on the diaries. These show who was watching and at what times. If any discrepancy between the meter and the diaries is detected, such as someone viewing when the set is switched off, data from that source is not used for that week. In addition, the household is regularly checked thereafter.

Though some households remain on the panel for a number of

years, research conducted by JICTAR shows no evidence that this has any undue influence on the accuracy of the data obtained from them. There are also two safeguards to maintain standards. Firstly, JICTAR employs an independent research company to collect the data. Secondly, JICTAR represents both the sellers of advertising time and the buyers. While the former are looking to make sure there is no understatement of audience sizes, the latter are looking to make sure there is no overstatement.

Activity

This activity is designed to illustrate the differences between the sampling methods described in the last two chapters.

Take four sheets of A4 graph paper. (If you haven't got any, you can rule up some plain or lined paper to give the same results.) On each, draw a rectangle containing 60 large squares (i.e. 6 × 10) each of 100 small squares. This represents sixty geographical areas which are themselves subdivided into 100 smaller areas. A five per cent sample of these smaller areas is required, i.e. 30 of them.

Allocate the numbers 0 to 59 to these large squares. The smaller squares can be identified as follows. The top row of the small squares in any large square is row 0, the one below that is row 1 and so on until row 9. Similarly, the leftmost column of small squares in any large square is column 0, the next one to the right is column 1 and so on until column 9. Each small square can be identified by first of all saying which large square it is in and then giving two digits. The first of these specifies which row the small square is in. The second specifies the column. So in figure 9 the shaded small square is number 47 within the large square, 20, as shown.

A random sample

To obtain a simple random sample of small squares, use your local telephone directory. Open a page at random. Use the last four digits of *successive* telephone numbers to pick out the small

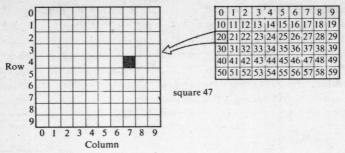

Figure 9

squares as follows. The first two digits are used for the big square. The next two then indicate the small square, within that big square. For example, the small shaded square in figure 9 corresponds to the four digits 2047. And, for example, **(a)** 2360, **(b)** 0071, **(c)** 3205, would give these squares:

(a) small square in seventh row (row 6) and first column (column 0) of big square 23;
(b) small square in eight row (row 7) and second column (column 1) of big square 0;
(c) small square in the first row (row 0) and sixth column (column 5) of big square 32.

This is shown in figure 10.

Self-check

Why do you think that this method yields a random sample?

It does so because there is no reason to assume that the telephone numbers are in any particular order; the names are, of course, but there is no relationship between the name and the corresponding number.

Self-check

There are two possible snags that you might run across when using this method to select a sample. Can you say what they are?

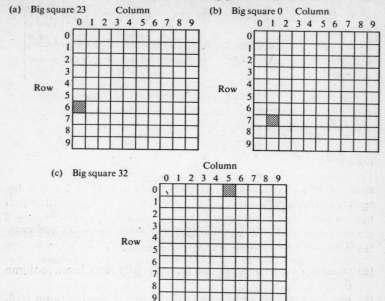

Key: selected small squares are shown shaded

Figure 10

First, there are only sixty big squares. What happens if we get a telephone number which gives big square sixty or more?

Self-check

Well, what do you think could be done?

The simplest thing to do is to ignore that number and move on to the next one. (If you said subtract 60 from the number obtained this would be wrong. It would give squares 0 to 39 (i.e. 60 – 60 and 99 – 60), an unfair advantage as you could not get squares 40 to 59 in this way.)

So, for example, (a) 3279, (b) 6961, (c) 0474, would give these small squares:

(a) the small square in the eighth row and tenth column of big square 32;

(b) no square – since the big square number 69 does not exist;

(c) the small square in the eighth row and fifth column of big square 4.

The second problem that could arise is that, when selecting a small square, the same last four digits may occur in another telephone number, giving the same square again.

Self-check

What do you think could be done if that happens?

Once again the easiest solution is to ignore that number.

In fact, as noted earlier, statisticians have devised tables of 'random numbers' which may be used in exactly the same way as the telephone numbers are used here. The same problems arise with these and the solutions are also the same.

Repeat the process of selection described above until thirty small squares have been chosen, colouring or filling in each one as it is selected.

What squares did you get? Did you get two or more small squares within one big square? You should be able to see a random pattern of shaded or coloured squares. However, you may have, by sheer chance, obtained a pattern which does not look random. Did you?

A proportional stratified random sample

To obtain a stratified sample, we need to decide on some strata. Let's use the columns. That is, suppose we need to have the numbers of squares in the sample, lying in some given column number, in the same proportion as in the population.

Self-check

What number of squares in the sample of thirty should lie in each column number?

There should be three small squares in each of the different columns in the sample, i.e. ten per cent in each as in the population as a whole. Of course, these do not all have to be in the same big square. To select this sample, we can use a similar method to that for the random sample. But here, we ignore the last digit in the telephone numbers. The first three selections are assumed to be all column 0, the next three all column 1 and so on. In each case the particular big square and the row is obtained from the telephone number. For example: **(a)** 4023, **(b)** 3256, **(c)** 4051, at the start of the selection process, would give the three column 0 squares of

(a) big square 40, row 2, column 0 (ignoring the 3);
(b) big square 32, row 5, column 0 (ignoring the 6);
(c) big square 40, row 5, column 0 (ignoring the 1).

The column 1 squares are then chosen in a similar way, and so on.

The same problems can arise as with the simple random sample and the same solutions employed. Select the sample of thirty, shading or colouring in the selected squares as before. Use a separate sheet to that of the random sample.

What sort of results did you get? Did you notice that the pattern is more regular this time? Did you get more than one small square in one large square? There was no reason why you shouldn't have had such a result, the strata only ensure an even spread across the columns, not across the big squares or even the rows.

A multi-stage sample

In a multi-stage sample, the big areas can be regarded as the first stage units. The small squares can be the second, and here final, stage units. Notice that to get a sample of thirty, a decision has to be made as to how many first stage sampling units will be picked. In a realistic situation, cost would dictate that there were as few as possible. So let's take six. This now determines how many small squares (i.e. final stage sampling units) there can be in each big square in the sample.

Self-check

How many could there be?

Since there should be thirty small squares in the whole sample, there must be five in each of the big squares in that sample, if they are to be spread evenly about the big squares. In this case, as all the large squares are similar, this would seem the best method. But note that this is not a necessity in general. There could be 2 from 5 big squares and 20 from the other, for example.

Self-check

Can you see how the first stage sample can be selected if it is to be a simple random one?

This can be done using exactly the same technique as with the simple random sample, with the two digits representing the small squares ignored. So (a) 3489, (b) 4567, (c) 3250, would give big squares (a) 34, (b) 45, (c) 32, and the last two digits in each case would be ignored.

Now select six big squares using this method. You should have a fairly scattered selection. Though once again, by sheer chance, you may not have.

Now what about the final stage sample? Let's see how we can select another random selection of five small squares from each large one selected.

Self-check

How would you do it?

The same system as was used earlier would do. The last two digits of successive telephone numbers could be used.

Now, for each large square selected for the first stage sample, choose five small squares within it as outlined above. When you have done so, colour or fill in the corresponding squares on a sheet of your graph paper. What sort of pattern did you get? Compare it with those you obtained for the simple random and the stratified random samples.

Now here we have taken simple random samples at each stage. There is no necessity for this. We could, for example, have used a stratified sample at either stage. If we had done so at the first stage, we could have ensured that we had one big square from each column of big squares, for instance (since there are six of them). If we had done so at the second stage, we could have had one in each column of the big squares chosen at the first stage. At least, we could have done had the sample been larger.

Self-check

Why would the sample have needed to have been larger? What size would it had to have been at minimum?

With only five small squares per big square, it does not give enough for one in each of the ten columns. We would have needed at least ten. This would have meant a sample of sixty small squares in total. (We could, of course, have chosen only three big squares at the first stage, and had ten in each of these to keep the same sample size.)

It would also have been possible to use a stratified sample at each stage. This would have ensured that the sample of small squares was representative of both the columns of large squares and of the column numbers of the small squares, for example.

Cluster sampling

Suppose now the *third* stage of a multi-stage sample is a cluster. We can imagine that the rows of each large square are similar. That is, in any one square, row 0 is very much like row 1, which is very much like row 3 and so on. So, in the first stage, big squares will be selected as before. In the second stage, one row is selected from each of these. In the third, and last, stage, the 'sample' consists of *all* the small squares in these rows.

Self-check

If we still want a sample of thirty small squares, can you suggest how many large squares there should be in the first stage sample?

Since there are ten small squares in one row, we need only three large squares. These can be chosen at random as before. Select these three squares. They should be scattered fairly widely. Are they? Of course, by sheer chance, they may not be. Now we need to select the one row from each.

Self-check

How can we do this do you think? Could we stratify by column?

The simplest method would be another random sample. It would prove difficult *not* to stratify by column as each row contains one small square from every column. Thus a reasonable sample will be obtained by using a random method to select the rows. The last digit in successive telephone numbers could be used here (with any repeats *not* being ignored, as each row would be in a different big square).

Using the method suggested, select the rows for the sample. Colour, or shade in, the selected squares. Compare this result with the others. There is an obvious difference in that the small squares chosen here appear in clusters.

A quota sample

It is rather difficult to show a quota sample on the same basis as the other kinds of sample. Unlike these other methods, it is not so much which 'small squares' are chosen but *how* they are chosen. If the quota sample goes well, it should be almost indistinguishable from a multi-stage sample with a simple random selection process at the final stage. However, if it doesn't it can be very unrepresentative. So to get a similar effect, we can take the *first* two digits of the telephone numbers, which do follow some pattern (i.e. they must not conflict with STD codes). These can be used to select, say, ten small squares from just three big ones, chosen at random as above.

Choose the three big squares at random. You should have got them widely scattered again. Though sheer chance may mean you have not. Now select ten small squares at random from each big square, using the *first* two digits in the telephone numbers.

What sort of results have you got? Can you see that they are not very random? Perhaps you can't. It isn't easy to see and, in any case, the difference might be fairly slight.

You have now seen how the major sampling methods operate and how their results differ.

Review

1 What sampling scheme would you recommend for obtaining a sample of supermarket check-out operators in the UK, for a survey on job satisfaction?

2 In the scenario, what technique do you think was used for first stage sampling in the concept testing phase of the new product? What assumptions have you made about the channel of distribution? What would happen with a different channel of distribution (or mixture of the two)?

ANSWERS

1 Here, cost must be a large factor. This implies that some form of cluster sampling would be best. There would also be a likelihood that attitudes would differ from one part of the country to another and depend, to a certain extent, on the prevailing socio-economic class of families in the area. It would most certainly depend on the size of the supermarket, this means that, to get a reasonably representative sample, some stratification needs to be employed. So some multi-stage sampling process is required.

At the first stage, the sampling units should be geographical areas. A stratified sample of these should then be selected, using region and socio-economic grouping of the area as strata. Some measure such as rateable value could be used for the latter.

The second stage units would be the supermarkets. The sampling method here would be to get clusters. This would be to cut down the cost of travel from store to store. That is, all the supermarkets in the selected areas would be visited. Different sizes of supermarket would then be included automatically. If this is not thought good enough, the average size of supermarket in the area could be included in the strata when selecting the areas.

The third stage units would be the check-out operators themselves. Since it would be wasteful to visit a supermarket and not interview all the operators there, a cluster sample is the obvious choice at the third stage. If you said a simple random sample, just think of the difficulties in getting a sample frame for the operators. Indeed, it would be costly, or wasteful, to have a random sample at *any* stage. For example, a simple random sample of supermarkets would involve a great deal of travel.

A quota sample of stores is not possible, while one of the check-out operators would waste opportunities.

2 If Baby Gourmet sells direct to the stores and shops, then it will have a good sampling frame from which to choose the stores to visit. However, if stratification is used, some further information, on the store size, etc., is required. The firm would have sales figures of Baby Gourmet foods for each of the stores and shops and would have a geographical area for each of them as well. This would probably be in terms of the sales areas. And stratification would be needed to get a good social mix at least.

In practice, since the interviewers are only interested in those customers buying a jar of Baby Gourmet food, the sampling frame would be reduced to only those stores big enough to have enough of this type of customer to make visiting it worth while. The information on sales would be ideal for this purpose. This may well, of course, distort the results somewhat.

The sampling process would be something like this then. First of all the big stores would be selected from the sampling frame. Then a stratified random sample of areas would be chosen, using socio-economic class of area as strata. Then, since the interviewers will not need to travel from store to store, a simple random sample of the big stores within each area would be taken. Interviewers would be sent to each of these, to interview anyone buying a jar of Baby Gourmet food.

If the company used a wholesaler, then it would need to get

a number of different sampling frames, one from each of these. Rather than try to combine them, it would take a sample of big stores, i.e. in terms of sales of Baby Gourmet food, from each *separate* frame. Apart from this, the sampling scheme could be the same.

Don't worry if you didn't think of the point about the big stores only being visited. It is not an obvious one. Your answers should have included a general multi-stage scheme along the lines suggested. If you said that a simple random sample of stores/shops could be used, then you were technically correct. There is, after all, a good sampling frame. However, think of the possibility of getting them all in London. If you mentioned quota samples in relation to the customers, then think of how many such customers there are likely to be. It would be very difficult to set a quota, wouldn't it?

Part 3
Making sense of
the data collected

earlier, the figures that Kevin collects are not exact. For one thing, despite the great care put into compiling them, some errors are almost bound to occur. It would be surprising if they didn't with such a mass of them. And the birth figures themselves are not reported down to the nearest one. Who would want them that detailed anyway? They are thus approximations.

But what effect will errors and approximations have on how the data is used? Will they invalidate our results? These are the kinds of question treated in the next two chapters. These questions can be divided roughly into two types. Ones concerning methodology are considered mainly in Chapter 6. There the question of how errors and mistakes occur, and how to avoid them, will be covered. Chapter 7 is concerned with questions about what the effect of using approximate figures will be on our calculations.

After having studied these chapters you ought to be familiar with the ways in which figures can be affected by errors and approximations, and be able to deal with their effects. You should also know how to cut down the errors in your own statistical work.

6 | How far can we rely on the data collected?

Types of statistical data

Statistics is concerned mainly with 'variables'; that is to say, with things such as people's heights, the weights of jars of Baby Gourmet food, the way people intend to vote in a general election, the UK's gross national product, people's opinions on a new product and so on. These all vary from person to person, from jar to jar or from time to time. What a variable varies over, e.g. people, jars, time, is called the 'domain' of that variable. We must always be clear about what domain we have in mind. For example, a *child's* height will vary from *time to time*, and *children's* heights at, say, the age of eight, will vary from *child to child*. These are thus separate variables.

Self-check

What variables appear in the scenario? What are their domains?

Those which can be found in the scenario, together with their domains, are:

- school rolls from school to school;
- a school's roll from year to year;
- the birth rate over time;
- the sales of the company's baby foods over time;
- the number of births per annum;
- the year itself (e.g. 1980, 1981), where the domain is time.

A 'constant', on the other hand, is exactly what its name implies, something that stays constant over some domain, nearly always time. In general, though statistics makes use of constants, it is not concerned with determining their values. Two examples are the number of minutes in an hour and the ratio of the circumference of a circle to its diameter (π). The first is determined by man. We could decide to have 100 minutes in an hour if we wanted to, provided there was general agreement. Time is one of the few things that hasn't yet been metricated! The second constant is a natural one. Man can't change that however hard he tries, though there is a story that one of the state senates in the southern United States once tried to enact a law that made π equal to 3 (which it isn't). An example of a constant with a domain other than time is the number of ears a human being has. Its domain is the human population of earth.

There are two major categories of variables and constants, numeric and non-numeric. An example of a non-numeric constant is the direction in which a ball-bearing would fall under the earth's gravity, i.e. downwards. Non-numeric variables are often called 'attribute variables'. For example, car colour, bottle shape, product name, geographical location and the answer to a question in a questionnaire are all attribute variables in which a marketing executive may be interested. You should note that an attribute variable can sometimes have values which take the form of numbers, and yet still be non-numeric, for example the number of the house in which an individual lives. The distinguishing feature is that arithmetic can sensibly be performed with values of numeric variables. It would be meaningless to take a group of people and calculate their average house number, whereas we could reasonably find their average height. Actually numeric variables can be divided into further categories, and these are discussed in the second half of this chapter.

Self-check

Which of the following are constants and which variables? Say whether the variables are attribute or numeric ones and state their domains.

1 The population of the UK.
2 The statutory number of members of the House of Commons.
3 The number of books on loan from a given library.

4 The number of books on loan at some given time from any UK public library.

5 The sound of different door bells/chimes.

6 The distance from London (Hyde Park Corner) to Birmingham (Bull Ring).

7 The route number of a London Transport bus.

ANSWERS

1 Numeric variable. Its domain is time. That is to say, it varies over time. If you said that the domain was the UK you would be confusing the area for which the figure is given with the aspect over which it varies.

2 Numeric constant (while the present laws remain).

3 Numeric variable. Again the domain is time, i.e. this can vary from time to time. If you said the domain was libraries, you were forgetting that the question specified 'a *given* library'.

4 Numeric variable. Its domain is the UK public libraries. That is, it will vary from library to library. If you said time again, you missed the fact that the question specified 'some *given* time'.

5 Attribute variable. If you said numeric, you just try giving a numeric value to the sound a door chime makes! Its domain is the different door chimes available, i.e. the sound would vary from chime to chime.

6 Numeric constant. The distance never varies.

7 This is an attribute variable. If you said it was numeric, think if it would be sensible to add two such 'numbers' together. Its domain is the London Transport buses, i.e. it will vary from bus to bus.

Sources of error in statistical data

The term 'error' in statistics does not mean 'mistake'. It is defined as the difference between the 'true value' of a variable and the value we attach to it. The words 'true value' refer to the one that would be obtained if 100-per-cent accuracy were possible.

> ## Self-check
>
> Suppose that the true value for the number of babies born in the world in some year was 76,435,301. Do you think we could ever discover that this was so?

No. We certainly could not. There is no way we could account for every birth throughout the world for a start. Even if we could, we would probably make some slip in producing the final figure. 100-per-cent accuracy would just not be possible in this case. We might, however, come up with the figure of 75,000,000. This would represent an 'error' of $76,435,301 - 75,000,000 = 1,435,301$.

This numeric aspect of error will be covered in the next chapter. Here we will look at what can cause errors.

We can divide errors into two types and we will look at each of these separately.

> ## Self-check
>
> Suppose we are investigating the weight of trout in a trout farm. We have a set of scales with which we weigh each fish, but, unknown to us these are wrongly adjusted and so are out by 1.5 grams. What can we say about the consequent errors?

Well, we can say that they would all be in the same direction, either over or under. This would then bias our results; so 'bias' is what we call this type of error. It acts in a systematic way over the domain of the variable. That is to say, it is always in the same direction.

We have, in fact, seen examples of bias in earlier chapters, though we did not refer to them as such. These, and others, are listed below.

Bias may occur for many different reasons including:

- important data being omitted, e.g. non-response to a questionnaire, data being difficult to locate and therefore ignored;
- consistent misclassification of attribute data, e.g. colours of cars, opinions;

- inaccurate 'measuring' devices, e.g. wrongly adjusted scales, leading questions in a questionnaire;
- investigators' preconceptions influencing the data actually recorded, e.g. interpretation of respondent's answers in interviews, oversight of data not thought important;
- incorrect methodologies, e.g. wrong calculations, poor control over numeric data;
- incorrect sampling methods, e.g. non-random when random could have been used, poor control over investigators, unrepresentative sample;
- particular methodologies being forced on us by various constraints, e.g. sampling, and the use of non-random sampling.

As for the last point, we are often forced by shortage of resources, money, time, etc. to use techniques which can introduce bias. This is not to say that they are bad techniques. They are the only ones available to us, or at least the only feasible ones. Given the constraints which they have to be operated under, they are on the whole very good. The most obvious example is the use of non-random as opposed to random sampling. The reasons involved here have already been covered in the previous chapter. Another is the employment of agents, sometimes a great many of them. The reasons for this were discussed in Chapter 2.

To introduce the second type of error let's look at an example.

Self-check

A company is thinking of moving its head office and wants to sound out the views of the staff there. The manager decides to interview a simple random sample of them. Assume that the opinions on the move are equally divided. Will the sample necessarily faithfully reflect this division or could it give the manager the wrong idea? Would it exhibit bias, i.e. would it tend to give a result favouring one of these reactions only? (Think back to what was said about random samples in Chapter 5.)

We saw that random samples need not be fully representative of the populations when we were looking at them earlier. By sheer chance, we may get an 'unfair' proportion of those favouring the move in the sample. But also by sheer chance, we may have a sample with more of those against the move in. This then answers the second part of the question: there is no reason to suppose that there would be more of those against the move in the sample than those for it or vice versa. Any error in the sample, i.e. any deviation from the 'true' proportion of those for or against the move, would thus not act in any particular direction. Errors like this are called 'random errors'. If several samples were to be taken, the error in them would sometimes favour those against the move and sometimes those for it. That is to say it would act in a random way over the different samples.

This random error as the result of sampling is called 'sampling error'. This is extremely important in statistics and we will return to it later in the book. But it isn't the only kind of random error that there is. Random errors are often caused by human mistakes. The random omission of data, spurious data, questions in questionnaires which were not understood by the respondents, mistakes in arithmetic or in the copying of figures and so on would all cause errors of this type.

Activity

An activity should make the effects of bias and random errors clear.

Collect together ten $\frac{1}{2}$p coins and twenty 10p ones, with half of the 10p ones having one date and half another.

We are going to use these to simulate the sampling of staff opinion as above. First we will use the $\frac{1}{2}$p coins to represent those in favour of the move and ten of the 10p coins those against it. Put all of these in a bag and shake them up. Now put in your hand and pick out the first five coins you feel (don't try to get equal numbers of both coins, just pick the ones your hand finds first). Well did you find that you had nearly all 10p coins? Because they are bigger, they are found more easily. Have another go and see if it happens again.

Self-check

Is this an example of bias or random error do you think?

We have an example here of bias, because we always get more of the 10p coins.

Now take out the $\frac{1}{2}$p coins and replace them with the other ten 10p coins. This time it will be the date on the coin that determines whether it represents a pro-move or an anti-move person. Put all the 10p coins in a bag and shake them up. Put in your hand and pick out the first five coins you feel. Write down how many of each date you have. Repeat the process several times.

What kind of results did you get this time? You probably found that some of the time you had more of one date and some more of the other.

Self-check

Is this an example of bias or random error?

Since there are sometimes more of one date and sometimes more of the other, it is a random error.

As an example of where bias or random errors could occur, think of the birth figures collected by Kevin in the scenario.

Self-check

What do you think were the sources of bias or random error in the figures collected by Kevin in the scenario? Was he right to conclude on the evidence he had that, though he wanted numbers of babies aged three months to nine months, the birth figures were good enough?

Apart from the fact that Kevin may have copied them down wrongly, causing random errors, several other things could have effected the figures. The *Annual Abstract* states that the number of live births for England and Wales is not those registered but 'occurrences'. Certainly a few occurrences could have been missed, causing bias. The figures were only given in thousands, anyway, which introduced some random error. It is not impossible either that a few figures could have been lost or changed during the collection and collation of this data introducing further random error. But there is a further source of error and that is Kevin's choice of figures in the first place. There is at least some doubt as to whether he should have chosen just those for England and Wales. In addition, he wanted the figures for three-month to nine-month-old babies, but took those for births. Some of these, a distressingly high proportion in fact, would not have lived to three months. It is also possible that emigration and immigration would have affected the situation. All of thus would have introduced bias. So his conclusion that the birth figures were good enough was not warranted on the evidence he had. He should at least have looked at the deaths for young babies and the immigration and emigration figures to confirm thay they were not significant.

Self-check

Which of the following would cause bias and which random errors?

1 Using a watch which was slow in works study.
2 Using a rubber tape measure to measure people's waists.
3 Using a ruler marked in 1/10 inches to measure the thickness of paper.
4 Conducting a survey of people's cinema-going habits by telephoned interviews.
5 Performing masses of calculations by hand.

ANSWERS

1 As this would mean all times as measured would be longer than they really were, this is an example of bias.
2 This is a rather tricky one. If we assume that the tape when unstretched is correct, i.e. an inch then really is an inch, then it would introduce bias. If you said 'random error', then you were confusing the fact that the error would not be equal each time a waist was measured with the definition of a random error. The type of error is not determined by the magnitude of the error but the direction only. Bias may well vary in magnitude, as it does here, but it must act in a consistent direction, as it also does here. That is, any waist measurement taken with the stretched tape would tend to understate the waist size.
3 Since the smallest measurement that could be taken is 1/10

inch, this is an example of bias, i.e. all measurements would be too large.

4 It is highly likely that those with telephones have different cinema-going habits from those without. This means that the results would be biased towards these habits. Note, though, that we are not saying that every person who is contacted by phone will necessarily go to the cinema more (or less) times than any person without a phone, but that, overall, those with phones will behave differently to those without them. By asking only those with phones, then, we are ensuring that we get a 'biased' view of the situation. If you gave the answer 'random error', you were probably confused by this point.

5 This would cause random errors in general. Some would be in one direction and others in the other.

Self-check

What types of error do you think could have occurred in the scenario about the new product?

First of all there would have been errors introduced by the fact that the sample of purchasers of the Baby Gourmet foods was not random. Only a few retail outlets were covered anyway, and in each of these only those who were in a position to visit them at that time could be interviewed. For example, those parents who could not get to the shops because they were working would not be included. They may, indeed, have even sent somebody to do their shopping for them. If these people were interviewed, you would not be getting the opinion of the parent at all! Since there is every reason to suppose that the views of working parents would be very different from others (convenience could be high on their list, for example), there would be bias. The sample of babies would suffer from the same problems if it were not chosen in a random way.

The use of interviewers would also introduce some bias, unless very good controls were established over the operation. For example, the phrasing of the questions asked should be carefully chosen and the interviewers briefed on how to conduct the interviews. The danger is that there might be a tendency to say that the idea of Junior Gourmet foods is a good one, without really giving it much thought. It is well known that people being interviewed, or responding to questionnaires, have a tendency to agree with views expressed in the questions. This would apply even more so in the 'taste testing' phase. The parents involved there are given some free food and might feel obliged to say the baby enjoyed it just because it is free.

Random errors could arise in the selection of the sample for testing. There is no reason why such errors should not occur in addition to the bias discussed above. Further random errors could result from human error in copying results from one document to another, for example.

You may have other points not included here. If you have, check back with the text to make sure that you have got the right idea.

Ways of reducing error

Strictly speaking, very few errors of any kind are unavoidable. Sampling error can be removed by taking a census of the whole population, for example. However, in practice this is likely to be impossible, which is why sampling is used, of course. A great many statistical data collection methods, e.g. non-random sampling, are the result of efforts to come to terms with such problems. Except in very simple cases, the major trade-off is between effectiveness and cost. Consider quality control, for instance. Here the trade-off is between the chances of a defective item escaping detection and the cost of checking.

Cost is one of the most frequently ignored aspects of statistical theory, but it is really one of its most central. The correct use of statistics can produce great savings. But it should never be forgotten that a striving after what is imagined is statistical perfection is almost always unproductive unless a cost element is included. One of the most important ways of reducing the cost of collecting accurate data is to plan ahead. The design of documents can be crucial when gathering data from them at a later date, for example. If it has to be extracted from several different sources this will increase costs as well as give more opportunity for error.

It is important that, wherever possible, we know the extent of the error, otherwise one side of the cost-effectiveness equation is unknown. That is, we would have no idea what we would be getting for our money. In simple random and stratified sampling, there is a mathematical formula (given in Volume 2) for the effect of sample size, one of the major contributors to costs, on the sampling error. But in other cases we rely on experience to tell us what degree of control is necessary to reduce errors to an acceptable level. For example, quota sampling is nowadays an accurate method in certain well-known applications, provided that the established rules are adhered to.

Statisticians also provide low-cost methods of controlling errors in numeric variables. One increasingly popular way of checking for transcription errors, for instance, is to use a check digit. The most common example of this is the International Standard Book Number (ISBN), which now appears on all books published. It is a ten-digit number uniquely identifying that book. The one for Peter Drucker's *The Effective Executive*, published by Pan Books, is 0 330 02507 4, for instance. The first nine digits represent the number proper, while the tenth is a check digit, formed as follows:

Multiply the first digit (on the left) by 1, the second by 2, the third by 3, and so on until the ninth by 9;
add up the results;
divide the sum by 11 and take the remainder.

This is the check digit.

For example, with the number quoted we obtain

$(0 \times 1) + (3 \times 2) + (3 \times 3) + (0 \times 4) + (0 \times 5) + (2 \times 6) + (5 \times 7) + (0 \times 8) + (7 \times 9)$
$= 125$
$125/11 = 11 \text{ R } 4$

and the check digit is 4. Where the remainder is 10 an X is used. If a mistake is made in copying such a number, then the calculation shown above will almost always fail to produce the correct digit. The check only breaks down when two or more mistakes are made which compensate each other.

Activity

Go through the above checking procedure for the ISBN of this book.

In other cases, a variety of techniques may be used for reducing or detecting errors. So, for example, arithmetic may be checked by arriving at the result in a different way. A very simple application of this is in adding up a column of figures. The sum can be checked by just adding up the column in reverse order. Another common measure is to number documents sequentially. If any are mislaid, it is obvious because there will be a break in the sequence. Order form pads are usually pre-printed with a set of numbers, for instance, so that it can be seen if any one goes astray.

There are many more examples that could be given. In most of these, the technique is based on common sense. It is difficult to give rules which must be applied in all circumstances. Rather, it can be said that the detection and control of errors is a fundamental part of any statistical operation and should never be forgotten.

Self-check

How might the following errors be checked for, prevented or reduced in number?

1 Incorrect *totalling* of the attendance columns in a class register for each class meeting.
2 Incorrect copying of a part number from one form to another.
3 Losing one or more of a day's invoices.
4 Interviewers not adhering to the numbers given in a stratified quota sample, but reporting that they had.
5 Interviewers misclassifying respondents' answers.

ANSWERS

1 The usual way of dealing with this is to total the register student by student at the end of each term. The total of the student attendances should equal the total of the class attend-

ances: it does, after all, represent the same figure. This then
gives a check on the correctness of the class totals. Another
way of cutting down errors would be to count the number
attending each class to give one figure for a column total. This
could be checked by counting the number of absences marked
in the register for that meeting and subtracting this figure from
the number of possible attendances. This should, of course,
give the same result. If you had a different answer, check to
see that your solution would really prevent or discover totalling errors.

2 This is a case where a check digit would be useful. However, it
may be thought that the effort required to check up on this
digit every time a part number is copied would be excessive.
As a minimum precaution, the clerks who fill in the form
should be instructed to check back to see that they have copied
correctly. This could be backed up with some kind of system
for monitoring how many errors each clerk makes and, con-
ceivably, adjusting their pay accordingly. If you have a different answer, check to see that it would help reduce or detect
errors.

3 Here the sequential numbering of the invoices would ensure
that any missing one could be detected. An alternative method
would be to 'batch' the invoices together, i.e. to collect them
in one pile. The number of invoices in a batch could then be
written on a sheet attached to it. When the number of invoices
is counted, the result should match that on the sheet. You may
have a different answer, in which case check to see that it
would work.

4 One way of checking against this is to make random visits to
the interviewers while they are at work. Even so, it is very
difficult to stop an interviewer filling in a report form
fraudulently.

  One technique of finding out when an interviewer is doing
this is to put some check questions in the actual interview
schedule without the interviewer's knowledge. These questions would be designed to yield information on which strata
the respondent belonged to, though indirectly rather than
directly. This is because otherwise the interviewers could fill
in the answers themselves. You may have thought of a differ-

ent, but still effective, way of checking on this problem: check
to see that it would work.

5 One way round this is to give the interviewers explicit instructions on how to classify respondent's answers, and to train
them in their use. Of course, it would be better if the problem
could be avoided altogether. This could be done by getting the
interviewer to write down exactly what the respondent says.
This could only work where any such answer was reasonably
short. Again, if you have a different answer, check that it
really does work.

Self-check

The first nine digits of an ISBN are 0 330 24536. What is the
check digit?

The check digit is given by

$(0 \times 1) + (3 \times 2) + (3 \times 3) + (0 \times 4) + (2 \times 5) + (4 \times 6) +$
$(5 \times 7) + (3 \times 8) + (6 \times 9) =$
$0 + 6 + 9 + 0 + 10 + 24 + 35 + 24 + 54 = 162$
and $162 \div 11 = 14$ R 8, and so the check digit is 8.

Review

1 What kinds of data were collected in the concept testing
operation in the scenario on page 87 – attribute or
numeric, constant or variable? State briefly what errors,
if any, you think might have occurred in collecting the
data. What could have been done to reduce them?

2 A company has a plain paper copier which staff have free
access to. There is a form by the copier for entering the
number of copies made. The statistics from this form are
made up each week and sent to the office manager. What
type of data is collected, attribute or numeric, constant
or variable? How reliable do you think these statistics
would be? Could you improve their reliability? If so,
how?

3 Quality control in a factory involves checking the colour
of the product against a chart. What type of data is being

dealt with, attribute or numeric, constant or variable?
The checkers are paid piecework, i.e. according to how
many items they check in a given time. What errors do
you think occur? How could these be reduced?

ANSWERS

1 The data in the concept testing consisted of people's opinions
and so was attribute data. Remember, though, that in order to
perform statistical calculations on it, it has to be turned into
numbers, e.g. the number who said they thought Junior
Gourmet was a good idea. If you said numeric, it was only all
right if you meant that as above. If you meant that the actual
data collected was numeric, then what could this number
possibly represent? The data is not constant, of course, as it
varies from customer to customer.

   There are a number of places where errors could have
occurred. These would be mainly in recording the answers to
the interview questions. This would be especially true if they
were coded. There would also be bias resulting from the
sampling technique. Young working mothers may well be
under-represented, for example. There is not a lot that could
have been done to reduce these errors short of good planning
and training of the interviewers. Of course, spending a great
deal of money could have done this, but it would not have
been worth it.

   You could have come up with different errors. If you did,
just check over them carefully to make sure you were correct,
as far as you can.

2 The data in this case is numeric: it is the number of copies
made. If the person making the copy had to fill in his name
and department and so on, this data would be attribute. It is a
variable, as not everyone makes the same number of copies. It
is unlikely that these statistics would be very reliable. People
would forget to fill in the form and some may even be doing
their own private copying. The only way to change that
situation would be to exercise greater control over the machine. One very good way of doing this is to make everybody
take out a special key. There is a system where the key has a
counter in it. When it is returned, the new figure is recorded

against the name of the person returning it. Usage can then be determined by subtracting the previous reading from this figure.

You probably got the idea about the source of error, especially if you have ever worked in an office where this has happened. It is unlikely that you put in anything about special keys. This information was given as an illustration of how the usage of the machine could be controlled.

3 Colour is, as we have seen, an attribute variable. You cannot easily express it as a number (not one that people could easily use anyway). In this case we have constant colours on the chart, but the data being observed is the varying colour of the product. You should not have confused the two.

If anyone on quality checking is paid piecework it will lead to lax control. A worker will always try to work fast to earn his extra pay and will consequently make more errors. It is thus a practice to be avoided. Doing so should reduce dramatically, but never totally eliminate, such errors.

If you said colour is numeric, were you thinking of the wavelengths? It is very difficult for humans to recognize colour in terms of this number. It is generally only used by engineers and scientists.

The human element

In general, it is human beings that collect statistical data for use by themselves or others. This remains true even when measuring instruments are used, since these have to be read. One of the best-known characteristics of humans is that they make mistakes, especially when doing repetitive work. This means that mistakes will inevitably be made in collecting data and so cause errors in it. The modern trend is to let computers collect it. In the United States you can even vote by machine, for instance. This eliminates human error in one part of the operation. However, in most instances all this does is to transfer it elsewhere. The human element then appears in the putting of data into the machine ('inputting' data, as the computer people would say).

It is, therefore, very important that people who collect data and people who, as part of their job, input data to computerized systems, should be trained to carry out these tasks. Where input to the computer is by the 'public', the method of doing so should be as simple and as straightforward as possible. There should also be checks on these operations, performed by a computer wherever feasible. One point that should be stressed is that where payment is involved for this type of work, it should not be dependent on work rate. Either it should be based on time or, better, on a combination of speed and accuracy, with emphasis on the latter.

As well as being prone to make mistakes, human beings are inclined to be subjective. This remains true when they are collecting data. Let's have a look at an example.

Self-check

Suppose you were asked to go out and interview a quota sample of tall men. How tall would a man have to be before you would interview him? How would you know how tall he was anyway?

Because you are given no guidance on what is to be taken as tall, you have to apply your own subjective judgement. By this, it is meant that you would not necessarily reach the same conclusions as would someone else. For example, if you are tall, you would probably have a different idea of what a tall man is than if you were small, and vice versa. The same thing goes for your estimate of a man's height. As a contrast, if you were able to measure each man's height, this would be an objective measurement. Within a degree of possible accuracy, anybody else measuring these men's heights would arrive at the same answer.

So, wherever possible, the subjective element should be avoided in data collection. It is for this reason that interested parties should never be involved in statistical data collection, for example. Training can play a large part here too. People can be taught to apply subjective criteria in this operation. But they must have a system to use. This means that, when planning a data collection exercise, careful thought must be given to eliminating the subjective element wherever feasible. Objective criteria must be provided if this is to be achieved. Of course, it is neither possible nor desirable to remove all subjective judgement, but it should only be allowed in extreme cases.

Self-check

Give examples of situations, which could occur in data collection, where subjective judgement may lead to errors.

There are two major areas of data collection where subjective judgement could lead to errors if care was not taken. One is the choice of data. Bias can be introduced where the investigator is allowed some freedom in selecting the sample. This can also happen when data which doesn't fit preconceptions is rejected as faulty. The other area, which has already been mentioned in an earlier chapter, is 'measuring', i.e. classifying, the values of attribute variables.

For example, the colour of a car is an attribute variable. We cannot put a numerical value on it. If we are trying to find out which colour cars people like, we would run into difficulties with making sure that the data we collected from one person was compatible with that collected from any other. They may not agree as to the definition of green, for instance, in cases where it borders on blue. So very careful guidance must be given in such cases. With the colours, for example, the provision of colour charts would help a great deal.

There are several ways in which the element of subjectivity can be reduced, the major ones being:

- to give as clear a definition as possible of any technical terms, e.g. 'shrinkage' in stocks;
- to supply positive aids where possible, e.g. colour charts for when colours have to be classified;
- to give a clear guide as to the meaning of the different categories, e.g. socio-economic grouping (a standard could be used here such as that produced by the Institute of Practitioners in Advertising);

- vague terms should be avoided; e.g. 'large shops' should not be used but rather some strict definition;
- the use of the category 'other' should be avoided if possible; e.g. in the classification of jobs 'other' can cover a very wide range of work;
- terms used should be as neutral as possible; e.g. 'unofficial stoppages of work' is preferred to 'wildcat strikes';
- clear guidelines should be given on what to do in marginal cases, e.g. whether a given expenditure is capital or revenue.

If statistics are to be meaningfully compared, they must have been prepared on the same basis. Where classification is involved, it is thus very important that the same categories are used. Wherever possible, therefore, standard classifications should be employed. An example of one is the Standard Industrial Classification (SIC), which all government statistics use as a basis. The categories relate to similar products, processes and services, as can be seen in table 1 below.

TABLE 1. STANDARD INDUSTRIAL CLASSIFICATION (1968)

Order	Title	Minimum list headings*
I	Agriculture, Forestry, Fishing	001–003
II	Mining, Quarrying	101–109
III	Food, Drink, Tobacco	211–240
IV	Coal and Petroleum Products	261–265
V	Chemicals and Allied Industries	271–279
VI	Metal Manufacture	311–323
VII	Mechanical Engineering	331–349
VIII	Instrument Engineering	351–354
IX	Electrical Engineering	361–369
X	Shipbuilding, Marine Engineering	370
XI	Vehicles	380–389
XII	Metal Goods not specified elsewhere	390–399
XIII	Textiles	411–429
XIV	Leather, Leather Goods, Fur	431–433
XV	Clothing, Footwear	441–450

Order	Title	Minimum list headings*
XVI	Bricks, Pottery, Glass, Cement, etc.	461–469
XVII	Timber, Furniture, etc.	471–479
XVIII	Paper, Printing, Publishing	481–489
XIX	Other Manufacturing Industries	491–499
XX	Construction	500
XXI	Gas, Electricity, Water	601–603
XXII	Transport, Communication	701–709
XXIII	Distributive Trades	810–832
XXIV	Insurance, Banking, Finance, Business Services	860–866
XXV	Professional and Scientific Services	871–879
XXVI	Miscellaneous Services	881–899
XXVII	Public Administration, Defence	901–906

*The Minimum List Headings (MLHs) show the classification in more detail. For example, 419 is:

419 Carpets.
Manufacturing pile carpets, carpeting, rugs, mats and matting from wool, cotton and man-made fibres, whether by weaving, tufting or other processes. Needle-loom carpets are classified in Heading 429.

It can, however, be difficult to classify head office personnel when the company provides a range of goods/services which cover more than one of these categories. But the SIC is, nevertheless, an extremely useful aid. For example, the government publishes the numbers of businesses in each category, which can be used to estimate the size of various segments for industrial marketing.

Activity

Classify your friends, relations and fellow workers according to their hair colour. Use the categories Bald, White, Grey, Red, Brown, Black and Blonde. Note any problems that you encounter. Did you run into difficulties? The bald category is particularly difficult to use, isn't it?

Self-check

Draw up a set of instructions for allocating expenses incurred by an old people's home into capital and revenue.

The set of instructions you have drawn up should contain:

capital – should include all expenses which will benefit the home in the next accounting period as well as this one. For example, new beds, curtains, building alterations;
revenue – should only include those items which will be of no benefit to the home in the next accounting period. For example, food, medicine, fares, heating, lighting.

In practice, there would probably be a fairly exhaustive list of items that should be put into each category.

Self-check

Allocate the following to the various major categories (orders) in the Standard Industrial Classification system.

1 Globe-Mutual Life Assurance.
2 Grebe and Co., Printers.
3 Sherbournes, Wholesale Confectioners.
4 Chives, Chives, Chives and Smollett, Solicitors.
5 Pring Bros, Makers of Doors and Window Frames.

ANSWERS

1 XXIV – i.e. Insurance, banking, finance and business services.
2 XVIII – i.e. Paper, printing and publishing.
3 XXIIII – i.e. Distributive trades.
4 XXV – i.e. Professional and other services.
5 XX – i.e. Construction. You may have XVII, Timber and furniture, but in this case the purpose of the goods is what is important, not what they are made of, and so your answer would be incorrect.

Using someone else's data

Data collected first hand for some specific purpose is called 'primary data'. If this is later used for some other purpose it becomes 'secondary data'.

This should not be confused with 'secondary statistics' which are statistics derived from secondary data.

Self-check

Which of the following are primary data and which secondary data?

1 The previous year's revenue expenses when used to estimate this year's.
2 Figures on car breakdowns, classified by manufacturer, compiled by a motoring organization and used by one particular manufacturer to advertise its cars.
3 Polls on voting intentions published in newspapers.
4 Information on clock cards when used for making up wages.
5 Information on clock cards when used for estimating time lost through sickness.
6 Sales representatives' expenses sheets when used to estimate the mileage covered by their company cars.

ANSWERS

1 Secondary. Figures for the previous year's revenue expenses were not collected primarily so as to be able to predict next year's.
2 Again this is secondary data. The motoring organization certainly did not collect the figures so that the car manufacturer could use them in its advertisement.
3 This is primary data. It was collected specifically for the purpose. Note, however, that if we use it to predict the result of the voting, we are going beyond the meaning we can attach to the figures. We are making an assumption that people will vote as they say they will. If you said that the data was secondary, this is probably what you had in mind.

4 This is primary data. The whole point of collecting it is to be able to calculate the wages.

5 Here the same data is used but for a different purpose. So it is secondary data in this case.

6 Once again this is secondary data. The reason for the expense claims is not so that the mileage covered by the company cars can be found. If this data is required, it would be better to ask for that and to make random checks to ensure that the correct figure is being given.

Great care needs to be exercised when using secondary data, otherwise erroneous results may be obtained. A check needs to be carried out to ensure that any source of error is identified. The following questions, in particular, should be asked.

1 What was the purpose of the original data collection exercise? How does this relate to the present one? E.g. great care has to be taken when using an electoral register as a sampling frame for market research.

2 Who collected the original data? Was it a reputable organization or individual? Did they have an interest in obtaining a particular result? E.g. data collected by a company about its own, or a rival's, products must always be somewhat suspect.

3 Is the data actual, an estimate or a projection? E.g. sales forecasts are not the same as sales.

4 Is the data out of date? E.g. data on buying habits for a particular commodity may well be invalid if there has been a recent large price increase.

5 Is the data complete? Is there any spurious data? E.g. information on retail outlets may exclude small 'corner shops'.

6 Does the data contain any abnormal items? E.g. tourist figures for a country may cover a period when something exceptional occurred, such as the Olympic Games.

7 Are key terms defined? Do they conform to those in the present exercise? E.g. 'manufacturing industry', 'profit', 'income', and 'assets' all need careful definition.

8 Are the data collection methods clearly explained? E.g. the sampling method, if any, should be given.

9 Were the data collection techniques employed adequate?

(See the previous two chapters for guidance on how to tell this, as well as this chapter for likely errors). E.g. there should be adequate controls over interviewers.

10 Is the data internally consistent? Is it consistent with similar data from elsewhere? E.g. an opinion poll on voting intentions should not yield data drastically different from other similar polls.

Where suitable secondary data is available and satisfactory answers can be obtained to the above questions, a great deal of time and money can obviously be saved by using it. Very often it would have been impossible for the data to have been obtained otherwise. This is particularly true of statistical data produced by the government, the numbers of births as in the scenario, for instance.

Self-check

What are the answers to the above questions in the case of the birth statistics in the scenario? (Check with the *Annual Abstract* if necessary. You should find one in your local college or public library.)

Answers to the above questions are as follows.

1 The original exercise arose from the government's need for vital statistics on which to plan, for example, school provision. This is near enough to Kevin's requirement to be feasible.*

2 The government collected the data. It should, therefore, be quite accurate.

3 The historic figures are actual, though estimates are often provided on the basis of the latest available figures. The figures for up to 2001 are clearly projections. (As are the ones for the current year.)

4 There is the problem that the data is almost two years out of date. Projections from this are bound to be speculative. (It should be noted that use of the *Monthly Digest of Statistics*

---

*Of course, this is assuming that Kevin has chosen the right set of data.

would give more up-to-date figures than those in the *Annual Abstract*.)

5 The data should be reasonably complete.*

6 There does not appear to be any abnormalities. The big power black-out in the Eastern United States some years ago is reputed to have caused a baby boom later, but there has been nothing similar in the UK since the post-Second-World-War 'bulge'.

7 The figures are given for 'live' births. They are also 'occurrences', not registrations, for England and Wales.

8 It is clear that these figures are census ones, obtained through the legal obligation to report births.

9 The figures should be reasonably accurate as the census through legal obligation is an efficient method of data collection.

10 The birth figures are consistent with expectations based on other years and with population figures.

Self-check

Comment on the suitability of using the *secondary data* in the self-check on page 173, for the purposes stated.

ANSWERS

a While revenue expenses for one year may be some indication of what they will be the following year, they should be treated with caution. It might well, for instance, contain some abnormal items. In a very cold winter there would be a larger than usual fuel bill, for example.

b The motor manufacturer may well leave out some of the qualifications that were placed on the original figures. It is, at any rate, going to present these figures in the best light it can. We must therefore be very sceptical of them. Furthermore, what kind of sample do these figures form?

c This is a very poor use of the data in question. The reason for absence is not given on the cards and so paid leave and illness will both result in gaps on the card.

*This point has been treated earlier in this chapter.

d There is some reason to suppose that there may not be an exact relation between the car mileage and the expenses claim. Apart from a little exaggeration, the car may not have been used for all of the trips covered by the claim. It could have been broken down.

Review

1 You read in a paper that the government says that it is 'within realistic striking distance of achieving the target of reducing the money supply and the public spending borrowing requirement to acceptable levels'. You want to immediately go to the local college library to check that this is so, by consulting the published statistics. (See the appendix on sources.) What would you need to know before you could do so?

2 A poverty action group has produced a report which is said to show that over five per cent of the families in a town in the north of England are in a state of poverty. This report is based on a sample survey of the incomes and expenditures of families in the town carried out by the group. What questions would you want to see answered in the report before you were satisfied with its claims enough to use it in some research you were doing? (Don't go into too great detail – not as much as in the chapter.)

ANSWER

1 You would need to know exactly what was meant by all the terms used. There are two which are subjective as they stand, 'realistic striking distance' and 'acceptable levels'. Until these were defined specifically, in terms of monetary values, it would be impossible to check the statement.

In addition, you would need to know what measure the government was using to determine what the money supply is, as there are several possibilities. And lastly you would need to find out, if you didn't know already, what the exact definition of the public spending borrowing requirement is.

If you don't know that there are two or more measures for

the money supply, you should at least know that this term needs defining.

2 Here, too, the definitions are crucial. Just what is meant by 'in a state of poverty', for example? You would expect the report to define this very carefully.

As the report is prepared by a poverty action group, you should be on the look out for (unintentional) distortions of the data or false conclusions. So you should ask such questions as, 'When was the data collected? Are the data collection techniques clearly explained? Were they adequate? And is the data in agreement with any other available?

But you should also ask some questions of your own research. For example, are the figures relevant to it? The purpose for which they were collected should be in accord with that of the research. Also, the figures are for one town only. This does not allow us to apply the conclusions to elsewhere.

If you didn't mention the points in the last paragraph then this is reasonable, as they weren't strictly asked for.

7 | Using approximations

When complete accuracy is impossible

Self-check

Just how accurately could you tell the time, whatever it happened to be?

When we try to measure such things as time, length and weight, we come up against a problem. However accurately we may do it, in theory we could always have done it more so. When weighing out the ingredients to cook for canning, for example, we could be accurate to a kilogramme, a gramme, or a milligramme and so on. Numeric variables such as these are called 'continuous variables'. The strict definition is as follows:

A continuous variable is a numeric variable such that, given any two values it may take, there is always one in between these that it could also take.

A continuous variable is like a decimal fraction in this sense. Given any two decimal fractions, one can always be found that lies between them; just put a non-zero digit at the right of the smallest one. For example, if .70371 and .70372 are the initial fractions, then .703715 lies between the two.

Self-check

Before going on, stop and see if you can think of a few more continuous variables yourself. Go on from time, length and weight to similar variables.

Apart from time, length and weight, there are area, volume, speed, acceleration, temperature, angle and light intensity, all of which are continuous variables, together with many more. When we measure any of these, we must make a decision as to how accurate we are going to attempt to be.

For example, if measuring someone's waist for a pair of off-the-peg trousers, the nearest inch would probably be good enough. When measuring a component for a complex machine, on the other hand, a few thousandths of an inch could be crucial. It all depends, of course, on the use to which the measurements are to be put.

For instance, in the JICTAR TV audience survey mentioned in Chapter 5, the following degrees of accuracy are stipulated. The meter records accurately to one minute. This certainly seems good enough for the purpose. The diaries are kept in quarter-hour units. If anyone is in the room with the television on for at least eight minutes in that quarter-hour, it is marked off in the diary as a viewing period. This is obviously a compromise. It would be counter-productive to ask someone to mark off each minute in the diary. On the other hand, to use hours would give misleading results.

Self-check

Can you see where someone not familiar with the exact workings of the JICTAR survey might misinterpret the data from the diaries?

When interpreting the data in the diaries, two very important points should be borne in mind. Firstly, they show when people were in the room with the television on, not necessarily when they were watching. Secondly, even if they were watching, they might not have been watching for the whole quarter-hour, but just for eight minutes of it. Methodological difficulties in defining 'watching' and the constraints on accuracy, discussed above, necessitate this procedure for completing the diaries, however. So any conclusions about whether or not particular advertisements were watched, for example, must be based on other evidence in addition to that collected from the diaries.

When complete accuracy is very difficult

While complete accuracy is actually impossible with continuous variables, this is not the case with 'discrete variables'. These are basically numeric variables which can only take certain values. For example, the price of things can only be given in terms of the smallest unit of currency, halfpence in this country. It can be seen that complete accuracy is possible here. Indeed, prices in shops are usually given exactly: there would be a few complaints if they weren't. The strict definition of a discrete variable is as follows:

> A discrete variable is a numeric variable such that there are always to be found two values that it may take between which there is no other one that it may take.

A discrete variable is like an integer (whole number) in this sense. Take any two integers next to each other (i.e. such that one is 1 more than the other), then there is no other between them. No integer exists between 7 and 8, for instance. There is thus a relationship between discrete variables and counting. In general, a discrete variable represents something that can be counted. Price, for example, can be equated with counting out the money when we pay for something. Note that such counting does not have to be performed in whole units. In the case of price, we can use halfpence, for instance.

Self-check

What discrete variables appear in the scenario? Can you think of any more? Is age (of people) a continuous variable or a discrete one?

In the scenario, several discrete variables are mentioned, the number on school rolls, the sales of Baby Gourmet food (either by jars or by value), the number of births in a given year and, actually, the year itself. Whether or not the birth rate is discrete or not is considerably more difficult to say. In general, the ratio of two discrete variables is continuous unless the figure on the bottom lies within strict limits. E.g. the ratio of the minutes reading to the hours reading on a digital clock is discrete (in steps of 1/12, or 1/24 if it is a 24-hour clock). The population of Britain has no strict upper limit, so the birth rate is effectively a continuous variable.

Other discrete variables are the number of matches in a box, the number of bottles in a milk crate, the number of people in the UK who suffer from hayfever and, indeed, anything that could, in theory, be counted. This does not necessarily mean physically counted. For example, age *last birthday* is a discrete variable, although age, as such, is a continuous one. Here we count the number of years since birth. The words 'in theory' above are important. The number of blades of grass in a lawn is a discrete variable which could, in theory, be counted. In practice, this would be virtually impossible.

Self-check

Which of the following are continuous variables and which discrete?

1 People's weight.
2 The total weight of Baby Gourmet food produced a day.
3 The number of jars of Baby Gourmet food produced a day.
4 The number of matches produced worldwide in a year.

ANSWERS

1 Continuous. We could measure this as accurately as we liked (or as we were able to!).
2 and 3 While the total number of jars produced is discrete, the weight of food that fills them is not. Small variations in the filling of the jars mean that this is so.
4 This is discrete. If you said 'continuous' you were getting confused with the fact that it is a very large number and so difficult to measure.

Complete accuracy is very often difficult to obtain with a discrete variable, however. Two examples of this have been given above: they were the number of blades of grass in a lawn and, in the self-check, the number of matches produced worldwide.

Self-check

Do you think it would be easy to find the number of people in Britain who suffer from hayfever? If not, why not?

No it wouldn't. The difficulty would be in locating the data. This, then, is another example of not being able to get completely accurate data.

In fact complete accuracy cannot feasibly be obtained with a discrete variable if

- the numbers are so large as to be effectively impossible to measure accurately, e.g. the number of grains of salt per packet;
- the numbers involved are so large as to make human error occurring during the measuring almost a certainty, e.g. the number of babies born in England and Wales in a year;
- the population is not known exactly, or is difficult to locate, e.g. the number of people in the UK who suffer from hayfever;
- the population changes more rapidly than the time taken to measure it, e.g. the population of England and Wales.

It should be noted that it is for the above reasons, amongst others, that sampling methods are used.

Self-check

What problems do you think would prevent complete accuracy in measuring the following?

1 The number of votes cast for a parliamentary candidate in a general election.
2 The number of murders committed in the UK in a year.
3 The number of book titles in print at any given time, published in the USA or the UK.
4 The number of bees in a hive.
5 The number of small components held by a very large manufacturer of electrical goods.

ANSWERS

1 Sheer numbers of counters. Someone, sometime, is bound to make a mistake. That is why recounts are always requested when the result is close.

2 While the figures for recorded murders are available, there are probably ones which go undiscovered and are recorded as ordinary deaths.

3 There are a great many books in print. While most of these appear in a special directory, it is difficult to get hold of information on the latest ones. So here it is a case of the data changing more rapidly than the time taken to collect it. If you said that the information is not easy to locate, then you have a point. However, books are made to be bought, so every effort will be made to publicize any book printed. It should be possible, therefore, to get hold of the data. If you said that the numbers are so large that there is bound to be a human error, then once again this is not unreasonable. However, it is likely that there will be sufficient checks, and enough time to carry them out, so that this error will be reduced to a low level.

4 Here the population can be reached. The bees could, for example, be put to sleep to be counted. it is another case of there being bound to be human error during the counting. In fact, there would be so many that if you have said that the number would be so great as to make it effectively impossible to count them you cannot count this as an incorrect answer.

5 Once again there are really two factors which may both operate. The number would change so rapidly that a 100-per-cent accurate figure would be impossible. But even if it did not, it would be very difficult to avoid any human error.

When complete accuracy is unnecessary

Complete accuracy of measurement is seldom absolutely necessary in statistical work, even when possible. What is important is that the degree of inaccuracy (i.e. error) is acceptable. Now the true value of a numeric variable is the value we would obtain if we could measure it perfectly accurately. The degree of error in a measurement depends on how close to the true value is the value that we obtain. The 'absolute error' is defined as the value of the variable, *as taken*, less the true value. Where the true value is known exactly, so is the error. Where it is not, we can often specify the maximum possible error, or at least say what the chances of getting a large error are.

For example, if the true population of a town is 86,945 but we decide to record it as 86,900, then the absolute error is 86,900 – 86,945 = –45.

> ### Self-check
>
> What is the absolute error in the figure for the stocks of a component which is taken to be 56,680 when its true value is 56,675?

It is 56,680 – 56,675 = 5. If you got –5, you did the subtraction the wrong way round.

But why should we allow any error at all if the true value is known? The reason is that too great an accuracy can often just get in the way of appreciating the figures. For example, in the scenario, Kevin could have obtained the 'exact' figures for the number of births in England and Wales from the *Annual Abstract*. A different table, showing births by age of mother, would have given them. The figures for 1970–77 were, for instance, as given in table 2 below.

TABLE 2. NUMBER OF LIVE BIRTHS IN ENGLAND AND WALES 1970–77

Year	Live births	Live births (thousands)
1970	784,486	784
1971	783,155	783
1972	725,440	725
1973	675,953	676
1974	639,885	640
1975	603,445	603
1976	584,270	584
1977	569,259	569

Now the last three digits in the exact live births figures would be
of little use to Kevin and it would make for a clearer picture if
they were removed. This may be done by 'rounding' the figures
to the nearest thousand. These rounded birth figures are also
shown in table 2. It is rounded figures like these that Kevin
consulted in the *Annual Abstract*.

Rounding figures 'to the nearest' something

In the above table the rounding is to the nearest thousand.
Rounding need not be to the nearest thousand, of course. We
can round to any convenient number of decimal figures. Figure
11 shows the sequence of steps to be followed when rounding.

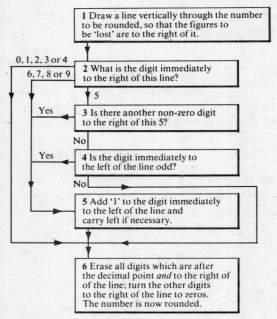

Figure 11. Steps in rounding 'to the nearest . . .'

The step taken when rounding from 5 ensures that approximately half the time rounding is upwards and half the time

downwards. To appreciate this, consider a petty cash book. Suppose a rule is adopted to always round down where $\frac{1}{2}$ps are involved. For example, $18\frac{1}{2}$p is entered as 18p and $19\frac{1}{2}$p as 19p. After a week, if a reasonable number of entries have been rounded down, the total error could be tens of pence. If the figures had been consistently rounded up similar error would have occurred in the opposite direction. Such errors are said to be cumulative, and they are examples of bias. But if the rule given in figure 11 is adopted, and $18\frac{1}{2}$p becomes 18p while $19\frac{1}{2}$p becomes 20p, for instance, the errors will tend to cancel each other out; that is, rounding errors are random or unbiased errors.

Some examples of rounding are given below:

1951 to the nearest 1000 is 2000;
1951 to the nearest 100 is 2000;
1951 to the nearest 10 is 1950;

.0535 to 1 decimal place is .1;
.0535 to 2 decimal places is .05;
.0535 to 3 decimal places is .054;
.0525 to 3 decimal places is .052.

Check through these using figure 11.

Self-check

Round the following figures as indicated:

a .4505 to 1 decimal place.
b .65 to 1 decimal place.
c 1.316 to 1 decimal place.
d 136.01 to the nearest 10.
e 7747 to the nearest 100.
f 713.05 to 1 decimal place.

ANSWERS

a .4/505 is rounded to .5. (Steps 1, 2, 3, 5, 6 in the diagram.) If you got .4, then you forgot that the 5 at the end means that you have to add 1 to the 4 (step 3 in the diagram).

b .6/5 is rounded to .6. (Steps 1, 2, 3, 4, 6.) If you got .7, then you went wrong at step 4, and added 1 to the 6, which you shouldn't have.

c 1.3/16 is rounded to 1.3. (Steps 1, 2, 6.) If you had 1.32 then you were rounding to the nearest 2 dp. and not 1 dp.

d 13/6.01 is rounded to 140. (Steps 1, 2, 5, 6.) If you got 136 then you were rounding to the nearest *unit* and not the nearest 10. If you had 130 then you overlooked the fact that at step 2 you should have gone to step 5.

e 77/47 is rounded to 7700. (Steps 1, 6.) If you had 7750, then you were rounding to the nearest 10 and not the nearest 100. If you got 7800 then you went wrong at step 2.

f 713.0/5 is rounded to 713.0. (Steps 1, 2, 3, 4, 6.) If you got 713.1 then you went wrong at step 4.0 is *even* and so you should have gone to step 6 after step 4. If you wrote down 713 as your answer then you did not do exactly what it says in step 6. It tells you to erase those digits to the right of the decimal point, but *only* those which are also to *the right of the line*. As the 0 following the decimal point is also to the *left* of the line, it must not be erased. Thus there is a convention that 45.0, say, is a number rounded to 1 decimal place, 45.00 to 2 decimal places and so on.

When a figure is rounded, it no longer equals its true value in general. The absolute error so introduced is often called the 'rounding error'. This is obtained by subtracting the true figure from the rounded one. So, in the table, the rounding errors in the figures for 1973 and 1976 are 676,000 − 675,953 = 47 and 584,000 − 584,270 = −270 respectively.

In cases where the true value of a variable is not known, neither is the absolute error. This is always so where continuous variables are concerned. We can, however, still state the *maximum possible* absolute error, provided that the *precision* with which the original measurements were made is known. Before looking at maximum errors, we must first examine precision, then. For example, suppose we are told that the length of a particular rod is 10 cm. What can we say about the maximum absolute error? The answer is nothing unless we know whether it was measured to the nearest centimetre, millimetre or what. Generally if it appears as 10.0 cm, for example, we can assume that this is the nearest millimetre. But it is better practice for the precision to be specified.

Similarly, with discrete variables we need to know how precise a given figure is. Suppose we are told that the stocks of a particular item stand at 10,000. Is this to the nearest 1, 10, 100 or even 1000? Sometimes you will see such a figure written as 10(000) meaning that it is to the nearest 1000 or 100(00) to the nearest 100 and so on. More usually, however, there is a separate statement. In the birth figutes in the *Annual Abstract* that Kevin used, for example, this appears at the head of the table.

Self-check

In each case below, say what the precision of the figure is, i.e. to the nearest ——, if the convention outlined above is adhered to.

a 10.000 m;
b 10.00 m;
c 10.0 m;
d 10 m;
e 1(0) m;
f 1(00) m;
g 1(000) m. (Note m is metres.)

ANSWERS

a To nearest thousandth of a metre, i.e. millimetre.
b To the nearest hundredth of a metre, i.e. centimetre.
c To the nearest tenth of a metre, i.e. decimetre.
d To the nearest metre. If you said nearest 10 metres, the figure on its own does not imply this. You would need a separate statement to warrant this conclusion, or the figure would have to be expressed as in (**e**).
e To the nearest 10 metres.
f To the nearest 100 metres.
g To the nearest 1000 metres, ie. kilometre.

Now once we know the precision of the original measurements, we can calculate the maximum absolute error. This can be done by looking at the possible range of true values that the figure

could represent. For instance, if the 10 cm rod was measured to
the nearest centimetre, it could have a true value of anywhere
between 9.5 and 10.5 cm. The maximum possible absolute error
would then be ± (plus or minus) 5 mm. If the rod was measured
to the nearest millimetre, the range would be 9.95 cm to 10.05
cm, and the error ± 0.5 mm. Note that, where true values are
unknown, we generally just use 'absolute error' for 'maximum
absolute error'. Figure 12 illustrates this point.

(a) Measuring a rod to the nearest centimetre and getting 10 cm.

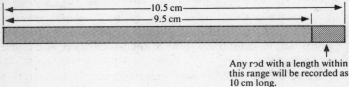

Any rod with a length within
this range will be recorded as
10 cm long.

(b) Measuring a rod to the nearest millimetre and getting 10 cm.

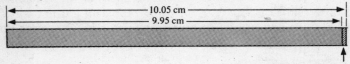

Any rod with a length within
this range will be recorded as
10 cm long.

Figure 12

Self-check

How would we go about finding out the rounding error in
the figures in table 2 on page 185?

Suppose we assume that we do not know the exact numbers of
births in England and Wales from 1970 to 1977. Then we cannot
calculate the actual absolute errors. But we can say that none
could have been more than 500 either way, or it would have been
rounded to a different figure. Thus for 1973, for instance,
anything outside the range 676(000) – 500 to 676(000) + 500, i.e.
675,500 to 676,500, would not have rounded to 676.

Self-check

A digital watch is used to time a number of trips made in a car one day. If there is a seconds readout, as well as hours and minute ones, but the time is recorded to the nearest minute, what is the maximum absolute error that can be obtained? Suppose there was no seconds readout, what would the maximum absolute error be then?

In the first case, the error would be a maximum of 30 seconds. This is because, for instance, a time of 2 hrs 32 mins and 30 secs would be recorded as 2 hrs 32 mins, giving an absolute error of 30 secs. If the seconds value had been a trifle more or a trifle less, this error would have been less. It must therefore be the maximum possible error.

In the second case, you may well have simply answered 'the same'. If you did you would have been wrong. When does the minute readout of a digital watch change? It changes when the seconds reach 60! So, if the seconds readout is not available, a recorded time of 2 hrs 33 mins could represent a true time of 2 hrs 33 mins and just coming up to 60 seconds. The error then would be one whole minute.

But the *absolute* error is sometimes misleading.

Self-check

A head of Engineering at a technical college works out his budget for the coming year at £16,672. To allow for inaccuracies, etc. he puts in for £17,000. The head of General Studies calculates his budget at £1672 and puts in for £2000. What is the absolute error in each case? Comment on your results.

You can see that the absolute error is the same in each case, i.e. £328. This doesn't seem right somehow. The head of Engineering seems hard done by!

The drawback with absolute errors is that the same error in two separate figures can have a different significance in each. This happens when one of them is considerably bigger than the other.

For example, suppose there are two packets of washing powder, with stated weights of 840 g and 2800 g, but actually weighing 845 g and 2805 g. Then the absolute error in both cases is 5 g. However, a cost accountant would have different reactions to each of these. 8400 g of washing powder should make either ten small or three large packets. But with 5 g error in each packet, it would take 50 g extra to produce the small packets, but only 15 g extra to produce the large ones.

It is for reasons like this that 'relative error' is used. This expresses the error as a percentage of the true value, if known. For example, the relative errors for the two packets of washing powder are $\frac{5}{840} \times 100\% = .60\%$ (to two decimal places) for the small and $\frac{5}{2800} \times 100\% = .18\%$ (to two decimal places) for the large. Note that the error is shown here as a percentage of the weight given on the packet. This is because this is regarded as the 'true' value. The error occurred in the weighing. When the true value is not known, the maximum relative error has to be estimated by expressing the maximum absolute error as a percentage of *whatever value is taken*. For instance, the relative error in the measurement of the '10 cm' rod is $\frac{5}{10} \times 100\% = 5\%$ if measured to the nearest centimetre and $\frac{.05}{10} \times 100\% = .5\%$ if to the nearest millimetre. As with absolute errors, however, even when the true value is unknown, we generally drop the word 'maximum' and just use the phrase 'relative error'.

Self-check

If the true time for a trip in the car of the self-check on page 191 was 20 mins and 6 secs, but was recorded as 20 mins, what was the relative error? If the time recorded had been obtained by rounding to the nearest minute, and it was 20 mins, what would we calculate the relative error as if we did not know the true time?

If we know what the true value is, we can calculate the relative error as

$$\frac{(20 \text{ mins} - 20 \text{ mins } 6 \text{ secs}) \times 100}{20 \text{ mins } 6 \text{ secs}}$$

or $\frac{-6 \times 100}{20 \times 60 + 6} = \frac{-600}{1206} = -.5\%$ to one decimal place, if we turn it to seconds. You may have missed the negative sign. This is not a serious mistake but it should be watched for. You may also have divided by the recorded time of 20 mins. You would have got the same result, because of rounding. That method is, however, wrong where the true value is known.

If we did not know the true time, and one of 20 mins was recorded, we would have to quote the maximum possible relative error. When rounding to the nearest minute, the maximum absolute error is 30 secs. The corresponding relative error is $\frac{30 \times 100}{20 \times 60} = \frac{3000}{1200} = 2.5\%$ if we turn all the figures into seconds. You should note that the figure on the bottom is the *recorded* value, since we do not know what the true value is. Actually this figure is $\pm 2.5\%$ since the error could be either way. If you got any other answer, read carefully through this answer to make sure you understand it.

Review

1 A jeans manufacturer wants to find out if teenagers' sizes have changed recently, so it wants to know waist, hip and leg measurements. What type of data is this? It is decided to collect data on colour and style preferences at the same time. What kind of data is this? Will the data collected be perfectly accurate? If not, why not?

2 The same manufacturer collects data from government sources on the number of teenagers in the population. What type of data is this? How accurate will it be?

3 Some of the measurements of the waist sizes of teenagers are 24.3 in, 27.8 in, 26.5 in and 27.5 in. What are these values when rounded to the nearest inch? Assuming the measurements to be accurate, what are the absolute and relative errors in the rounded figures? Which rounded figure is most accurate? Suppose the true values of the measurements were not known, but only the rounded ones. What would be the (maximum possible) absolute and relative errors then?

194   *Making sense of the data collected*

ANSWERS

1 The waist, hip and leg measurements are continuous numeric
  data. If you said they were discrete data, think whether you
  could ever expect the measurements to be accurate down to
  the smallest possible fraction of an inch. The data on colour
  and style is attribute data. If you said it was numeric, what
  number would be recorded if someone liked narrow, red
  jeans, for example? The data collected could never be completely accurate. Firstly, it would be out of the question to
  measure and interview all teenagers. Secondly, the numeric
  data, being continuous, can never be perfectly accurate, but
  can only be measured 'to the nearest ——'. The attribute data
  will need to be coded and classified, and some inaccuracy will
  almost certainly occur here too.

2 The data here is discrete and numeric. If you said it was
  continuous, then you would have such numbers as .1 of a
  teenager, for example! Because the government collected the
  figures, they would be reasonably accurate. However, they
  would be somewhat out of date, because of the time taken to
  collect and process the data. Also, it is likely that, with the
  great numbers involved, the figures would not be 100-per-cent
  correct even for the time they were collected. It is not likely,
  though, the inaccuracies would be anywhere near large
  enough to be of worry to the jeans manufacturer.

3 These values rounded to the nearest inch are 24 in, 28 in, 26 in
  and 28 in, respectively. If you got 27 in for the third one, you
  forgot the 'rule of evens', which says that you always round to
  the even number where a value exactly halfway between two
  possible rounded numbers occurs. If you got 27 in for the last
  one, you were applying a 'rule of odds' rather than a 'rule of
  evens'.

  The absolute errors in the rounded figures are:

  $24 - 24.3 = -.3$ in; $28 - 27.8 = .2$ in;
  $26 - 26.5 = -.5$ in; and $28 - 27.5 = .5$ in.

  If you got the signs wrong, you were subtracting the rounded
  figure from the true one and not vice versa as you should.

  The corresponding relative errors are:

$\frac{-.3}{24.3} \times 100 = -1.2\%$ (to one decimal place);

$\frac{.2}{27.8} \times 100 = .7\%$ (to one decimal place);

$\frac{-.5}{26.5} \times 100 = -1.9\%$ (to one decimal place);

and $\frac{.5}{27.5} \times 100 = 1.8\%$ (to one decimal place).

If you divided by the rounded figures, you were forgetting that we divide by the 'true' value, *where known*.

The most accurate of these figures is the second, which has a relative error of only .7%.

If the 'true' values were not known, the maximum absolute errors in *each* case would be ± .5 in. So the relative errors would be:

$\frac{\pm.5}{24} \times 100 = \pm 2.1\%$ (to one decimal place);

$\frac{\pm.5}{28} \times 100 = \pm 1.8\%$ (to one decimal place);

$\frac{\pm.5}{26} \times 100 = \pm 1.9\%$ (to one decimal place);

and $\frac{\pm.5}{28} \times 100 = \pm 1.8\%$ (to one decimal place).

If you divided by the true values here, you were missing the point. We were supposing that the true values were *not known*. In such cases we are forced into dividing by the recorded values.

Performing calculations with approximate figures

Self-check

Add up the figures in table 2 on page 185, both rounded and unrounded. Round the sum of the exact figures to the nearest thousand. What do you notice?

Care must be taken when performing arithmetic with rounded figures. For example, if the exact figures for the live births in the table are added up, the total is 5,365,893. If this is rounded to the nearest thousand, the result is 5,366(000). The sum of the rounded figures is, on the other hand, 5364. Statistical work generally involves arithmetic of this type. If the exact figures are known, as in the above case, the most exact rounded figure should be taken; here the 5366. But what if the exact figures aren't known? To help us examine this question, let us take an example of calculating accounting ratios: the current ratio and the acid test, in fact (see below).

Wilbow Trading imports integrated circuits and markets them in Britain. Its current assets and liabilities are as follows:

Current Assets
Cash at bank	£14,400 (to nearest £100)
Debtors	£ 9,200 (to nearest £100)
Stock	£11,200 (to nearest 100) circuits at £3.70 (to nearest 10p) each

Current liabilities
Trade creditors	£18,100 (to nearest £100)
Current tax	£780 (to nearest £10)

The current ratio is current assets/current liabilities.
The acid test ratio is (current assets–stock)/current liabilities.

First of all we need to total the current liabilities. We get £18,100 + £780 = £18,880.

But this figure will have an error associated with it too. How can we find what it is? To answer this, let's look at a slightly different problem.

Self-check

Suppose you have two rods, one which is 10 cm long to the nearest centimetre, and the other of which is 20 cm long to the nearest centimetre. If you join these two together, what is the longest *true* value that the resulting rod could have?

Well, it would be when each rod was its longest. The 10 cm one cannot be more than 10.5 cm, and the 20 cm one more than 20.5 cm. The longest joined rod would then be 31 cm. Figure 13 illustrates this point. The absolute error in the length of the joined rod is then: 30 – 31 cm = –1 cm.

By the way in which it is obtained, this error is thus the sum of the separate errors. We could, of course, have equally well used

Joining two rods together

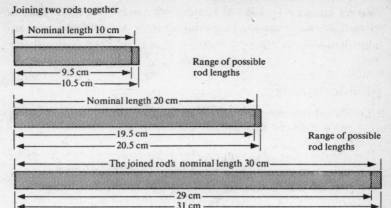

Figure 13. Joining two rods together

the smallest joined rod. This would have given the same numerical result, except that it would have been positive.

So how, then, can we use this method in the case of the ratios? Well, the absolute error in the 'trade creditors' figure is ± £50, while in the 'current tax' it is ± £5. The total error is thus ± £55, and occurs when both errors are in the same direction.

Self-check

What is the equivalent error in the sum of the 'cash at bank' and the 'debtors' figures?

In a similar way, the absolute error in the sum of the figures for the 'cash at bank' and 'debtors' is found from ± £50, for the 'debtors', and ± £50 for the 'cash at bank', giving ± £100.

The calculation of the relative error of a sum from the relative error of its parts is not so easy. For example, the relative error in the 'trade creditors' figure is $\frac{\pm 50}{18100} \times 100\% = \pm .28\%$ (to two decimal places) while that for the 'current tax' is $\frac{\pm 5}{780} \times 100\% = \pm .64\%$ (to two decimal places). We can calculate the relative error of the sum, since we know the absolute error from above.

We get, in fact, $\frac{\pm 55}{18880} \times 100\% = \pm .29\%$ (to two decimal places). It does not bear any obvious relation to the relative errors of its two components. Note, however, that it does lie *between* the two.

|| ### Self-check

|| What is the relative error in the sum of the 'cash at bank' and 'debtors' figures?

The simplest way of calculating the relative error in a sum, then, is to calculate the absolute error first. Thus the relative error in the sum of the figures for the 'cash at bank' and 'debtors' is $\frac{\pm 100}{23600} \times 100\% = \pm.42\%$ (to two decimal places).

|| ### Self-check

|| The car journey times collected in the self-check on page 192, by rounding to the nearest minute, are added together at the end of the day. What are the absolute and relative errors in this sum if there were eight journeys totalling 2 hrs 8 mins?

We saw earlier how the absolute error in each time is at most 30 secs. If you thought it was 60 secs, you were confusing rounding to the nearest minute with not having a seconds display on the watch. Now it is just possible that each of the times recorded was out by the full 30 seconds, *and in the same direction*. That is they were all either 30 secs over the time recorded or all 30 secs under. If this were so, the total absolute error would be $\pm 8 \times 30$ secs, i.e. ± 4 mins. The relative error in the sum is then

$\pm (\frac{4}{2 \times 60 + 8}) \times 100\%$ turning everything into minutes.

This is $\pm (\frac{4}{128}) \times 100\% = \pm 3.125\%$.

If you got an answer of 40% then you probably added the 8 mins to the 2 hrs, something that you cannot do: when you add like that, the numbers must all be in the same units. If you got an answer of 3200% then you had the fraction the wrong way round.

We now have most of the values we need to calculate the ratios. Just the value of the stock needs to be found. This requires multiplication. So how do we find the error in a product?

Self-check

Suppose we have a rectangular carpet with sides 10 metres and 20 metres, to the nearest metre. What is the largest value that the area of the carpet can take?

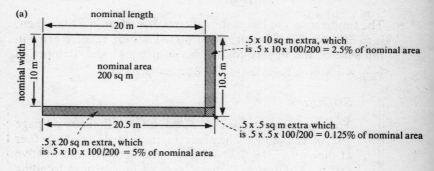

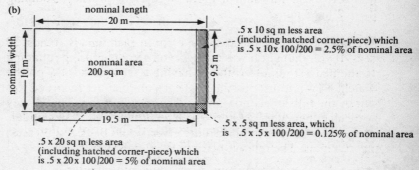

Figure 14. The area of a carpet

It is easiest to see with the aid of a diagram, so look at figure 14(a). The largest area will be when the length and the width are both their maximum. These are 20.5 m and 10.5 m, respectively. The area of the carpet is then 20.5 × 10.5 sq m. But look at how this is made up. We can write this area as $(20 + .5) \times (10 + .5)$ sq m $= 20 \times 10 + 20 \times .5 + .5 \times 10 + .5 \times .5$ sq m.

The first term here is the nominal area of the carpet. The second two terms are the strips at the edge, which are shown shaded in the diagram. The last term is the little piece at the corner, shown hatched in the diagram. The absolute error in this area is then the two shaded strips plus the hatched piece.

Now let's calculate the relative errors. That for the length is $\frac{.5}{20} \times 100\% = 2.5\%$ while that for the width is $\frac{.5}{10} \times 100\% = 5\%$. The relative error in the area can be expressed as

$$\frac{20 \times .5 + 10 \times 5 + .5 \times .5}{200} \times 100\%.$$

This can be split up into its three parts

$$\frac{20 \times .5}{200} \times 100 = 5\%, \quad \frac{10 \times .5}{200} \times 100 = 2.5\%,$$

and $\frac{.5 \times .5}{200} \times 100 = 0.125\%$.

That is, we have the two strips and the shaded piece expressed separately as percentages of the nominal area. This is shown on the diagram. But we can see that the first two of these three parts are exactly equivalent to the relative errors in the length and width, respectively. So, apart from the hatched piece, the relative error in the area of the carpet is the sum of the relative errors in the width and the length.

But what happens when we look at the smallest area? This situation is shown in figure 14(b). This smallest area can be written as

$$(20 - .5) \times (10 - .5) \text{ sq m} = 20 \times 10 - 20 \times .5 - .5 \times 10 + .5 \times .5 \text{ sq m}.$$

Once again, the first term is the nominal area of the carpet. The next two terms this time, though, are the strips at the edge, but *including the hatched piece in each*. This is why the area of this piece has to be added on again. By subtracting both strips, we take away the area of this hatched piece twice.

The absolute error in the area this time is (the negative of) the two shaded strips (each including the hatched piece) less the hatched piece. Its relative error is $\frac{-20 \times .5 - 10 \times .5 + .5 \times .5}{200} \times 100\%$.

Once again, this can be written as three parts

$$\frac{-20 \times .5}{200} \times 100 = -5\%, \quad \frac{-10 \times .5}{200} \times 100 = -2.5\% \text{ and } \frac{.5 \times .5}{200} \times 100 = 0.125\%.$$

That is, we have the strips (including the hatched piece each time) and the hatched piece expressed separately as percentages of the nominal area.

This is shown in the diagram. Here again the first two of these three parts are exactly equivalent to the relative errors in the length and width, respectively. These will be the same as before, but negative. So once more, apart from the hatched piece, the relative error in the area of the carpet is the sum of the relative errors in the width and the length.

We can say, then, as a rule that can be applied in all cases, that the relative error in a product is the *sum* of the relative errors of the numbers being multiplied.

So how can we apply this to the problem of the ratios?

Self-check

Use this rule to find the relative error in the value of the stock.

The relative error in the amount of stock is $\pm \frac{50}{11.200} \times 100\% = \pm.45\%$ to two decimal places; while that in the price of the stock, per unit, is $\pm \frac{.05}{3.70} \times 100\% = \pm1.35\%$ to two decimal places. The relative error in the value of stock is thus $\pm(.45 + 1.35)\% = \pm1.8\%$. We can check on this by finding the maximum and minimum possible stock value. To calculate the value of stock requires multiplication. The maximum errors in this will occur when we have £$(11,200 + 50) \times (3.70 + .05)$ or £$(11,200 - 50) \times (3.70 - .05)$, that is £42,187.50 or £40,697.50. Now the errors in each case here are actually different. They are, in fact, £41,440 − £42,187 = −£747.50 or £41,440 − £40,697.50 = £742.50. The relative errors in the product are thus $\frac{-747.50}{41.440} \times 100\% = -1.80\%$ (to two decimal places) or $\frac{+742.50}{41.440} \times 100\% = 1.79\%$ (to two decimal places). The relative error of the product is thus roughly equal to the sum of the relative errors of the stock levels and price.

Self-check

A box of matches contains 80 matches to the nearest 5. The

length of each is 40 mm to the nearest millimetre. The
nominal total length of matchwood in the box is thus
$80 \times 40 = 3200$ mm. What is the absolute and the relative
error in this figure?

First of all note that we have here a mixture of a continuous and
a discrete value. This is perfectly all right. Nothing that has been
said so far has applied only to one type or the other alone.
Indeed, examples of both have been used. The two worst errors
will occur when either
(a) there are 85 matches and they are all 40.5 mm long, or
(b) there are 75 matches and they are all 39.5 mm long.
    The absolute errors in the two cases are

(a) $3200 - 85 \times 40.5$ mm
    $= 3200 - 3442.5$ mm $=$
    -242.5 mm.
(b) $3200 - 75 \times 39.5$ mm $=$
    $3200 - 2962.5$ mm $=$
    237.5 mm.

If you calculated only the positive one, then that would give
only one end of the picture. The fact that we have two different
absolute errors is always awkward.
    The relative error in the above product can be found by adding
the relative errors in the number of matches and their lengths,
which are

$$\tfrac{\pm 5}{80} \times 100\% = \pm 6.25\%$$
$$\text{and } \tfrac{\pm 5}{40} \times 100\% = \pm 1.25\%$$

respectively.
    The required relative error is then
$$\pm(6.25 + 1.25) = \pm 7.5\%.$$

We can check this with the figures for the absolute errors as
follows. The relative error in the length of matchwood in the box
of matches is

$\tfrac{-242.5}{3200} \times 100\% = -7.58\%$ to two decimal places;

or $\tfrac{237.5}{3200} \times 100\% = 7.42\%$ to two decimal places.

This is in rough agreement with the relative error as calculated above. As mentioned earlier, there will never be perfect agreement in these cases. If you got a relative error of 5% you subtracted the relative errors in the number of matches and their length instead of adding.

We are now in a position to calculate the errors in the ratios. Consider the acid test ratio first. This is equal to

$$\frac{\text{current assets} - \text{stock}}{\text{current liabilities}} = \frac{£23,600 \pm 100}{£18,880 \pm 55}$$

using the absolute errors calculated earlier.

It can be seen that the maximum error will occur when we have either

$$\frac{£23,600 + 100}{£18,880 - 55} = 1.259 \text{ (to three decimal places)}$$

or $\frac{£23,600 - 100}{£18,880 + 55} = 1.241$ (to three decimal places).

The figures themselves give a ratio of $\frac{£23,600}{£18,880} = 1.25$.

The absolute errors in the ratio are thus $1.25 - 1.259 = -.009$ or $1.25 - 1.241 = .009$, i.e. $\pm.009$ (to three decimal places). If we look at relative errors, the relative error in the ratio is

$$\frac{\pm.009}{1.25} \times 100\% = \pm0.72\%.$$

We have already calculated the relative errors in the components, .42% for the assets and .29% for the liabilities. We can see that the same law that worked for multiplication can apply here. That is, the relative error of the ratio (or quotient) can be taken to be equal to the sum of the relative errors of the components. The slight discrepancy here is due to the fact that, as with the product, the rule is not exact.

 ‖ *Self-check*

 ‖ Calculate the current ratio and determine the maximum relative error in it.

To calculate the current ratio we need to add in the stock. The maximum absolute error in the total current assets is $\pm$ {£100 (for the sum of the 'cash at bank' and 'debtors') + £745 (midway

between the two extremes of the absolute errors in the stock
value of £747.50 and £742.50)} = ± £845.

Now the total current assets equal £14,400 + £9,200
+ £41,440 = £65,040. The relative error in this is thus
$\pm\frac{845}{65,040} \times 100\% = 1.30\%$ (to two decimal places) and the
current ratio is

$$\frac{£65,040}{£18,880} = 3.44491525437. . .$$

with a relative error of ±(1.30 + .29)% = ±1.59%. Now since
there is that much error, it is totally pointless to go to so many
decimal places in the answer. This is called 'spurious accuracy'.
It gives the appearance of being very accurate, when in fact it
isn't. Indeed, not even the second decimal place is accurate! We
should thus record this answer as 3.4. This is quite accurate
enough for our purposes and shows that the accuracy of the
figures involved in the self-check on pages 201–2 *was adequate*.

Self-check

A firm is to go into liquidation and has assets of £12,500
and liabilities of £20,000, to the nearest £100 in each case.
Assuming that the money from the assets will be shared
equally among each pound owed, what will creditors get
per pound in repayment? What is the relative error in this
figure?

Each creditor will get $\frac{£12,500}{20,000} = £.625$ (i.e. $62\frac{1}{2}$p) in the pound.
Now the absolute error in both the assets and the liabilities is
£50, since they are both given to the nearest £100. The relative
errors are thus *

$\frac{50}{12,500} \times 100\%$ for the assets = .4%
and $\frac{50}{20,000} \times 100\%$ for the liabilities = .25%.

The relative error in the $62\frac{1}{2}$p is then the sum of these two, i.e.
.4 + .25 = .65%.

We have not yet touched on subtraction, and for a very good
reason. It is here that high relative errors can occur. The difference between two inaccurate figures is far less accurate than
either, if they are of comparable size. To illustrate this, suppose

that we knew only that the current assets were £65,000 to the
nearest thousand and that of this the stocks contributed £41,000
to the nearest thousand. To calculate the acid test ratio we would
have to subtract the stock value from the total current assets. We
would obtain £24,000. But what would be the error?

Self-check

What values of those two figures would give the worst
possible error?

The worst case would be either (£65,000 + £500) −
(£41,000 − £500) = £25,000 or (£65,000 − £500) − (£41,000 +
£500) = £23,000. So the absolute error of the difference is
± £1000.

As with the sum of two numbers then, the absolute error of a
difference is the *sum* of the absolute errors in the separate
numbers.

Self-check

What would be the relative error in the difference between
the total current assets and the stock value corresponding
to the absolute error calculated above?

This is a relative error of $\pm\frac{1000}{24,000} \times 100\% = \pm4.17\%$ (to two
decimal places). The relative errors in the components were only
$\pm\frac{500}{65,000} \times 100\% = \pm.77\%$ for the total current assets and
$\pm\frac{500}{41,000} \times 100\% = \pm1.22\%$ (to two decimal places)! Extreme
care should be taken when subtracting rounded figures,
therefore.

Self-check

The population of a country is estimated at 15 million (to
the nearest million). Of these 4,300,000 (to the nearest
hundred thousand) live in cities. Calculate the number of
people in the country who live outside of cities. What is the
relative error in this figure?

The number of people who live outside the cities is

$$15,000,000 - 4,300,000 = 10,700,000.$$

This is only an approximate figure, though. At worst it could be either

$15,500,000 - 4,250,000 = 11,250,000$ (i.e. 550,000 more), or
$14,500,000 - 4,350,000 = 10,150,000$ (i.e. 550,000 less).

If you didn't get this you may not have seen what the absolute errors in each number were, or not realized what the relationship should be between them to give the worst case. Because the country's population is to the nearest 1,000,000, the absolute error is ±500,000. The cities have a population given to the nearest 100,000, and so the absolute error here is ±50,000. The worst errors would occur when the first of these was its greatest and the second its *least* or vice versa (so giving the biggest possible difference). These are the values given above.

The relative error in each of these cases is the same, namely

$\frac{550,000}{10,700,00} \times 100\% = 5.14\%$ to two decimal places.

If you got a different relative error, you probably had the fraction upside down, or forgot to multiply by 100, or both.

To summarize:

● when adding rounded numbers, the absolute error in the sum is the sum of the absolute errors in these numbers;
● when subtracting rounded numbers, the absolute error in the difference is the *sum* of the absolute errors in these numbers;
● when multiplying rounded numbers, the relative error in the product is (very nearly equal to) the sum of the relative errors in these numbers;
● when dividing rounded numbers, the relative error in the quotient is (very nearly equal to) the sum of the relative errors in these numbers.

Review

1 The distances between the towns on a journey are, to the nearest mile:

A to B   9 miles
B to C 11 miles
C to D   6 miles
D to E 14 miles

What is the relative error in the total distance from A to E? A town, F, on the route is 4 miles from E, to the nearest mile. How far is it from A? What is the relative error in that distance?

2 A new factory is being built. A workforce of 200 men (to the nearest ten) will be handling dangerous material that will require them to go through a decontaminating procedure, taking 10 minutes (to the nearest minute). If there was only one decontamination chamber, which would deal with only one man at a time, how long would it take to decontaminate the whole workforce? What is the relative error in the answer? If the total decontamination time is not to exceed one hour, plus or minus 5 minutes, how many booths would be needed? What is the relative error in the answer? How many booths would be needed to ensure that the target is met?

ANSWERS

1 The total distance is $9 + 11 + 6 + 14 = 40$ miles. But, at worst, each figure could be $\frac{1}{2}$ a mile out. So this figure could actually be 38 or 42 miles, with an absolute error of ± 2 miles. The corresponding relative error is

$$\frac{\pm 2}{40} \times 100 = \pm 5\%.$$

If you divided by 38 or 42, remember that we do not know that either of these is the correct mileage; they are just the worst cases. So we have to divide by the recorded value.

Town F is, nominally, $40 - 4 = 36$ miles from A. The absolute error in this distance is $\pm 2\frac{1}{2}$ miles, though. That is, the distance could be $42 - 3\frac{1}{2} = 38\frac{1}{2}$ miles, or $38 - 4\frac{1}{2} = 33\frac{1}{2}$ miles. The corresponding relative error is

$$\frac{\pm 2\frac{1}{2}}{36} \times 100 = \pm 6.9\% \text{ (to one decimal place)}.$$

Note that, again, we have to divide by the nominal distance, as we don't know the true one.

2 The nominal time for the workforce to pass through one decontamination chamber would be $200 \times 10 = 2000$ minutes. But there is some error in this figure. The relative error in the number of men is

$$\tfrac{\pm 5}{200} \times 100 = \pm\, 2.5\%.$$

In the decontamination time it is

$$\tfrac{\pm .5}{10} \times 100 = \pm\, 5\%.$$

The relative error in their product is the sum of these two, namely $\pm\, 7.5\%$. Remember, you don't multiply the relative errors but *add* them.

To obtain the number of booths we have to divide this decontamination time by 60; not by 1, notice. The above time is in minutes, so we must convert the one hour to these also. The answer we get is

$$\tfrac{2000}{60} = 33.3 \text{ booths (to one decimal place).}$$

We found the relative error in the 2000, it was $\pm\, 7.5\%$. The relative error in the 60 is

$$\pm\tfrac{5}{60} \times 100 = \pm\, 8.3\% \text{ (to one decimal place).}$$

So the relative error in the number of booths is

$$\pm(7.5 + 8.3)\% = \pm 15.8\%.$$

Notice again we add the relative errors. We *don't* divide or subtract them.

To make certain that the specification is met, the number of booths should be

$$33.3 + 15.8\% \text{ of } 33.3$$
$$= 33.3 + \tfrac{15.8 \times 33.3}{100}$$
$$= 33.3 + 5.3 \text{ (to one decimal place)}$$
$$= 38.6$$

So it would require at least 39 booths. Notice, it can't be left at 38.6, since the number of booths is a discrete variable. Also, only the plus error is used; less booths would make the situation worse.

Scenario 5
Late for work

As you read through this scenario, make a mental note of the occasions on which Brian Kelly needs to reduce a mass of data to a simpler form. You could also try to decide how you would go about doing that if it were your problem.

There had been an increasing number of complaints about the time-keeping of some of the workers at the Baby Gourmet plant and, in particular, Elsie Hall. Elsie worked on the machine that put the food in the jars. Brian Kelly, the personnel officer at the plant, was going to have to examine her record and make a decision, in conjunction with Elsie's foreman and chargehand. But he would also have to look at the situation with regard to the other poor timekeepers.

When hourly paid employees arrived late for work there was generally a good explanation for it, since they had money stopped from their wages if they were more than five minutes late. The system in operation was that if someone clocked in between six and fifteen minutes late they had a quarter-hour's wages deducted. If they were even later then they had a further quarter-hour's wages deducted. A minute extra could mean another quarter-hour. For example, clocking in 31 minutes late resulted in a loss of 45 minutes' wages.

Brian wanted first to check on just how big a problem timekeeping was. He thought he should start by looking simply at the number of times employees had been late over the previous quarter, i.e. 13 weeks. These statistics were fairly easy to obtain from the files. But it was difficult for Brian to get the overall picture from a mass of figures. So he sorted them out in order to be able to see the pattern clearly. What emerged was that quite a number of people had been late once or twice over this period, more than he would have expected, in fact. There were also a few who had been late an even greater number of times and, of those, one or two who had been late quite often. Elsie Hall had the worst record.

Brian decided to investigate why so many workers were being late. On talking to one or two employees, including office staff, he discovered that many of them blamed the buses. The service as a whole had deteriorated over the last six months, so they said. The plant was on an industrial estate with good routes from the town centre. But many of the workers had to catch another bus to get from home to the town centre and back. It was these workers who were having the greatest difficulty and it was the women who were particularly hard hit.

Elsie Hall, and a couple of other workers whose records were not very good either, now remained to be dealt with. Brian decided that he would get figures for each of these on exactly how late they had been. If it was a matter of only being a few minutes late each time, and they lived on a bad bus route, then there was at least some excuse. However, he would tell them that they would have to make an effort to catch earlier buses.

When Brian examined these figures, after putting them into some kind of order, he found that Elsie had often been up to a half-hour late or more. She had already been warned several times by her chargehand and foreman about this lateness. It looked very much as though he was going to have to dismiss her. Brian wasn't looking forward to this at all. He made up his mind that he would ask the foreman to give a 'pep' talk to the other two poor timekeepers. If they didn't improve he might have to see about them as well.

In this scenario, Brian collects information on timekeeping by the workforce. But the amount of figures collected is too large for their relevance to be really appreciated. In order to cut down the amount of data to a manageable level, Brian needs to reduce it to its essentials. Just how this can be done is the subject of the next two chapters.

One way is to sort the data into order, and to combine similar data. Exactly how to do this is covered in Chapter 8. Working on the principle that 'a good picture is worth a thousand figures' (the statistical equivalent of another well-known saying), the other method is to represent the data graphically. This is discussed in Chapter 9.

In both cases we are not just concerned with presenting the data. We are largely interested in processing it to produce conclusions. The presentation of statistical data for showing to others will be covered in a chapter in Volume 2.

After you've studied these two chapters you should be able to take unprocessed sets of figures and reduce them to manageable levels, using graphical and other methods. You should also understand why such processing is necessary.

8 | Amalgamating data

The need to reduce data to manageable levels

We saw in the last two chapters how primary data could be collected. But consider what we might end up with as a result of such an exercise. It may well be just a lot of figures written down as they were gathered. These are called 'raw data'. So, for example, in the scenario, the raw data on the number of times employees were late could have been as follows:

TABLE 3. NUMBER OF TIMES EACH HOURLY PAID EMPLOYEE WAS LATE IN ONE QUARTER

2	7	0	1	0	0	0	1	3	0
0	0	1	6	4	1	3	1	0	2
0	1	0	2	0	0	2	0	0	1
0	0	1	0	5	0	0	3	1	13
2	0	4	9	0	0	0	0	3	1
1	0	0	3	0	1	0	2	4	0
0	5	1	0	1	0	0	10	6	0
0									

A glance at this display is sufficient to see that the figures are difficult to assimilate when shown like this. We can't immediately say what the largest or smallest is, for example, or what sort of pattern they form. In fact there are only a few figures here in comparison to what statisticians normally have to deal with. Just imagine how hard it would be to make sense of a jumble of hundreds of figures, let alone thousands. One of the first things to do after collecting data, therefore, is to extract some pattern out of it, to reduce it to a manageable level, as Brian had to in the scenario. There are several ways of doing this. The ones described in this chapter are those which might well be used in the early phases of a larger exercise; that is to say, when the data may be processed further.

Activity

This activity will be used throughout this, and the next, chapter. At this point, you will be generating some data on which to work.

Get a watch with a second hand (or display, if it is digital). Time how long it takes you to multiply two three-digit numbers together. Repeat this operation twenty-times with different numbers, at random. You can use the last three digits of successive telephone numbers from your local directory. These will be fairly random. Try to get the times to the nearest second. Note these times down for later use in this and succeeding chapters.

Sorting out the repetitions

Self-check

Can you think of any way(s) of arranging the data in table 3 so that it is more immediately comprehensible?

One way of producing some pattern in the above figures would be to list them in order (ascending or descending). This results in what is called an array. For example, with the figures above we would have the following.

TABLE 4. NUMBER OF TIMES HOURLY PAID EMPLOYEES WERE LATE IN ONE QUARTER (ARRAY)

0	0	0	0	0	0	0	0	0	0
0	0	0	0	0	0	0	0	0	0
0	0	0	0	0	0	0	0	0	0
0	0	0	0	0	1	1	1	1	1
1	1	1	1	1	1	1	1	1	2
2	2	2	2	2	3	3	3	3	3
4	4	4	5	5	6	6	7	9	10

13

Activity

List the times you obtained for your multiplications in an array.

Does this help you to see the pattern a little better? The author tried this exercise and got an array of

20 21 22 22 23 24 25 25 25 26 27 27 28 29
30 30 30 30 31 32

Though this helps slightly, it is still difficult to grasp the picture without studying the figure in some detail. But an improvement can be made. Notice that, in table 4, some figures recur. We need write each one of these down only once and by its side the number of times it occurs. This number is called the 'frequency'. We have then cut down on the amount of data displayed while still conveying all the same information.

Self-check

What are the frequencies of the figures for late arrivals given above?

The frequencies of the figures for late arrivals, given above, are shown in the 'frequency table', table 5 overleaf. Note that the total frequency should equal the number of items of raw data, in this case the number of hourly paid employees.

Activity

Are there any multiplication times, from the activity on page 212, which occur more than once in your data? Draw up a frequency table for this data.

As you can see by looking at the author's results given earlier, he did get some repeats. His frequency table was as shown in the 'multiplication times' table overleaf.

TABLE 5. NUMBER OF TIMES EACH HOURLY PAID EMPLOYEE WAS LATE IN ONE QUARTER

Number of times late	Number of employees late this number of times
0	35
1	14
2	6
3	5
4	3
5	2
6	2
7	1
8	0
9	1
10	1
11	0
12	0
13	1
	Total 71

MULTIPLICATION TIMES

Time (secs)	Frequency
20	1
21	1
22	2
23	1
24	1
25	3
26	1
27	2
28	1
29	1
30	4
31	1
32	1
	Total 20

Self-check

Produce a frequency table for the following raw data, on the number of employees off work in a factory each day over a quarter.

301121150210432204 61
00113 6544411100 21000
3 33112111176611 00111
3 3222

The answer to this question should have been arrived at in a similar way to what follows.

First of all the different digits that appear in the array are written down. These are 0 1 2 3 4 5 6 7. There are none above 7.

Now the frequency of each of these is determined by counting how many of them there are. The answers are then written in the frequency table, which is thus

NUMBER OF EMPLOYEES OFF WORK OVER THE QUARTER

Number of absentees	*Number of days on which there were this number absent*
0	13
1	23
2	9
3	8
4	5
5	2
6	4
7	1
	Total 65

The total frequency should add up to the number of working days in the quarter as it does.

Notice the headings. They should always be included. Also, it is better to write what the frequency represents rather than just 'frequency', if there is likely to be any confusion whatsoever. It might be possible to be confused in this instance, for example.

Perhaps you were? If you wrote as headings, 'Number of days absent' and 'Number of employees absent for that number of days', or something similar, then you misread the data. It showed the number of employees off work each day over a quarter.

If you started off by producing an array you were not wrong.

Frequency tables can be obtained without the intermediate step of the raw data being written down, by using the tally method described on page 49. Brian would probably have done this in the scenario. The possible number of times late would have been written down first and, as each one of them was encountered, a tally mark would have been made in the appropriate place. We can also use this method to get from the raw data, in table 3, to the frequency table, in table 5, by working systematically through the figures. The tallies for the first few figures here, for example, would be as follows:

0	~~HHT~~ ~~HHT~~ ~~HHT~~ ~~HHT~~ ~~HHT~~ ~~HHT~~ ~~HHT~~	35
1	~~HHT~~ ~~HHT~~ ~~HHT~~	14
2	~~HHT~~ /	6
3	~~HHT~~	5

Self-check

Tally the frequencies of the different rates of absence in the previous self-check (page 215).

You should have started out in the same way as in the self-check on page 213, writing down all the possible values. Then you should have worked through the raw data item by item. As you met each item, you should have put a tally mark in the appropriate place, i.e. against the corresponding figure in the tally table. In this way, *you only need to go through the raw data once.* You would have gone through it eight times in the self-check on page 215 if you had done it as in the answer given. Having completed the tally table, the total frequencies should then have been entered, giving the following result:

NUMBER OF EMPLOYEES OFF WORK OVER A QUARTER

Number of absentees	Number of days on which there were this number absent	
0	∦∦ ∦∦ ///	13
1	∦∦ ∦∦ ∦∦ ∦∦ ///	23
2	∦∦ ////	9
3	∦∦ ///	8
4	∦∦	5
5	//	2
6	////	4
7	/	1
		Total 65

Keeping running totals

A running or 'cumulative total' is often useful. For example, the cumulative total of late arrivals by Elsie Hall in the scenario on page 209 could be used to give a picture of her timekeeping to date. Her figures might have looked like this:

TABLE 6. NUMBER OF TIMES LATE PER WEEK FOR ELSIE HALL

Week No.	Times late	Cumulative total
1	1	1
2	0	1
3	1	2
4	1	3
5	0	3
6	1	4
7	2	6
8	1	7
9	0	7
10	1	8
11	1	9
12	1	10
13	3	13
	Total 13	

The entries in the cumulative total column are obtained by adding together the number of times Elsie had been late *to date*. So, for week 1 the cumulative total is equal to 1, i.e. the number

of times Elsie was late in week 1. In week 2, the cumulative total
is still 1, because Elsie was not late during the second week. In
week 3 it is 2, because the total number of times Elsie was late up
to *and including* the third week was 2. You don't have to keep
adding up from the beginning each time, though. All you need
to do is to take the previous cumulative total and add in the value
for the current week; e.g. the cumulative total for week 7 is
found by adding 2, the number of times Elsie was late in week 7,
to 4, the number of times Elsie was late up to then, i.e. to the
cumulative total for week 6. Note that the final cumulative total
must equal the total of the single-week figures. Also, the difference between two successive cumulative totals is the figure for
the later single week . For example, the cumulative totals for
weeks 7 and 6 are 6 and 4 respectively. The difference between
the two is 2, which is the single-week figure for week 7.

Where, as here, the figures that are being totalled are frequencies, the figures in the cumulative total column are called 'cumulative frequencies'. The idea of a cumulative total can, of
course, be used in other cases such as in keeping track of costs,
but this aspect is not covered here. Note that cumulative frequencies don't have to be cumulative over time. This would only
be so if each frequency were for a different time period. In the
figures for late arrivals by the hourly paid workers in table 5, for
example, frequencies are of the number of employees late for
each *different number of times*.

Self-check

What are the cumulative frequencies for the figures in table
5?

The cumulative frequency table for these figures is as shown
opposite. You can check your answer by making sure that the
last cumulative frequency is equal to the total frequency, here
71.

If you look at the table in the answer to the previous self-
check, you can see that we can, with very little difficulty, find the
answers to such questions as, how many employees were late less
than nine times during the quarter? This is precisely the kind of
thing that cumulative frequencies tell us. We can answer this

NUMBER OF TIMES EACH HOURLY PAID EMPLOYEE WAS LATE IN
ONE QUARTER

Number of times late	Number of employees (frequency)	Cumulative frequency
0	35	35
1	14	49
2	6	55
3	5	60
4	3	63
5	2	65
6	2	67
7	1	68
8	0	68
9	1	69
10	1	70
11	0	70
12	0	70
13	1	71
Total 71		

question by looking at the cumulative frequency corresponding
to the number of times late of *8*. Notice that it is not the one
corresponding to the number of times late of 9.

Self-check

Why not?

It is because the cumulative frequency for some week gives the
total up to *and including* that week. The answer to the question
is thus 68.

Self-check

Use the table in the last-but-one self-check to find the
following:

1 the number of workers late less than four times;
2 the number of workers late more than three times;
3 the number of workers late more than five but less than
  eleven times.

ANSWERS

1 The answer is 60. If you got 63, you forgot about the point made in the previous self-check.

2 The answer is 11. If you got 55, then you did not notice that the question asks for *more* than 3 times. Now it is not possible to get this from the table direct. It must be worked out by finding how many workers were late *less* than 4 times, i.e. less than or equal to 3 times. This was 60. That figure then has to be subtracted from the total number of employees, i.e. 71, giving 11. If you got 8, then you most probably found how many workers were late less than *or equal* to 4 times, i.e. 63, and subtracted this from 71.

3 The answer here is 5.

You can get the answer using the cumulative frequencies by finding out how many workers were late less than 11 times, and subtracting from it the number of employees who were late less than 6 times. Notice it is less than 6 because the figure for 6 itself is to be included in the answer. The answer is thus $70 - 65 = 5$. If you got 3, then you are still not taking into account the point made in the last-but-one self-check.

Grouping like data

When looking at how late Elsie Hall actually was, Brian had two possible approaches. The most obvious way of finding out how late she was would have been to use the wages sheets to see how many quarter-hours she had been docked. This data may have been as below, for example:

TABLE 7. QUARTER-HOURS' WAGES LOST THROUGH LATENESS IN ONE QUARTER FOR ELSIE HALL

1 5 2 1 3 1 3 2 1 4 1 2 2

These figures would be better expressed in a frequency table as shown in table 8 opposite. Now this table is an ordinary ('ungrouped') frequency table.

But Brian could also have looked at the clock cards and found out the clocking on times. From these he could have determined

TABLE 8. QUARTER-HOURS' WAGES LOST THROUGH LATENESS IN
ONE QUARTER FOR ELSIE HALL

$\frac{1}{4}$ hours lost	Frequency
1	5
2	4
3	2
4	1
5	1
	Total 13

how late she was, to the nearest *completed minute*. Say the raw
data was as follows:

TABLE 9. MINUTES LATE (TO NEAREST COMPLETED MINUTE) IN
ONE QUARTER FOR ELSIE HALL

   13 69 24 12 39 11 43 28 11 50 10 24 27

Now if we put this into a frequency table, we would get very little
change. It would look like this:

TABLE 10. MINUTES LATE (TO NEAREST COMPLETED MINUTE) IN
ONE QUARTER FOR ELSIE HALL

Minutes late	Number of times Elsie was that late
10	1
11	2
12	1
13	1
24	2
27	1
28	1
39	1
43	1
50	1
69	1
	Total 13

Now such a table is of little use, as nearly all the frequencies are 1. Indeed, if we put in all the intermediate values like 14, 15, . . ., minutes late, the vast majority of the frequencies would be zero. But this data is essentially the same as that in Table 8, in which there are reasonable frequencies.

Self-check

Can you see how we might turn table 10 into one with frequencies like table 8?

What we can do is to group the times together and give frequencies for each group. If you look at table 8, you can see that $1 \times \frac{1}{4}$ hr lost covers 10, 11, 12 and 13 mins late, i.e. the first four times in table 10, $2 \times \frac{1}{4}$ hrs lost covers the next three, and so on. These groups can then correspond to the $\frac{1}{4}$ hrs lost on table 8. When such groups are used to make a table, it is called a 'grouped frequency table'. The one for the data above is shown below:

TABLE 11. MINUTES LATE (TO NEAREST COMPLETED MINUTE) IN ONE QUARTER FOR ELSIE HALL

Minutes late	Frequency
6–15	5
16–30	4
31–45	2
46–60	1
61–75	1
Total	13

Notice that the first group is 6–15 and not 1–15.

Self-check

Can you see why?

It is because a worker is not considered to be late unless he or she is more than five minutes past clocking on time.

In this particular instance there are not many different times and so a grouped frequency is not vital, though it is convenient. In very many cases in practice, there may be a large number of items each with their own different frequency and a grouped frequency table becomes virtually a necessity.

Activity

Take the multiplication times that you obtained earlier (page 212). Produce a grouped frequency table from them by using the groups 0–4 secs, 5–9 secs, 10–14 secs, etc.

The author's figures produce the grouped frequency table below:

MULTIPLICATION TIMES

Time (secs)	Frequency
20–24	6
25–29	8
30–34	6
Total	20

NB. Those groups with frequency of zero are not shown.

It is evident that in a grouped frequency table, some of the information conveyed by the original figure is lost. For example, although we know there is one time between 46 and 60 minutes in table 11, we don't know what it is from this table alone. Care must be taken in choosing the groups, therefore. This point is treated in the next few sections.

Self-check

Using the ungrouped frequency table below, produce a grouped frequency one with the following groups: 1–5 cigarettes a day, 6–10, 11–20, 21–30, 31–50, 51–100.

NUMBER OF CIGARETTES SMOKED A DAY BY A SAMPLE OF FIFTY SMOKERS

Number of cigarettes a day	Number of smokers
1	2
2	3
5	7
8	1
10	18
12	1
15	2
20	8
25	3
30	1
40	2
50	1
60	1
	Total 50

The grouped table is as below:

NUMBER OF CIGARETTES SMOKED EACH DAY BY A SAMPLE OF FIFTY SMOKERS

Number of cigarettes a day	Number of smokers
1–5	12
6–10	19
11–20	11
21–30	4
31–50	3
51–100	1
	Total 50

If you had frequencies of 5, 8, 21, 11, 3 and 2, then you were including 5, 10, 20, 30 and 50 cigarettes a day in the wrong group.

Review

1 In what circumstances might the sequence of figures in the raw data *as collected* have some interest to us? Give examples.

2 The following figures show the petty cash totals in pounds for the fifty-two weeks in a particular financial year.

18.70	17.84	17.16	19.27	17.39	18.26	16.93
17.67	18.56	18.78	19.39	19.04	16.73	15.07
17.21	16.54	13.72	13.00	13.93	12.18	11.97
12.04	15.72	18.05	17.67	16.83	18.18	18.53
17.84	18.31	19.16	19.84	17.27	18.13	17.62
17.70	16.93	16.03	10.14	12.17	12.52	16.37
17.84	19.40	13.12	18.12	17.04	17.62	14.92
16.00	15.19	19.14.				

Using the groupings

10—11.99
12—13.99
14—15.99
16—17.99
18—19.99

draw up a frequency table and cumulative frequency table for these figures.

ANSWERS

1 The raw data might be collected over a period and this sequence might be of interest in itself. For example, the figures for lateness, above, are given in the table in order of how late workers were. It cannot be determined from this table alone at what dates these late arrivals occurred. At some later date this may be of interest, e.g. to check pay for a given week.

Another case in which the sequence may be of importance is if it represents a physical change of location. For example, it may represent the different storage areas in a stock room, different branches of a firm, and so on.

If the sequence is of interest, the original data may be kept in order. Alternatively, the date, location, or whatever, can be recorded separately together with the data.

2 The frequency table may be compiled by using the tally system. The results of this are shown below:

Petty cash total (£)	Tally	Frequency	Cumulative frequency
10–11.99	//	2	2
12–13.99	+++ ///	8	10
14–15.99	////	4	14
16–17.99	+++ +++ +++ +++ /	21	35
18–19.99	+++ +++ +++ //	17	52
	Total	52	

Grouped data and accuracy

When we group data, we must allocate each recorded value of the variable in question to one of a number of groups or 'classes'. The minimum and maximum values that would be so allocated to a class are called its (nominal) lower class limit and upper class limit respectively. It is these that, in some form or other, should appear in the grouped frequency tables. They should not be specified to a greater degree of accuracy than was the data from which the table is derived. Thus there will never be any doubt as to which class items should belong.

Self-check

Suppose we have decided on classes of 100–109 cm, 110–119 cm, 120–129 cm, etc. for rod lengths. Given that the lengths of three rods are 109 cm, 119 cm and 129 cm, to the nearest cm, and that this data is to be entered in the table, which classes would they go in? Would we be able to decide which classes the data should go in if the lengths of the rods were rounded to the nearest 10 cm, as 110 cm, 120 cm and 130 cm?

In the first case there is no real problem. The three lengths would be allocated to the first three classes, respectively. But if these lengths were rounded to the nearest 10 cm there would be difficulties. We wouldr't know, from the rounded lengths alone, if the 110 cm rod really belonged to the second class, i.e. 110–119 cm, since it could have a true value of, say, 106 cm or one of, say, 114 cm.

When the variable is continuous, or is discrete but the figures are rounded, the *true* value of a figure allocated to a given class could lie outside of these limits even if they are correctly specified. For example, in table 11, on Elsie's timekeeping, the class limits 6–15, 16–30, 31–45, 46–60 and 61–75 minutes accord with the fact that times are recorded to the nearest completed minute. But the range of *true* values (i.e. the exact times, which aren't known) of the times that this could be placed in these classes are different.

Self-check

What is the maximum true value of a time recorded to the nearest completed minute as 30 minutes? In which class interval in table 9 would such a value be placed? Does its true value necessarily lie within the class limits for that class, then? If it doesn't, does it lie within the limits of *any* class?

A time recorded as 30 minutes, could be very nearly 31 minutes. Because it was recorded as 30 minutes, though, it would be put in class 16–30 minutes. So its true value does not necessarily lie in that class. But it can't lie in any other class. The next one begins at 31 minutes, and is thus more than the maximum true value. What happens, in fact, is that the true value can lie in the gaps between classes. If we look at the ranges of *true* values that will be placed into the various classes, we get 6–16, 16–31, 31–46, 46–61 and 61–76 respectively. These are called lower and upper 'class boundaries' and are defined as the minimum and maximum *true* values of the variable that would end up being allocated to that class. Actually, of course, the upper class boundaries in the above example aren't exactly 16, 31, 46, 61 and 76. Because time is a continuous variable, they are these minus the smallest possible fraction of a second. It is 6–16, 16–31 and so on that are used, however, as it would otherwise be very awkward to specify the boundaries.

'The nearest completed minute' is rather like 'age last birthday', and would be treated in the same manner. For example, class limits of 15–19 years would correspond to class boundaries of 15–20. It is more usual to find figures rounded to the nearest thousand, to three decimal places, or whatever. In such cases both the upper *and* lower class boundaries are outside the class limits.

Let's have a look at an example. Suppose we are making a grouped frequency table of the lengths of rods and that the groups are 85–89 cm, 90-94 cm, 95–99 cm, 100–104 cm, 105–109 cm and 110–114 cm. The rod lengths will be given in cm to fit in with these. We can see which class any rod will be allocated to. For example, a rod of 94 cm would be put into the second group while one of 95 cm would be put into the third group. But what about the true values of such rods? Figure 15 shows the relationship between these and the class limits.

The first rod lies just short of 99 cm so it goes in class 95–99 cm. The second is between 99 and 99.5 cm. This, then, goes in class 95–99 cm too, since it must round to 99 cm. The third rod is between 99.5 and 100 cm. It would round to 100 cm and so would be placed in class 100–104 cm. The fourth rod is just over 100 cm long and so will be put in class 100–104 cm also.

Self-check

What classes do the fifth and sixth rod belong to?

You must use the same principle. The fifth one is between 104.5 and 105 cm. Its rounded length is thus 105 cm and so it must go in the class 105–109 cm. The last rod lies between 109 and 109.5 cm. This would round to 109 cm and so would go into the class 105–109 cm.

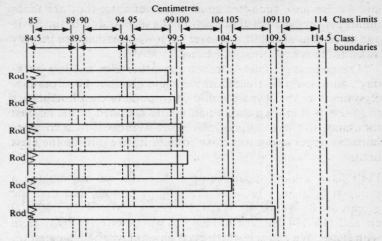

The first two rods lie in the class 95-99 cm. The second two rods lie in the class 100-104 cm. In which classes do the fifth and sixth rod lie?

Figure 15. Class boundaries and class limits

Self-check

In table 12, below, what are the class boundaries corresponding to the given class limits?

TABLE 12. AVERAGE TIME TAKEN TO PERFORM A PARTICULAR OPERATION BY 100 MACHINE OPERATORS (TO NEAREST SECOND)

Time for operation (seconds)	Frequency
360–379	3
380–399	7
400–419	15
420–439	28
440–459	26
460–479	13
480–499	6
500–519	2
Total	100

Here times have been measured to the nearest second. The class
limits reflect this, i.e. there is a gap of one second between the
upper class limit of one class and the lower class limit of the next
higher. Referring back to the discussion on rounding in the last
chapter, the class *boundaries* are thus 359.5–379.5, 379.5–399.5,
and so on. Note that there are no gaps here; i.e. the upper class
boundary for one class is the lower class boundary for the next
higher one. But what class would a measurement like 379.5 have
been put in? Well, if it really was 379.5 as far as could be
ascertained, and not 379.51 or 379.49, it would have gone into
whichever class the rounding rule adopted put it in. For example,
if the 'rule of evens' had been used, as explained in the previous
chapter, then it would have been included in the 380–399 class.
This is because it would have been rounded to 380, the nearest
even number, and not to 379, the odd one.

It can be seen that, in fact, even an apparently ordinary (ungrouped) frequency table is really a grouped one if it refers to a
continuous variable. Suppose, for instance, that twenty people
of similar height are measured to the nearest inch and the
following results obtained:

TABLE 13. HEIGHTS OF A GROUP OF TWENTY PEOPLE (TO NEAREST
INCH)

Height (ins)	Frequency
68	3
69	4
70	4
71	6
72	3

Then, actually, 68, for example, is a class with both class *limits*
equal to 68 and class boundaries 67.5 and 68.5.

Self-check

The contents of a number of bottles of skin cream, nominally 350 ml (millilitres) are carefully measured to the
nearest 1 ml. The results are entered in a grouped fre-

quency table with classes 345–349, 350–354, 355–359 and 360–364 ml. What are the corresponding class boundaries? Would these class limits still be suitable if the volumes were measured to the nearest .1 ml?

The best way to find the class boundaries from the class limits is to proceed outwards (i.e. away from the middle of the class) from the class limits until true values are found that no longer round to the class limits. Where the change occurs is the class boundary. So, for example, starting with 345 ml and moving further away from the class, i.e. to smaller figures, we pass through values like 344.9, 344.65, 344.55 and 344.51, which all round to 345 ml, and eventually reach 344.5 ml. If this figure is passed, the volumes no longer round to 345 ml but to 344 ml. So, for example, 344.499. .99 ml rounds to 344 ml. 344.5 ml is thus the class boundary corresponding to the limit of 345 ml. The same kind of reasoning can lead to the class boundaries for the other classes. An answer is obtained of class boundaries of 344.5–349.5, 349.5–354.5, 354.5–359.5, and 359.5–364.5 ml. If you had an answer of 345–350, 350–355, 355–360, 360–365 ml, then these would not have fulfilled the criteria of class boundaries. 350 ml is not, for example, on the *borderline* of true values that round to either the upper limit of class 345–349 ml, that is 349 ml, or to the lower limit of class 350–354 ml, that is 350 ml. 349.9 ml will, for example, round to 350 ml but it is on the 'wrong' side of the supposed class boundary for this to be correct.

If the volumes are measured to the nearest .1 ml, then we must see if there is a rule which will uniquely allocate any rounded volume to a particular class. If there isn't, then these class limits are not suitable. So look at a recorded volume of 349.5 ml, for example. Can we say what to do with this? Well, as it stands we can't. We would first have to round it to either 349 or to 350 ml. How we did this would depend on what rounding rule we were following for dealing with these halfway cases. The rule of evens would have rounded it to 350 ml, and so put it in class 350–351 ml. Had the true value been, say, 349.45 ml, this would have been wrong.

So the class limits, while not being wrong, would require the data to be rounded to the nearest 1 ml before they could be used.

If the volumes are not required to this accuracy for any other reason, then it appears that they might as well have been taken to the nearest ml in the first place. In fact, it is even stronger than this. They *must* be measured to the degree of accuracy required by the class limits, here 1 ml, or errors will be introduced, as with the 349.45 ml previously. If more accurate figures need be kept, for some separate reason, these must be recorded *in addition* and *not* rounded for the purposes of tabulation.

We can now look at frequency tables with data from discrete variables. Suppose we take the figures in table 5 (page 214) and group them. We could do this as follows:

TABLE 14. NUMBER OF TIMES EACH HOURLY PAID EMPLOYEE WAS LATE IN ONE QUARTER

Number of times late	Frequency
0–1	49
2–3	11
4–5	5
6–7	3
8–13	3
	Total 71

These classes would have been chosen to enable Brian to see the overall pattern of late arrivals. If there was some company rule about a worker being late more than so many times in a given period, this would obviously be one of the class limits. In practice, this table would have been constructed as the data was collected, using the tally method described earlier. The tallies would be for the classes rather than the individual figures. As Brian would not have known what upper limit to expect he would probably have used 8 *and over* for the end class. Note that it is, in any case, bigger than the other classes. These points will be returned to in the next section.

Now, here, the class limits and the class boundaries are the same. This means that there are gaps of 1 unit between the latter. This is because the data relates to a discrete variable and is recorded without rounding. That is, the figures on which this table is based are *true* values. In this case, class boundaries are replaced by 'mathematical limits'. The mathematical limits are obtained by extending the class boundaries (or class limits since they are the same here) by ½ a unit. Thus the upper mathematical limit of one class equals the lower mathematical limit of the next higher, since the gap between the corresponding boundaries is one unit. For example, take the data in table 14.

Self-check

What are the mathematical limits of the classes in table 14?

The class boundaries and equivalent mathematical limits of the class here are as follows:

Class boundaries	Mathematical class limit
0–1	–0.5–1.5
2–3	1.5–3.5
4–5	3.5–5.5
6–7	5.5–7.5
8–13	7.5–13.5

The –0.5 looks rather strange, but it is, in fact, perfectly acceptable.

Self-check

The numbers of matches in a box are recorded in a grouped frequency table with classes 70–74, 75–79, 80–84, 85–89 and 90–94. What are the corresponding mathematical limits?

The mathematical limits are $\frac{1}{2}$ a unit outside the class limits. So here they are $69\frac{1}{2}$–$74\frac{1}{2}$, $74\frac{1}{2}$–$79\frac{1}{2}$, $79\frac{1}{2}$–$84\frac{1}{2}$, $84\frac{1}{2}$–$89\frac{1}{2}$ and $89\frac{1}{2}$–$94\frac{1}{2}$. If you got $70\frac{1}{2}$–$74\frac{1}{2}$, $75\frac{1}{2}$–$79\frac{1}{2}$, $80\frac{1}{2}$–$84\frac{1}{2}$, $85\frac{1}{2}$–$89\frac{1}{2}$ and $90\frac{1}{2}$–$94\frac{1}{2}$, then you were not going *outside* the class limits at the lower limits. Adding to the lower limits takes you further into the class. The result is that your mathematical limits at the upper end of one class do not match with the lower ones of the next class up as they should.

Suppose now we had a discrete variable but the figures were rounded, what would happen then? Consider the data in table 15 below, for example:

TABLE 15. NUMBER OF TOWNS AND VILLAGES OF DIFFERENT POPULATION IN A GIVEN REGION

Population (1000s)	Frequency
1–5	10
6–10	5
11–20	5
21–30	1
31–50	0
51–70	0
71–100	3
101–150	1

The figures from which this table was compiled were rounded to the nearest 1000. Again, the class limits reflect this. (They are, in fact, given in 1000s.) There is a gap between upper class limits of one class and the lower ones of the next higher of 1(000). The class limits of 71–100(000), for example, thus correspond to class boundaries of 70,500 and 100,500. Here we see that rounded values of a discrete variable behave very much like values of a continuous variable. There are, for example, no gaps between the class boundaries. This is because the digit 5 will sometimes cause rounding up and sometimes rounding down. As with a continuous variable, too, an 'ungrouped' frequency table for rounded figures from a discrete variable is in effect a grouped one. Each value, in fact, represents a range of values within the limits of the absolute error.

   A diagram would be of some help here. Look at figure 16. This shows the data at the edge of a class for a discrete variable rounded to the nearest 10. The data is the numbers of bricks out of samples of 1000 that are found defective after having been dumped on building sites. The three particular results shown are 43, 45 and 47 which, when rounded to the nearest 10, give 40, 40

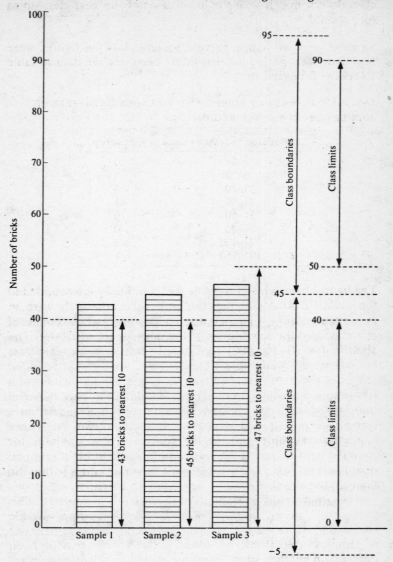

Figure 16. Number of defective bricks in a sample of 1000

(using the rule of evens) and 50. The classes that are used for
these numbers of bricks are

$$0\text{–}40, 50\text{–}90, 100\text{–}140, \text{etc.}$$

The corresponding class boundaries are thus

$$-5\text{–}45, 45\text{–}95, 95\text{–}145, \text{etc.}$$

(As before, the −5 is acceptable.) Notice that, since we are
rounding to ten bricks, there are gaps of ten between the upper
class limit of one class and the lower class limit of the next class
up.

> ### Self-check
>
> What class would a sample of bricks with 95 rejects be put
> in?

95 rounds to 100 (by the rule of evens). So it would be put in
class 100–140.

> ### Self-check
>
> What are the class boundaries in a table which shows the
> number of watches sold by salesmen to the nearest ten
> watches, where the classes are 50–90, 100–140, 150–190,
> 200–240, 250–290 and 300–340?

If we look at a true figure near the middle of the 'gap', between
two classes, for example, 90 to 100, then we can see that it can be
placed in either of the surrounding classes depending on its exact
value. So 94 would be placed in 50–90 while 96 would be placed
in 100–140. It is the figure ending in 5 that forms the boundary
between classes. They will sometimes be put in the higher one
and sometimes in the lower, according to what rule is followed
for rounding. The class boundaries are then:

$$45\text{–}95, 95\text{–}145, 145\text{–}195, 195\text{–}245, 245\text{–}295 \text{ and } 295\text{–}345.$$

If you got 50–100, 100–150, 150–200, 200–250, 250–300 and
300–350 then you are forgetting that the boundaries are concerned with figures *before* they are rounded. 100, for example,
cannot be a boundary because it is in a form in which it has to be

capable of being allocated to some class as it stands. That is, it corresponds to a rounded number and must lie within some class limits somewhere.

Choosing the groupings

In the case of the data used above, showing how many minutes late Elsie Hall was, the grouping was determined by the way the system operated, i.e. in quarter-hours. This sort of situation does sometimes occur. More often the investigator has to decide on his own groupings, as we did with table 14 for example. The first step in doing this is to find the range, that is the difference between the maximum and minimum recorded values of the variable concerned. For instance, look at the data in review 2 on page 225. Here the range is £19.84 − £10.14 = £9.70. Obviously the groups or classes into which the values of the variable are divided must between them cover at least this range.

In many cases, a rough estimate of the 'class width' may be obtained by dividing the range by the number of classes required. The class width is strictly defined as the difference between the upper and lower class *boundaries*. In grouped frequency tables for unrounded figures from a discrete variable, this definition needs modifying, however. It is then taken to be the difference between the mathematical limits. So, for example, the class width of the highest class in table 14 is $13.5 − 7.5 = 6$. Note that this actually equals the number of different values covered by that class, which agrees with common sense.

A note should be made here about the term 'class interval'. It is commonly used to mean the same as class width. In this book, however, we shall reserve it to mean the range of values in a class, which is another interpretation commonly put on it. Thus we can talk about a class interval of 13–16, or 20.5–21.5, but we could not say a class width was 13–16 or 20.5–21.5. For these two instances the class widths would be 4 (assuming unrounded values of a discrete variable) and 1 (assuming a continuous variable) respectively.

Self-check

What are the class widths of all the classes in tables 14 and
15?

In table 14, the class widths are not constant. That of the first
class is $1.5 - (-.5) = 2$, i.e. the difference between successive
mathematical limits. For the second it is $3.5 - 1.5 = 2$; and for
the third and fourth it is again 2. For the last one it is, as you saw,
6. If you got an answer of 1 and not 2, you did not use the
mathematical limits as you should have.

In table 15, the class widths are not constant either. They can
all be calculated by taking the differences between successive
class *boundaries*, as shown below:

Class limits	Class boundaries	Class width	
1–5	.5–5.5	5.5–.5	5
6–10	5.5–10.5	10.5–5.5	5
11–20	10.5–20.5	20.5–10.5	10
21–30	20.5–30.5	30.5–20.5	10
31–50	30.5–50.5	50.5–30.5	20
51–70	50.5–70.5	70.5–50.5	20
71–100	70.5–100.5	100.5–70.5	30
101–150	100.5–150.5	150.5–100.5	50

If you got answers for the class widths of 4, 4, 9, 9, 19, 19, 29 and
49, then you found the differences between the class limits and
not the class boundaries as you should.

To return to the question of choosing the groupings, however:
we have assumed so far that the number of classes required is
known. As a general rule, there should not be less than 5, nor
more than 20 of them. Occasionally, however, the number of
classes are predetermined for us, as with Elsie Hall's timekeeping figures. 10 is a convenient number if it can be used. However,
it also helps a great deal in later calculations if we have class
widths of 5 or 10, rather than 3 or 7. In fact, this is more
important, on the whole, than the number of classes. But there

are no hard and fast rules and common sense must always prevail.

Self-check

Why do you think the class intervals given in review 2 on page 225 were chosen as they were?

5 classes were chosen because 10 would have effectively been just rounding to the nearest pound and would still be too fine. Any number of classes between 5 and 10 would have given unsuitable class widths. Less than 5 would have been too few, as any pattern would have been obscured. So 5 was chosen. This number quite clearly reveals this pattern. Dividing the range by 5 we obtain $£\frac{9.70}{5} = £1.94$, and a class width of £2 would be chosen, as £1.94 is an awkward value to use.

Let's look at another example. A magazine dealing with holidays has compiled a list of recommended hotels in a seaside resort. The numbers of hotel bedrooms in these hotels were as follows:

TABLE 16. NUMBER OF BEDROOMS IN RECOMMENDED HOTELS AT A SEASIDE RESORT

121	125	69	98	94	107	60	66	53	66	50	28	56	41	51	62	20	45
58	120	120	31	68	41	65	38	71	17	40	50	25	35	39	44	46	37
85	36	30	17	10	23	90	38	52	45	61	97	100	58	19	48	27	102
24	20	15	90	66	100	80	93	102	115	37							

Self-check

Draw up a grouped frequency table for the above data, choosing your own class widths.

To draw up the grouped frequency table for this data we must first decide on the class intervals. The range is $125 - 10 = 115$. If we want between 5 and 20 classes of equal class width, we should choose one between 23 and 6. The two natural choices in this range are 10 or 20. So how do we choose between them? Well, a class width of 10 would probably still give too fine a picture. There would only be around 6 or 7 figures in each class, too. So six classes of width 20 seems best. However, just to see what they both look like, they are given below.

TABLE 17

(a) NUMBER OF BEDROOMS IN RECOMMENDED HOTELS AT A SEASIDE RESORT

Number of bedrooms	Number of hotels
10–19 ++++	5
20–29 ++++ //	7
30–39 ++++ ////	9
40–49 ++++ ///	8
50–59 ++++ ///	8
60–69 ++++ ////	9
70–79 /	1
80–89 //	2
90–99 ++++ /	6
100–109 ++++	5
110–119 /	1
120–129 ////	4
	Total 65

(b) NUMBERS OF BEDROOMS IN RECOMMENDED HOTELS AT A SEASIDE RESORT

Number of bedrooms	Number of hotels
10–29 ++++ ++++ //	12
30–49 ++++ ++++ ++++ //	17
50–69 ++++ ++++ ++++ //	17
70–89 ///	3
90–109 ++++ ++++ /	11
110–129 ++++	5
	Total 65

Note that the tally marks are shown in the tables just to indicate how they were formed. They never appear in such tables if they are printed or distributed. Here it is evident that the pattern (of very few hotels having 70–80 bedrooms) is quite clear in the second table and, possibly, not even quite as clear in the first.

Self-check

The prices of a number of shares on the stock exchange one day were 278, 292, 410, 183, 85, 88, 232, 225, 168, 102, 416, 312, 163, 428, 362, 98, 141, 263, 121, 382, 409, 427, 94, 192 and 465 pence. Draw up a grouped frequency table for them.

The range is $465 - 85 = 380$. A suitable set of classes would be either 16 (or so) of width 25, or 8 (or 9) of width 50, with 4 of width 100 a possibility. With the few prices given, 16 classes would be too many. If you chose that solution, look at the frequencies you have. The four of width 100 could well lose detail. If you have this, look at the picture you get. The 8 (or 9) of width 50 are probably the best bet. The corresponding table is shown below:

Share prices (pence)	Number of shares
50–99	4
100–149	3
150–199	4
200–249	2
250–299	3
300–349	1
350–399	2
400–449	5
450–499	1

Notice that, in fact, 9 classes were used so as to make the class limits convenient values. To get them in 8 would have needed classes of, say, 75–124 . . . 425–474. While not incorrect, these classes are somewhat inconvenient.

If you used classes of 100 then that is quite reasonable in this case also. The ones of width 25, though, would really give too small frequencies.

Another point to be borne in mind is that although, ideally, equal class widths should be used, very often this would create more problems. Occasionally, the data may be already classified in unequal intervals, e.g. 16–21 as an age group or in Elsie Hall's timekeeping figures. But there may be other reasons.

Self-check

What problems do you think would be involved in having equal class widths in a grouped frequency table of gross income of employees in a large company? (That is, the frequency is the number of incomes in a given range.) Can you see what additional difficulty might present itself in connection with class widths?

Think of the statistics on the gross salaries paid to employees in a large company. While there would be a great many bunched at the lower end, there would be very few thinly spread at the top. This would make it very awkward to have equal class widths. If a small width were used, near the top end the frequencies would be very low and a great many of them even zero. If a large width were used to make the frequencies at the top end reasonable, most of the detail at the lower end would be lost. So variable widths would be used.

But there might be an additional problem. Salaries at the top end may be so high as to be quite disproportionate to all the others, so that an 'open-ended class' would be better. This would be a class interval of, say, £50,000 *and above*, where no upper class limit is specified. Another reason for having an open-ended class is that if the classes were determined before the figures were collected, the upper limit may not be known. We try to keep the frequency for an open-ended class interval as low as possible consistent with the above considerations. So, for the salaries mentioned earlier, we might have a table like table 18.
Note the way in which the limits are specified. This is an alternative which avoids many of the problems with rounding. 'Under 3' and so on can allow for various degrees of accuracy.

Self-check

What class intervals would you suggest for recording the petrol consumption of cars?

There is some freedom in how this may be answered. However,

TABLE 18. GROSS SALARIES (PER ANNUM) IN A LARGE COMPANY
(INCLUDING PART-TIME WORKERS)

Salary (£1000)	Number of incomes
under 2	95
2 and ,, 3	1126
3 ,, ,, 4	5208
4 ,, ,, 5	10,216
5 ,, ,, 6	13,412
6 ,, ,, 8	4099
8 ,, ,, 10	2163
10 ,, ,, 15	812
15 ,, ,, 25	107
25 ,, ,, 50	11
50 and above	3
Total	37,252

the general pattern ought to be as below. The lower and upper
ends should have open classes, as you won't know what the limits
would be. It would not be wrong to have a class like 0–20 mpg to
start with, but it is perhaps better not to start at zero, as it is
rather obvious in this context that it is not possible to get such a
value. To have a definite upper limit is wrong. There just may be
a car better than you think! So a possible answer is:

under 20 mpg
20 and under 30 mpg
30 and under 40 mpg
40 and under 50 mpg
50 and under 60 mpg
over 60 mpg

If you had different sized classes, as well as open ones, then this
would be all right provided that the larger class widths were
where there were the least number of cars.

Activity

Look at the data on your multiplication times. Do you
think that the classes given earlier can be changed in the
light of later information? Would the display benefit from

244 Making sense of the data collected

having one or more open classes, do you think? If you were going to do some more calculations, would this influence your answers to these questions.

The author's data fitted all right into the classes as given. If there were to be more calculations, however, then two other classes would cater for any times outside the limits of the old classes. At the start an under-20 class would be useful and at the end, a 35-and-over class might be needed.

Review

1 What are the class boundaries for the class intervals 15–19, 20–24 when these figures represent
   a number of hotels – exact?
   b population – in thousands?
   c journey times by bus – nearest minute?
   d age last birthday?
2 The following figures represent the number of photocopies produced on a single machine each day over a quarter. Produce a grouped frequency table which preserves the essential pattern in these figures and yet is not too detailed:

497	436	501	486	523	395	439	423	479	525
507	415	497	522	468	407	441	522	502	456
443	506	479	530	449	440	385	393	476	553
375	374	546	431	536	499	461	423	351	441
412	538	533	555	482	519	406	452	433	453
375	513	384	438	496	367	476	522	488	524
470	440	388	458	375					

3 The following table shows trade union sizes in 1970:

Number of members			Number of unions
under 100			90
100 and under		500	116
500 ,, ,,		1000	50
1000 ,, ,,		2500	59
2500 ,, ,,		5000	50
5000 ,, ,,		10,000	30
10,000 ,, ,,		15,000	13
15,000 ,, ,,		25,000	21
25,000 ,, ,,		50,000	13
50,000 ,, ,,		100,000	16
100,000 and above			23

Why haven't the compilers used a constant class width?
Why did they use open-ended classes?

ANSWERS

1   **a** 15–19 and 20–24. As they are exact there is no difference.
If you said 14.5–19.5 and 19.5–24.5 you were getting confused
with the mathematical limits.

    b 14,500–19,500 and 19,500–24,500. Because the limits are
rounded to the nearest 1000, the true population could lie
within the above boundaries. If you said 15–19 and 20–24
thousand, because the data was discrete, you were forgetting
that it was also rounded.

    c 14.5–19.5 and 19.5–24.5 minutes. As it is continuous data,
true values can lie in that range. If you said 15–20 and 20–25,
you were getting confused with 'to the nearest completed
minute'.

    d 15–20 and 20–25. As it is age *last* birthday, any age from
19 exactly up to 20 (less a very small fraction of time) will be
recorded as 19, and so for the other classes.

2 Looking through the list, the range is $555 - 351 = 204$. Class
widths of 10 or 20 would give 20 classes or 10 classes, respectively, or thereabouts. Widths of 25 or 50 would give 8 or 4
classes, respectively, or thereabouts. With 65 items of data in
all, more than 10 classes would give too small frequencies. Just
4 classes would lose detail. The choice, then, can be narrowed

to class widths of 20 or 25. There is not a great deal to choose
between them. The author tends to prefer 25, but you certainly
are not wrong if you chose 20.

Using 25, then, the table is as below:

Number of copies in the day	Tally	Frequency
350–374	///	3
375–399	++++ ///	8
400–424	++++ /	6
425–449	++++ ++++ //	11
450–474	++++ //	7
475–499	++++ ++++ /	11
500–524	++++ ++++ /	11
525–549	++++ /	6
550–574	//	2
	Total	65

Did you remember that, since the frequencies are exact, the
limits are 350–374 and so on?

3 The compilers wished to have classes with frequencies that
were very roughly equal. Furthermore they wanted to em-
phasize certain aspects, particularly in the smaller numbers,
which would have been obscured had larger class widths been
used there. If small class widths had been used all the way
through, there would have been too many of them though.

The class 'under 100' was used as a 'catch all' for very small
unions. It looks better than putting 1–100 (or 0–100), as a
union with 1 or so members is hardly likely. The '100,000 and
above', equally, was used to cover all unions with membership
in the very high range, rather than put some upper limit on the
membership.

9 | Representing data by graphs

Why use graphs?

The word 'graph' is used in this chapter rather loosely to mean any method of displaying data which utilizes the two-axis system and coordinates. In this chapter, we will be concerned mainly with graphs constructed with further processing in mind. The use of graphs to display data for others is treated in Volume 2. In some cases the graphs will require work to be carried out on the raw data first, e.g. to produce a grouped frequency table.

Statistical data may be processed in two basic ways, arithmetically or graphically. It is the first that is most commonly used. However, graphical methods can yield reasonably accurate results fairly quickly. Some special techniques will be left to later chapters, but basic principles are covered here. First, though, a general word about these methods. Basically, they involve drawing graphs of various kinds and making measurements on them to obtain different statistics.

There are two ways in which graphs can prove especially useful. These are called 'interpolation' and 'extrapolation'. The first term means (using a graph) to determine values of a variable *in between* the values that we already have, by examining the patterns in the data. The second term means (using a graph) to determine values of a variable *outside of* the range of values that we already have, by assuming that the patterns in the data persist outside that range.

An example should make this clearer. Suppose we have some data on the prices of rival brands and on their sales which, if we plot it, looks something like the graph in figure 17 overleaf.

We now draw a line or curve through the points and make it as good a fit as we can. Perhaps it might then look like figure 18.

Then we could use this graph to find out what sales we would

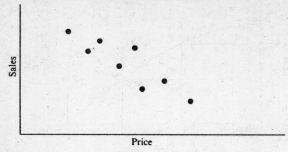

Figure 17

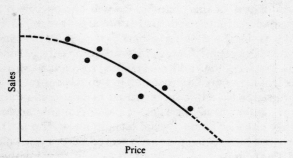

Figure 18

expect at a price other than the ones we have plotted. We do this by drawing straight lines through the prices we are interested in, e.g. A, B, C and D below, and see where they cut the curve. We then draw horizontal lines from here to cut the sales axis, e.g. E, F, G and H. See figure 19.

When we have done so, we read off the sales corresponding to the price selected. Where the lines drawn cut the curve in the continuous line portion, e.g. B, C, this is interpolation. Where they cut it in the dotted line, e.g. A, D, it is extrapolation.

Self-check

The following data is plotted on the graph in figure 20. It shows the productivity per man, measured in some suitable way, for several different sized firms, in a given industry:

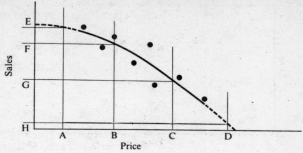

Figure 19

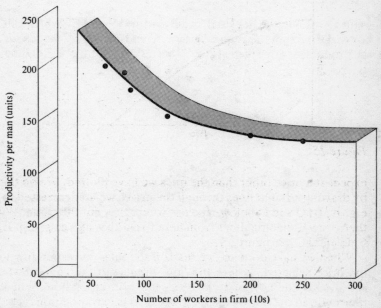

Figure 20

Number of workers in firm (10s)	Productivity per man (units per day)
60	210
70	? (to be found by interpolation)
80	200
90	180
120	160
200	140
250	135
300	? (to be found by extrapolation)

Use figure 20 to estimate the productivity of firms with 70 and 300 workers.

Figure 21 shows the lines AB and BC with DE and EF which can be used to obtain the required data. C and F give the values for the productivity of a firm of size 70 and 300 respectively. Reading

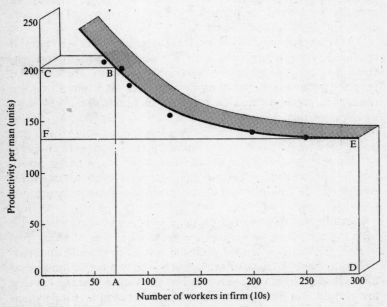

Figure 21

from the graph, these are 204 and 134. However, if you have got 205 and 135, this will do. You may have rounded to the nearest 10, and have answers of 200 and 130. This rounding is actually unwarranted from the data given. If you read the values as 205 and 135 and then rounded to 210 and 140, then this is not correct practice.

Graphing the data collected

If the data we collect is for only one variable, such as the heights of a sample of men, then it is called 'univariate' data. If we collect pairs of *corresponding* figures, e.g. the heights and weights of the same men, then this is 'bivariate' data. If we collect a set of corresponding figures, say the heights, weights and ages of the men, we have 'multivariate' data. It should be noted that some data which might appear superficially to be univariate is actually bivariate. For example, sales figures for a given company. Here the other variable is time. That is we actually have a pair of figures, the time (year, month or what-ever) and the sales for that time.

As far as plotting raw data goes, there is no way we can plot univariate data as such, since there is nothing to plot it against. Bivariate data (provided both variables are numeric) may be graphed with one variable along one axis, and one along the other. The sales graph in the previous section (page 249) was an example of this. Multivariate data may be graphed pairwise as for bivariate data. In all these cases the graphs will exhibit any patterns of relationships in the data clearly. Subsequent chapters will be dealing with this in detail. However, it is worth mention-ing the special case where we have collected data which varies over time, i.e. the domain of the variable we are measuring is time.

Plotting the values of a variable over time is excellent for bringing out the patterns. It is a very common way of doing this, in fact, especially when we want the record constantly updated. You only have to think of sales charts, the subject of innumera-ble cartoons. In many cases it is not the values themselves that are plotted, but the cumulative values. For example, total expen-diture to date on a project could be plotted so that control could be exercised over budgets and so on. In the scenario (on page 209), Brian might have kept a graph showing cumulative numbers of late arrivals and taken action when these exceeded a given limit in any period.

In some sense, producing an ungrouped frequency table can be thought of as converting univariate data into bivariate. In particular, having done this we can plot the values of the variable against their frequencies. If we do this, and join up the points with straight lines, we obtain what is called a 'frequency polygon'.

Self-check

Plot the frequency polygon for the data in table 19 below.

TABLE 19. NUMBER OF $\frac{1}{4}$ HOURS WAGES LOST BY ELSIE HALL

$\frac{1}{4}$ hours lost	Frequency
1	5
2	4
3	2
4	1
5	1
	Total 13

Table 19 repeats the data on Elsie Hall's timekeeping, given in the last chapter. The frequency polygon for this data is as shown in figure 21 (a).

Note that, conventionally, we bring the polygon down to zero at either end by, effectively, plotting two extra points, here (0, 0) and (6, 0).

Activity

Would a frequency polygon of your multiplication times from the previous chapter show anything useful, or are the frequencies in the ungrouped table, like the author's, too small?

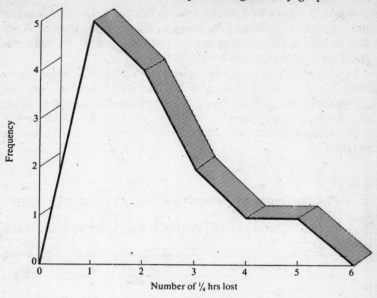

Figure 21 (a)

Self-check

Plot the frequency polygon for the data below.

NUMBER OF STRIKES IN A GIVEN INDUSTRY BY LENGTH OF STRIKE

Length of strike (days)	Number of strikes of this duration
1	14
2	8
3	4
4	2
5	8
	Total 36

The polygon for this data is shown in figure 22. Did you remember to 'tie down' the ends by bringing them down to zero? Also, you should have the frequencies always vertical. To draw the polygon the other way round is incorrect.

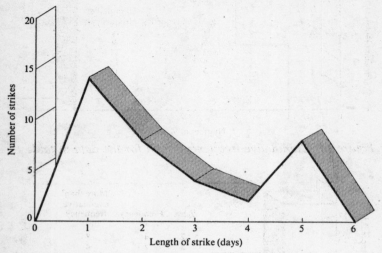

Figure 22. Frequency polygon

We may also plot cumulative frequency against the values of a variable. If, again, we join the points up, although this time in a special way, we obtain what is known as a 'cumulative frequency graph' or 'ogive'. For the same set of figures we get the graph shown in figure 23.

The graph is sometimes called a 'less than cumulative frequency graph', because it shows the number of times Elsie was less than (*or equal to*) so many $\frac{1}{4}$ hours late. There is also a 'more than – or greater than – cumulative frequency graph'. For the above figures it would be as shown in figure 24.

Note that when no 'less than' or 'more than' is specified it is the former that is understood.

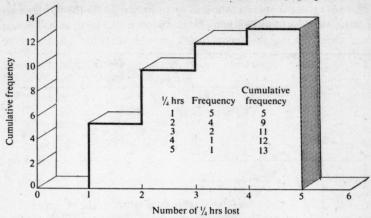

Figure 23. Cumulative frequency graph for the data in table 19

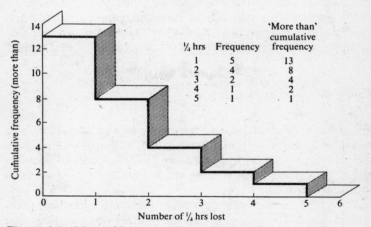

Figure 24. 'More than' cumulative frequency graph for data in table 19

Self-check

Plot the 'less than' and 'more than' cumulative frequency graphs for the data in the last self-check.

The two graphs are shown in figures 25 and 26 respectively. The cumulative frequencies are shown below:

Length of strike (days)	Frequency	Less than cum. freq.	Greater than cum. freq.
1	14	14	36
2	8	22	22
3	4	26	14
4	2	28	10
5	8	36	8
Total	36		

Check to see that you have the two graphs the correct way round. If your graphs have the same shape as those given, but they appear to be shifted sideways, then you are probably not plotting the cumulative frequencies against the right value for the length of the strike. Don't forget that the cumulative frequencies give the number 'less than *or equal to*', or 'greater than *or equal to*', the value of the length of strike to be plotted against.

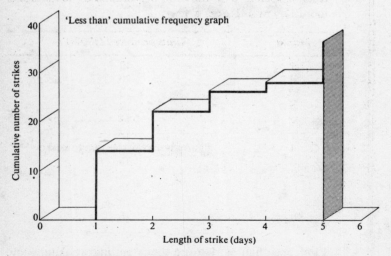

Figure 25. *'Less than' cumulative frequency graph*

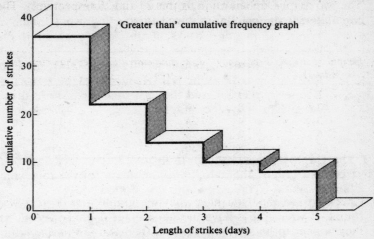

Figure 26. 'Greater than' cumulative frequency graph

Review

1 The following figures represent the data collected by a trade association on the total production of its members month by month over a year:

Month	Units produced (1000s)
J	19
F	20
M	20
A	19
M	18
J	17
J	figures not available due to strike
A	16
S	17
O	20
N	20
D	18

Plot these figures, leaving space for extrapolation into the January of the next year.

By interpolation, find the missing figure for July. By extrapolation, find a figure for the following January. What are the drawbacks of obtaining each of these figures by these methods?

2 Using the figures given in table 5 (page 214), for late arrivals for work at the Baby Gourmet plant, draw the frequency polygon and the 'less than' and 'more than' cumulative frequency graphs.

ANSWERS

1 The graph for this is shown in figure 27. The July figure is, from this graph, about 16.4 and the figure for the following January about 16 thousand units (see dotted lines).

The drawback with these methods is that, unless the curve is very smooth, because there are a great many points on it, and unless there are not likely to be any sudden changes, inaccuracy can occur. So, for example, it is quite possible that, in the July, the whole set of firms give their workers a fortnight's holiday, in which case the interpolated figure is likely to be a long way out. The extrapolated figure is, in effect, based only on *two* figures, those for November and December. It is not very likely to be correct since the Christmas holidays will have depressed production and it should go up again.

These problems are treated later in Volume *2*; there a partial solution to the problem of fluctuations is offered.

You should have plotted the graph with the months along the bottom and the production along the side. It is not the practice to plot such figures the other way round.

2 The graphs are shown in figure 28(a), (b) and (c). Did you remember to tie down the end of the frequency polygon? The left hand end has to be tied to a negative point, but this is perfectly acceptable. And did you remember *not* to join up the points on the cumulative frequency graphs by straight lines but by *steps*?

Graphing grouped data

The simplest way of displaying grouped data is by way of a

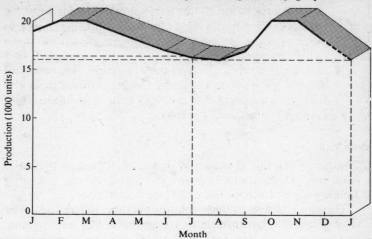

Figure 27. Production figures

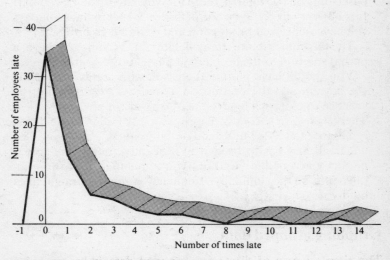

Figure 28 (a). Frequency polygon

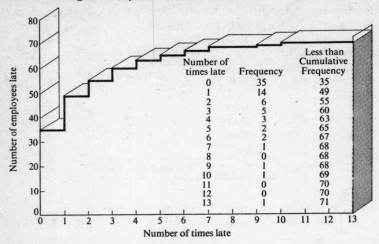

The table within graph (b):

Number of times late	Frequency	Less than Cumulative Frequency
0	35	35
1	14	49
2	6	55
3	5	60
4	3	63
5	2	65
6	2	67
7	1	68
8	0	68
9	1	68
10	1	69
11	0	70
12	0	70
13	1	71

(b). 'Less than' cumulative frequency graph

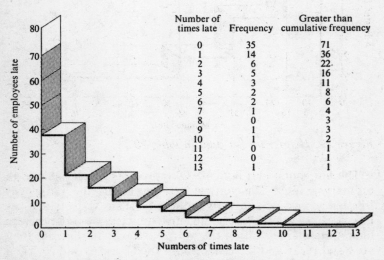

The table within graph (c):

Number of times late	Frequency	Greater than cumulative frequency
0	35	71
1	14	36
2	6	22
3	5	16
4	3	11
5	2	8
6	2	6
7	1	4
8	0	3
9	1	3
10	1	2
11	0	1
12	0	1
13	1	1

(c). 'Greater than' cumulative frequency graph

'histogram'. That for the data on Elsie's timekeeping is shown below. The data is repeated in table 20:

TABLE 20. MINUTES LOST FOR LATENESS BY ELSIE HALL

Minutes late	Frequency
6–15	5
16–30	4
31–45	2
46–60	1
61–75	1
	Total 13

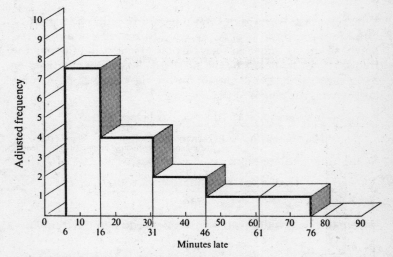

Figure 29. Histogram for data in table 20

The horizontal axis in figure 29 represents the variable as in ordinary graphs. The vertical axis represents the (adjusted) frequency. Just what exactly 'adjusted' means is explained below. To construct a histogram, first the class boundaries (*not* limits) are marked off on the horizontal axis. In this case they are 6 and 16, 16 and 31, 31 and 46, 46 and 61 and 61 and 76. Then one of the class widths, almost always the one that occurs most often, is chosen as standard *for this particular histogram*. Here it would be 15 (minutes). On the standard width classes, rectangles are drawn up from the boundary values equal in height to the frequency for that class. So the rectangle for the class interval 16–31 is 4 units high.

Self-check

Look back at the data in table 20. Work out *all* the class widths. Can you see what problem is going to arise in finding the heights of the rectangles in the histogram?

There is one class width that is less than all the others. This must be treated specially.

When the class width is not the standard (for that histogram) a different procedure must be adopted to that given above. The height of the rectangle in such cases is given by multiplying the frequency for that class by the *standard* class width and dividing by *its* class width. For example, for the class interval 6–16 in the above data, the height of the rectangle is

$$\frac{5 \text{ (the frequency)} \times 15 \text{ (the standard class width)}}{10 \text{ (the width of class interval 6–16)}} = 7.5.$$

So the 'adjusted' frequency is

$$\frac{\text{frequency} \times \text{standard class width}}{\text{class width}}.$$

Where the class width is standard, this is equal to the frequency.

Self-check

The width of a rectangle in a histogram is equal to the class width, and its height is equal to the 'adjusted' frequency, as defined above. What, then, is its area? Can you simplify this statement at all?

The *area* of each rectangle is given by class width × adjusted frequency. But, by above, this is equal to frequency × standard class width. Since the standard class width is a constant for the histogram, this means that *the area of each rectangle in the histogram is proportional to its class frequency*. It is only when all class widths are equal that the *heights* of the rectangles are proportional to the frequency. For this reason, the height of a rectangle (the 'adjusted' frequency) is often termed the 'frequency density' for that class. It should be noted that where there is an open-ended class no rectangle can be drawn. No histogram is possible in such cases, therefore, unless that class is, somewhat arbitrarily, closed at some value.

Self-check

Look carefully at the histogram below. There are thirty workers who earn between £90 and £100 a week. Which of the classes has the highest frequency? Which has the lowest? Use the numbers in the rectangles to identify them.

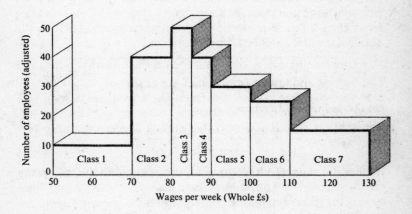

Since the height of any rectangle is, as outlined in the text, given

$$\text{by } \frac{\text{frequency} \times \text{standard class width}}{\text{class width}}$$

we can see that the standard class width in the above histogram is 10. This is because it is given that the frequency of class 5 is 30, and this is also the height of the rectangle for that class. As can be seen, this means that the width of this class must equal the standard.

From this we can calculate the frequencies for all the classes. For each, the frequency will be found by dividing the area of the rectangle by the standard class width. The results are then:

Class no.	Frequency	
1	$\frac{20 \times 10}{10} = 20$	← Joint lowest
2	$\frac{10 \times 40}{10} = 40$	← Highest
3	$\frac{5 \times 50}{10} = 25$	
4	$\frac{5 \times 40}{10} = 20$	← Joint lowest
5	$\frac{10 \times 30}{10} = 30$	
6	$\frac{10 \times 25}{10} = 25$	
7	$\frac{20 \times 15}{10} = 30$	

The highest and lowest frequencies are as shown.

If you said that class 3 had the highest frequency, then you forgot that it is the *area* of a rectangle that matters, not its height. The same is true if you said that class 1 *alone* had the lowest frequency.

If we wish to draw a histogram for a discrete variable when the values have not been rounded, care has to be taken. If we were to use the class boundaries there would be gaps between the rectangles. This is considered undesirable. The problem may be overcome by using the mathematical limits.

Self-check

Draw the histogram for the data in table 21 below, on lateness at the Baby Gourmet plant.

TABLE 21. TIMEKEEPING AT BABY GOURMET PLANT OVER A QUARTER

Number of times late	Frequency
0–1	49
2–3	11
4–5	5
6–7	3
8–13	3
	Total 71

With the data on lateness at the Baby Gourmet plant given in table 21 above, the mathematical limits are as follows:

Class limits	Mathematical limits
0–1	$-\frac{1}{2}$–$1\frac{1}{2}$
2–3	$1\frac{1}{2}$–$3\frac{1}{2}$
4–5	$3\frac{1}{2}$–$5\frac{1}{2}$
6–7	$5\frac{1}{2}$–$7\frac{1}{2}$
8–13	$7\frac{1}{2}$–$13\frac{1}{2}$

The histogram is then as shown at the top of page 266.

Note that the standard class width is taken as 2 (e.g. $3\frac{1}{2} - 1\frac{1}{2}$) but that the highest class has width 6 (i.e. $13\frac{1}{2} - 7\frac{1}{2}$). The height of the rectangle for that class is thus $\frac{3 \times 2}{6} = 1$.

Activity

Draw a histogram for your data on multiplication times. Don't forget that you can't leave open ended classes as they are.

The author's times are shown in the histogram halfway down page 266.

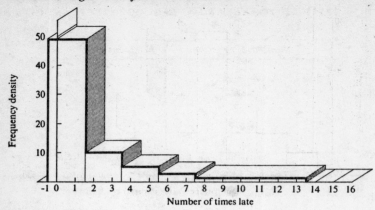

Histogram for data in table 21

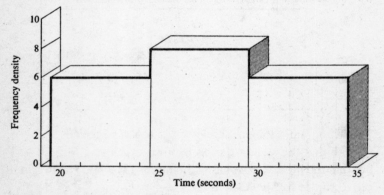

Author's multiplication times

Self-check

1 Draw the histogram for the data in table 12 in the last chapter.
2 Draw the histogram for the data in the table given in the answer to the self-check on page 223 in the last chapter.

ANSWERS

1 The answer is given in figure 30. Did you remember that there

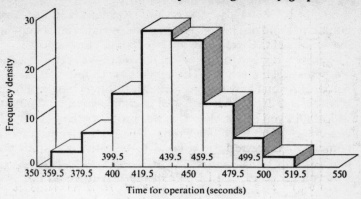

*Figure 30. Average time taken to perform a machine operation
by 100 machine operators*

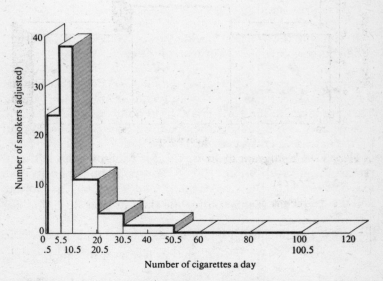

*Figure 31. Number of cigarettes smoked each day by a sample
of fifty smokers*

must not be any gaps between the rectangles and use class
boundaries and not limits? As these class widths are all equal,
the heights of the rectangles are equal to the frequencies.

2 The answer is given in figure 31. Did you remember to use the
mathematical limits here? This time, the class intervals are not
equal. Did you allow for this and adjust the rectangle heights
accordingly? Note that you had a choice for the standard
width. Did you choose 10? This was probably the best, but if
you chose 5 you were not wrong. Given no obviously more
numerous class width, it is usual to take the one from the
middle of the table.

If you chose 10, the heights of the first two and last two
rectangles can be found as follows:

Class 1–5: width $5.5 - .5 = 5$ Height of rectangle $= \frac{12 \times 10}{5} = 24$

Class 6–10: width $10.5 - 5.5 = 5$ Height of rectangle $= \frac{19 \times 10}{5} = 38.$

Class 31–50: width $50.5 - 30.5 = 20$ Height of rectangle $= \frac{3 \times 10}{20} = 1.5.$

Class 51–100: width $100.5 - 50.5 = 50$ Height of rectangle $= \frac{1 \times 10}{50} = .2.$

If you got the fraction upside down, you would have got
heights of 6, 9.5, 6 and 5 instead of these.

Frequency polygons for grouped data may be drawn by joining
the mid-points of the top of each rectangle in the histogram.
They are taken to the horizontal axis at points half a class width
outside each end rectangle, the operative class width being that
for the particular end rectangle. For the data in table 20 (on page
261) and its histogram in figure 29, for example, the leftmost
rectangle has width 10, i.e. $16 - 6$. So a point on the horizontal
axis 5 to the left of this rectangle, i.e. at $6 - 5 = 1$, is plotted
and the frequency polygon ended there.

‖ *Self-check*

Draw the complete frequency polygon for this data.

Your answer should have looked like this:

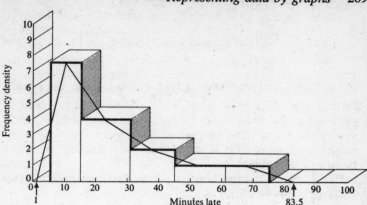

Figure 32. Frequency polygon for data in table 20

Note that the right hand end is 'tied' to zero at 76 + 7.5 = 83.5.

Actually, for reasons which are beyond the scope of this chapter, the frequency polygon as drawn like this is strictly only correct where there is a constant class width. In one particular case, there is a method of avoiding the problem. This is when we have all class widths a multiple of the standard class width chosen for that histogram. Here we can treat the rectangle concerned as a number of different rectangles, each of a standard class width. It is the mid-points of these that are then used to draw the frequency polygon.

For example, consider the following data:

TABLE 22. AREAS OF 33 PARKS IN A GIVEN DISTRICT (NEAREST ACRE)

Acres	Number of parks
1–5	3
6–10	14
11–15	7
16–20	5
21–30	4
	Total 33

Self-check

Draw the histogram and frequency polygon for the data in table 22.

The histogram and frequency polygon for the above data would be as follows:

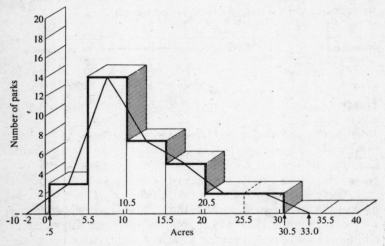

Figure 33. Frequency polygon for data in table 22

The rightmost rectangle has an area equal to frequency × standard class width (see above), i.e. $4 \times 5 = 20$. Since its base is 10 (i.e. $30.5 - 20.5$) it must be 2 units high. If we assume (and this is slightly doubtful) that the four parks are distributed equally over two class intervals 21–25 and 26–30, then we can make these two separate ones each of frequency 2. We have then effectively got a histogram with equal class intervals and can draw the frequency polygon as shown. Note that the left hand end point is negative. This does not matter, although it has no real interpretation in terms of park areas. Also, since we have divided up the 20.5–30.5 rectangle, the rightmost point of the frequency polygon is only 2.5 to the right of the histogram.

Self-check

From the data given in the answer to the self-check on page 223 of the last chapter, draw a histogram taking class width 5 as standard. Draw the frequency polygon on this.

With a standard class width of 5, the other classes can, as was detailed above, all be divided into classes of this width and the frequencies shared out accordingly. So we get:

New class	Mathematical limits	Frequency
1–5	.5–5.5	12
6–10	5.5–10.5	19
11–15	10.5–15.5	$\frac{11}{2} = 5.5$
16–20	15.5–20.5	$\frac{11}{2} = 5.5$
21–25	20.5–25.5	$\frac{4}{2} = 2$
26–30	25.5–30.5	$\frac{4}{2} = 2$
31–35	30.5–35.5	$\frac{3}{4} = .75$
36–40	35.5–40.5	$\frac{3}{4} = .75$
41–45	40.5–45.5	$\frac{3}{4} = .75$
46–50	45.5–50.5	$\frac{3}{4} = .75$
51–55	50.5–55.5	$\frac{1}{10} = .1$
etc. until		
96–100	95.5–100.5	$\frac{1}{10} = .1$

The frequency polygon can now be obtained by joining the mid-points of the tops of each rectangle in the histogram. It is shown in figure 34 overleaf.

Did you remember to divide the frequencies by the number of standard widths (5's) in the original classes? If you didn't you

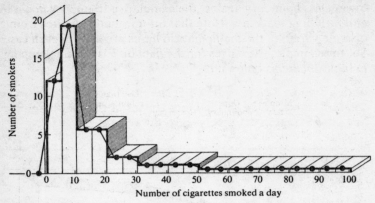

Figure 34. Number of cigarettes smoked a day from sample of fifty

would have had, for example, a frequency of 11 for classes 11–15 and 16–20, instead of only 5.5 in each. Did you also remember to 'tie down' the ends of the frequency polygon? Since all the new classes are of width 5, the polygon should be brought down to zero at the points

$.5 - \frac{5}{2} = .5 - 2.5 = -2$
and $100.5 + \frac{5}{2} = 100.5 + 2.5 = 103.$

If you put the frequency polygon down to zero at a point $\frac{50}{2}$ from 100.5, i.e. at 125.5, then you were forgetting that the class 51–100, of width 50, had been divided up into ten classes of width 5.

What proportion of the data has values below a given one?

We can also graph cumulative frequencies for grouped data, i.e. we can produce an ogive. What we actually plot is the upper class *boundary* of each class interval against the cumulative frequency up to and including that class. When we join these points together by straight lines we have the 'less than' cumulative frequency graph. To obtain the 'greater than' one, we plot the lower class boundary against the cumulative frequency *down* to and including that class. Note that for unrounded figures from a discrete variable, the mathematical limits are used in each case. So, for example, the ogives for the data on Elsie's timekeeping, in table 20, are as follows:

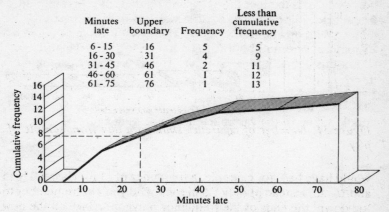

Minutes late	Upper boundary	Frequency	Less than cumulative frequency
6 - 15	16	5	5
16 - 30	31	4	9
31 - 45	46	2	11
46 - 60	61	1	12
61 - 75	76	1	13

Figure 35. (Less than) cumulative frequency graph for data in table 20

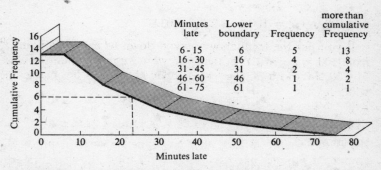

Minutes late	Lower boundary	Frequency	more than cumulative Frequency
6 - 15	6	5	13
16 - 30	16	4	8
31 - 45	31	2	4
46 - 60	46	1	2
61 - 75	61	1	1

Figure 36. (Greater than) cumulative frequency graph for data in table 20

Note that the ogives always start or end at zero, i.e. in the 'less than' case we start by plotting zero cumulative frequency for the

lowest lower class boundary, while in the 'greater than' graph
the zero occurs for the highest upper class boundary. Thus the
ogive for grouped data shows how many items of data lie below
(or above) any value of the variable. For example, in the above
graphs, suppose we draw a line up from the value 25 on the
horizontal axis to meet the ogive and read off the corresponding
frequency. This tells us that Elsie was less than (or equal to) 25
minutes late on about 7 occasions (and greater than or equal to
25 minutes late on about 6). Reference to the original figures
shows this actually to be correct. This is a further example of
interpolation.

The ogive for data in which the greater frequencies are for the
middle values of the variable tends to be as in figure 37.

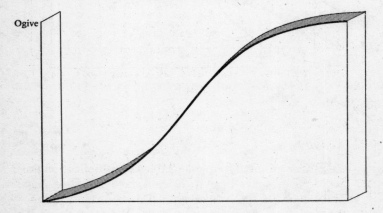

Figure 37

It is this shape, in fact, that gives the ogive its name. The
greater the number of class intervals, the more the straight lines
look like a curve. Consider the data in table 12 (page 229) on the
times taken by machine operators on a particular operation.

Self-check

Draw the (less than) ogive for the data in table 12.

Your answer should look like figure 38. Note how similar this is to the smooth curve above. Often, in fact, rather than using straight lines for the ogive, a smooth curve is drawn through the points.

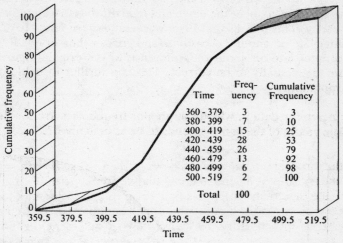

Time	Freq- uency	Cumulative Frequency
360 - 379	3	3
380 - 399	7	10
400 - 419	15	25
420 - 439	28	53
440 - 459	26	79
460 - 479	13	92
480 - 499	6	98
500 - 519	2	100
Total	100	

Figure 38

Activity

Take your grouped frequency table of multiplication times and draw an ogive from it. Does it have the ogive shape? The ogive for the author's times is shown in figure 39 overleaf. This certainly does not have the ogive shape. The increase here is uniform, which shows a fairly even distri-bution of frequency.

Self-check

Draw both the 'less than' and the 'greater than' cumulative frequency graphs for the data in table 15 of the previous chapter.

The two graphs are shown in figures 40 and 41. If you get a graph

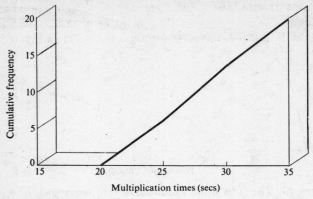

Figure 39

of the same shape, but moved sideways, then you took the wrong
boundary to plot against the cumulative frequencies. Remember, the 'less than' graph has figures up to and including those
for the class plotted against the upper boundary of that class.
The 'greater than' graph has figures down to and including those
for the class plotted against the lower boundary of that class.
And did you get the boundaries right? They are 500 less than,
and 500 more than, the lower and upper limits respectively.

This means that the 'less than' graph is plotted with population
values, in 1000s, of:

population	0.5	5.5	10.5	20.5	30.5	50.5	70.5	100.5	150.5
cumulative									
frequency	0	10	15	20	21	21	21	24	25

The equivalent figures for the 'greater than' graph are:

population	0.5	5.5	10.5	20.5	30.5	50.5	70.5	100.5	150.5
cumulative									
frequency	25	15	10	5	4	4	4	1	0

Very often, too, ogives are drawn using cumulative relative
frequencies. The relative frequency is the ordinary frequency
divided by the total of all the frequencies for that data. In the
case of the data in figure 38 on page 275, for example, the relative

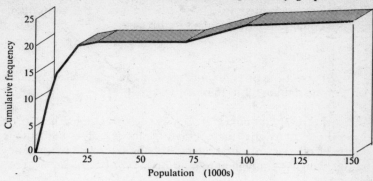

Figure 40. The 'less than' cumulative frequency graph

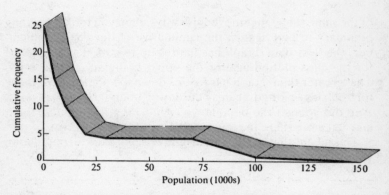

Figure 41. The 'greater than' cumulative frequency graph: Population of a group of towns and villages

frequencies are $\frac{3}{100}$, $\frac{7}{100}$, $\frac{15}{100}$ and so on. Most of the time these relative frequencies are actually expressed as a percentage.

Self-check

What are the relative frequencies of the data in figure 38 expressed as percentages?

278 Making sense of the data collected

Since the total frequency is 100, the percentage relative frequencies are equal to the frequencies in this case.

Self-check

What are the ordinary and percentage relative frequencies of the data in table 15 of the last chapter?

There the total frequency is 25. So each frequency has to be divided by 25 to give the relative frequency. The percentage relative frequency is found by multiplying the *relative* frequency by 100, which is equivalent to multiplying the frequency by 4. So we get:

Class	Frequency	Relative Frequency	Percentage Relative Frequency
1–5	10	$\frac{10}{25} = .4$	$.4 \times 100 = 40$
6–10	5	$\frac{5}{25} = .2$	$.2 \times 100 = 20$
11–20	5	$\frac{5}{25} = .2$	$.2 \times 100 = 20$
21–30	1	$\frac{1}{25} = .04$	$.04 \times 100 = 4$
31–50	0	$\frac{0}{25} = .0$	$.0 \times 100 = 0$
51–70	0	$\frac{0}{25} = .0$	$.0 \times 100 = 0$
71–100	3	$\frac{3}{25} = .12$	$.12 \times 100 = 12$
101–150	1	$\frac{1}{25} = .04$	$.04 \times 100 = 4$

Total 25

When ogives are plotted using relative frequencies they can be directly compared. For example, the three overlaid ogives in figure 42 opposite are obviously very different.

Self-check

What differences are revealed by these three ogives?

The 'dashed' ogive represents high frequencies in the lower values and low frequencies in the higher values. The 'dotted'

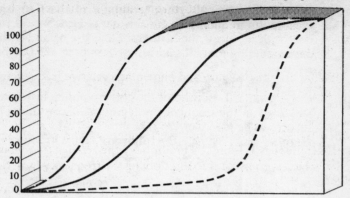

Figure 42. Three ogives

ogive represents the reverse. The middle one is the case discussed above in which the frequencies are highest in the middle.

Activity

Take your multiplication times and draw a percentage relative frequency ogive. On the same graph plot the author's figures. How alike are they?

Review

1 The salaries of the 200 office workers, junior management and other salaried employees of a small firm are as follows:

Salary (per annum)	Number of employees earning that salary
under £5000	16
£5000 and under £7500	38
£7500 and under £10,000	74
£10,000 and under £15,000	48
£15,000 and over	24
Total	200

What difficulty would you encounter if you tried to draw
the histogram and ogive for this data? How would you
deal with it? Draw the histogram and the ogive for this
data assuming that all salaries are less than £25,000 per
annum.

2 Convert all the class widths in the data in review 1 to a
single standard width, plot the corresponding histogram
and draw in the frequency polygon (again assuming all
salaries to be less than £25,000.)

3 Another small firm has the following salary structure:

Salary (per annum)	% of employees earning that salary
under £6000	10
£6000 and under £8000	40
£8000 and under £10,000	30
£10,000 and under £14,000	15
over £14,000	5
Total	100

By plotting percentage cumulative frequencies of this
data and of the data in review 1 together, compare the
salary structure of the two firms (assume all salaries are
less than £25,000 in the first firm and £24,000 for the
second).

ANSWERS

1 The difficulty lies in the fact that there is an open-ended class,
£15,000 and over. Without any upper limit, it is not possible to
draw either the ogive or the histogram. The solution is to
arbitrarily set an upper limit to the class or, if the class
frequency is very small relative to the others, it might be
ignored, but the other method of dealing with the problem is
the one usually adopted. The histogram and the ogive are
shown below (see figures 43 and 44). The heights of the
histogram rectangles are based on a standard class width of
£2500. While you would not be wrong if you used a different
standard, this one, being the smallest, is the most convenient.

The new high class, the adjusted frequencies for the histogram and the cumulative frequencies for the ogive are as follows:

Salary	Frequency	Adjusted frequency*	Cumulative frequency
Under £5000	16	$\frac{16 \times 2500}{5000} = 8$	16
£5000 and under £7500	38	$\frac{38 \times 2500}{2500} = 38$	54
£7500 and under £10,000	74	$\frac{74 \times 2500}{2500} = 74$	128
£10,000 and under £15,000	48	$\frac{48 \times 2500}{5000} = 24$	176
£15,000 and under £25,000	24	$\frac{24 \times 2500}{10,000} = 6$	200

Total 200

These graphs are shown in figures 43 and 44 overleaf. Note that, in the ogive, the cumulative frequencies are plotted against the *upper* boundaries of the class intervals. If you drew a smooth curve instead of the straight lines then this is acceptable, though there are really two few points to do this with confidence.

2 The frequencies for the new classes can be obtained from the old ones by dividing up the class widths into sections of standard width. Since £2500 is the smallest class width, it is this that will be used as standard. The frequencies must then be divided the same number of times. So the frequency for the class £15,000–£25,000, which is divided into 4 equal classes of £2500, is also divided into 4. This gives 6. Actually, as you can see, the frequencies for the new classes are equal to the adjusted frequencies for the class from which they are obtained. So they do not all have to be recalculated. Did you spot this? This histogram and frequency polygon are shown in figure 45. Did you remember to 'tie down' the frequency

*Adjusted frequency makes allowances for the different class widths: it is equal to frequency × standard class width/class width.

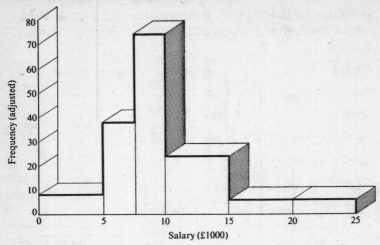

Figure 43

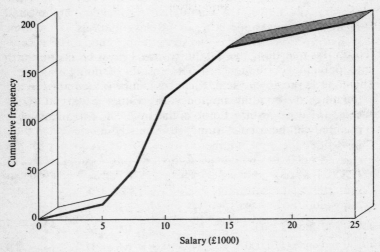

Figure 44

polygon ends? The left hand side has to be tied down to a negative value, but this is acceptable. Remember that the 'tie points' are *half a rectangle's width* away from the edges of the outside rectangles.

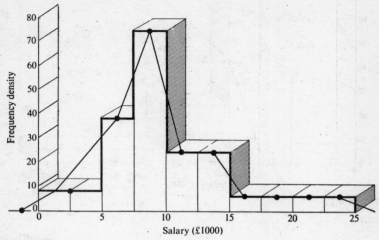

Figure 45

3 To do this question, the data in review 1 must be converted into percentage frequencies. The results of doing this are shown in figure 46 overleaf. Each frequency is expressed as a percentage of the total frequency. Since that is 200, all that needs to be done, in effect, is to divide by 2. The data in review 3 is already in the correct form.

Salary	Frequency	% of total frequency	Cumulative %
under £5000	16	$\frac{16}{200} \times 100 = 8$	8
£5000 and under £7500	38	$\frac{38}{200} \times 100 = 19$	27
£7500 and under £10,000	74	$\frac{74}{200} \times 100 = 37$	64
£10,000 and under £15,000	48	$\frac{48}{200} \times 100 = 24$	88
£15,000 and under £25,000	24	$\frac{24}{200} \times 100 = 12$	100
Total 100			

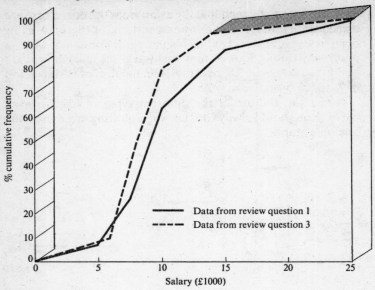

Figure 46

The percentage cumulative frequencies for the data in review 3 are:

Salary	% frequency	Cumulative %
under £6000	10	10
£6000 and under £8000	40	50
£8000 and under £10,000	30	80
£10,000 and under £14,000	15	95
£14,000 and under £24,000	5	100
Total 100		

The ogives are as below. Because the salaries of the second firm do not go up as far as £25,000, an extra line is added in the graph for that data, to make the two ogives meet at the upper end. Once again, if you drew smooth curves it is acceptable, but there are really too few points to do this accurately. From the graph, it can be seen that the salaries in the second firm are concentrating more in the lower end than in the first, as its ogive rises more steeply at its beginning. If you said it was the other way round, look at how many salaries in each firm are below £10,000, say. There are 64% in the firm of review 1 and 80% in the one of review 2.

Note, too, the use of the different types of line for each ogive. You should always do this when plotting more than one line on a graph.

Scenario 6
A dispute about
wages

The next two chapters are concerned with taking a lot of information and 'boiling it down' to just a few figures. As you read
through this scenario, make a mental note of those places where
one figure is used to represent many different figures and look at
the difficulties that can arise when such a figure is used.

This scenario took place during a period when there was a lot of
grumbling in the country about wages being kept down and prices going
up. It also happened to coincide with a time when there was a fairly
militant shop steward representing many of the women at the Baby
Gourmet plant. Her name was Jenny Wright. There was an article in
one of the national papers one morning announcing that wages had
'soared to a new high' and that the average was now £42 a week. Jenny
read this. On comparing that figure with the money received by the
women she represented, she came to the conclusion that they were
being hard done by. Their standard wage was £16.70. As the annual
wage round was only a short time away, she decided that some action
was required.

After talking to the workers, Jenny went to see Brian Kelly, the
personnel officer at the plant. She told him that her women wanted a
twenty-per-cent pay rise this time. She mentioned the figure of £42 a
week for the average wage that she had seen in the newspaper. Brian
gently pointed out that you had to be very careful with statistics obtained
from newspapers. He had seen the original figures, he said, and the £42
applied to men workers, both manual and non-manual, over the age of
twenty-one. Moreover, it included about £8 for overtime, shift working,
bonuses and so on.

'All right,' said Jenny, 'but it also said in the paper that the same
figure last year was £37. That's a thirteen-per-cent increase, and we only
had eight per cent.' Brian replied that other factors had to be taken into
account, such as what the pay levels had been prior to that, productivity,
profits and so on. He warned Jenny that, with the company performing
as it was, they would be lucky to get eight per cent this year.

So Jenny got together with the other shop stewards, representing the engineers, cooks and so on, to prepare a case for a substantial rise. They contacted their unions for advice on how to deal with the statistics. On the day of the meeting between management and shop stewards to agree new wage levels, Jenny presented a good case for the women. She showed that figures for wage levels of women doing manual work in the food, drink and tobacco industries indicated that Baby Gourmet paid below average wages.

The management, on the other hand, were very frank about the state of the company and were able to convince the shop stewards that too high a wage settlement could only harm the situation. It was only after a long and protracted discussion that agreement on the actual wage increase was arrived at, however. It was fourteen per cent. Jenny was reasonably pleased, and so were the women. Management were also quite satisfied. Some other companies had had a lot more trouble and had ended up giving considerably more.

We saw in the two previous chapters how the sheer bulk of the data could be reduced. But very often this is not enough. In the scenario, Jenny wants to compare wages in the factory with those elsewhere. Imagine trying to do this with even the grouped frequency tables of Chapter 8.

What we need to be able to do is to 'boil down' the data even further to just a few figures. One such figure is, in fact, met in every day life, and is called an average. What the scenario shows is that there can be a great deal of misunderstanding about averages. Just why this should be so is investigated in Chapter 10.

But the average on its own is usually not enough. Suppose you were told that the average adult male height of a race of beings from another star system was 15 ft. Would you be surprised to see a 12 ft one? You can't say, because you've no idea how much these beings can vary in height. Chapter 11 investigates how we can measure how much things vary, so that a figure can be given to indicate this.

After studying Chapters 10 and 11 you should be able to define what figures can be used as summaries of data and be able to calculate them. You should be capable of using these figures to make comparisons and be aware of problems associated with doing so.

10 | On the average

What do we mean by average?

We saw in the last chapter how a large amount of data could be reduced in quantity by producing (grouped) frequency tables, graphs and so on. But very often we want to convey this information even more simply. An 'average' is a *single figure* that sums up the data we have collected. It is a measure of 'central tendency'; that is, it tells us what value the figures tend to centre on. In the scenario, for example, the average wage is a figure which indicates broadly what level of wage people earn in general. An average tells us something about the overall picture. We can ask questions, as they did in the scenario, about whether a particular figure is above or below average, for instance.

But just how do we go about obtaining this average figure? Well, there are, in fact, many different ways and not just one figure. One of the objectives of this chapter is to help you decide which one is appropriate in given circumstances. The emphasis here will be on understanding rather than on calculation. It is, however, necessary to include a fair amount of arithmetic to put across the ideas involved.

The arithmetic mean – the point about which the figures balance

The most commonly used average is the 'arithmetic mean', or just simply the mean. To calculate this, what you basically have to do is to add together all the figures you want the mean of and divide by the number of figures there are. For example, suppose a wholesaler carries five different brands of tinned tomatoes (14 oz) priced $10\frac{1}{2}$p, 11p, $11\frac{1}{2}$p, 12p and $12\frac{1}{2}$p. Then the mean price of tins of tomatoes is $\frac{(10\frac{1}{2} + 11 + 11\frac{1}{2} + 12 + 12\frac{1}{2})}{5} = \frac{57\frac{1}{2}}{5} = 11\frac{1}{2}$p.

> *Self-check*
>
> Suppose the prices were 10p, $10\frac{1}{2}$p, 11p, $12\frac{1}{2}$p and $13\frac{1}{2}$p. Calculate what the mean would be then. What do you notice about it?

The mean would be the same, i.e.

$$\frac{(10 + 10\frac{1}{2} + 11 + 12\frac{1}{2} + 13\frac{1}{2})}{5} = \frac{57\frac{1}{2}}{5} = 11\frac{1}{2}\text{p}.$$

But in this case there is no brand priced at $11\frac{1}{2}$p. So the mean does not have to correspond to one of the actual figures.

> *Self-check*
>
> Suppose the prices were $10\frac{1}{2}$p, 11p, $11\frac{1}{2}$p, 12p, $12\frac{1}{2}$p and 13p. Calculate what the mean would be in this case. What do you notice this time?

The mean price would then be

$$\frac{(10\frac{1}{2} + 11 + 11\frac{1}{2} + 12 + 12\frac{1}{2} + 13)}{6} = \frac{70\frac{1}{2}}{6} = 11.75\text{p}.$$

In this case we see that the answer could not be the price of a tin of tomatoes anyway. We don't have a coin for .75p. This is typical of the means of discrete variables. It's like the statistic that the average number of televisions owned, or rented, by people in Britain is $\frac{1}{3}$ of a set – a statistic which is obtained by dividing the total number of sets by the population.

> *Self-check*
>
> Suppose that the wholesaler carries a super-luxury brand of tomatoes priced at 20p a tin, as well as others priced $10\frac{1}{2}$p, 11p, $11\frac{1}{2}$p and 12p. Calculate the mean of these. What do you notice about it?

Once more, suppose one price was very much more than all the

others, say 20p. If the rest are priced at $10\frac{1}{2}$p, 11, $11\frac{1}{2}$p and 12p.
The mean then becomes

$$\frac{(10\frac{1}{2} + 11 + 11\frac{1}{2} + 12 + 20)}{5} = \frac{65}{5} = 13\text{p}.$$

Here we see that the mean price is higher than four of the five
prices. Extreme values, such as the 20p, can influence the mean
to a considerable extent.

The principle here is very much like the one that operates in a
balance. Suppose that we hang the tins of tomatoes (which are of
equal weight) on a beam, as shown in figure 47. The distances
away from the balance point are to equal the differences between
the prices and their mean (-ve being to the left). The weights will
then balance.

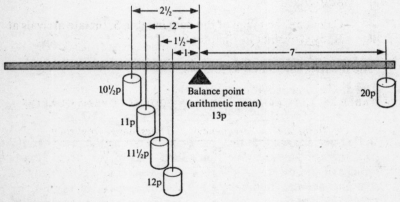

Figure 47

This shows that the mean acts as a balance point. Values a
long way away from it have a greater effect than those near it, in
the same way that weights placed further away from the balance
point of the beam have a greater effect than those near it.

Finally with the tomato prices, suppose we had some brands
which had the same price. Say we had 1 brand at $10\frac{1}{2}$p, 2 at 11p,
3 at $11\frac{1}{2}$p, 2 at 12p and 2 at $12\frac{1}{2}$p. The figures themselves are the
ones used in the initial example, but the mean in this case is

$$\frac{(10\tfrac{1}{2} + 11 + 11 + 11\tfrac{1}{2} + 11\tfrac{1}{2} + 11\tfrac{1}{2} + 12 + 12 + 12\tfrac{1}{2} + 12\tfrac{1}{2})}{10} = \frac{116}{10} = 11.6\text{p}.$$

However, it would obviously be easier to calculate this as

$$\frac{(1 \times 10\tfrac{1}{2} + 2 \times 11 + 3 \times 11\tfrac{1}{2} + 2 \times 12 + 2 \times 12\tfrac{1}{2})}{10}.$$

That is, multiply each value by its frequency and add then divide by the total frequency. Note that we divide by 10 because there are ten brands, even though there are only five different prices. This time the mean is not $11\tfrac{1}{2}$p because, although the same prices are involved, they occur with different frequency.

The above indicates a way of finding the means of data in ungrouped frequency tables.

Self-check

Calculate the mean of the data in table 5, on late arrivals at Baby Gourmet in Chapter 8.

The mean is calculated as follows:

TABLE 23. LATE ARRIVALS AT BABY GOURMET OVER A QUARTER

Times late	Frequency	Times late × frequency
0	35	0
1	14	14
2	6	12
3	5	15
4	3	12
5	2	10
6	2	12
7	1	7
8	0	0
9	1	9
10	1	10
11	0	0
12	0	0
13	1	13
Total 71		114

Mean times late $= \frac{114}{71} = 1.6$ (to one decimal place).

If your answer was $\frac{114}{14} = 8.1$ (to one decimal place) then you divided by the number of different possible times late and not by the total frequency as you should.

What do we do if the data has already been amalgamated?

When data is grouped, we have to select one figure to represent each class and which is then multiplied by the frequency for that class. This figure is the 'class mid-point' – that is, a point exactly halfway between the class boundaries. Figure 48 illustrates this for various cases. Let's have a look at an example. Review 2 on page 225 of Chapter 8 had a class of £12–£13.99. Since this is discrete data, the class boundaries are the same*. The class mid-point is thus

$$\frac{£12 + (£13.99 - £12)}{2} = \frac{£12 + £1.99}{2} = £12.99\frac{1}{2}.$$

Figure 48(d) illustrates this point. Actually, the same result can be obtained rather more easily by just adding together the two class boundaries and dividing by 2. So here we get

$$\frac{£(12 + 13.99)}{2} = £12.99\frac{1}{2}*.$$

> *Self-check*
>
> Calculate the class mid-points, for the first class only, in the following cases:
>
> **a**   10–19, 20–29 inches
> **b** class 10–19, 20–29 times a week
> **c** limits 10–19, 20–29 age last birthday
> **d**   10–19, 20–29 population to nearest 1000.

*Note that the upper boundary is given as £13.99 because in petty cash $\frac{1}{2}$ps are ignored. However, when the mid-point is calculated, the $\frac{1}{2}$p is necessary because we are now dealing with the mathematical aspects of the matter. As with the mean, which sometimes gives 'impossible' results, like .03 of a dog per family, we must treat this as a mere number.

(a) Continuous data (rounded to the nearest ...)

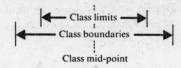

(b) Discrete data (not rounded)

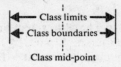

(c) Discrete data (rounded to nearest ...)

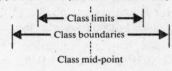

(d) Discrete or continuous data (disregarding the fractional part - e.g. 12.9 becomes 12)

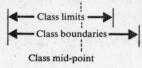

Figure 48. The class mid-point

a Because the data is continuous, the class boundaries are 9.5–19.5, 19.5–29.5. The class mid-point for the first is thus $\frac{9.5 + 19.5}{2} = 14.5$ inches.

If you said 15, you didn't apply the formula.

b This data is discrete and so the class boundaries are the same as the class limits, 10–19, 20–29. The class mid-point of the first is thus $\frac{10+19}{2} = 14.5$ times a week. Notice that, like the mean, a 'nonsense' answer can be obtained with discrete data. It is also the same answer as for the inches. This is because in both cases there is symmetry about the mid-point. If you got

14 or 15 as an answer, you may have rounded to get a 'sensible' answer. This is, in fact, incorrect.

c This is a case where there is no symmetry. The lower class boundary is the same as the class limit, but the upper one is not. The class boundaries are, in fact, 10–20 (all but the smallest fraction of time), 20–29 (all but the smallest fraction of time). The class mid-point of the first is thus $\frac{10+20}{2} = 15$ years. If you said the boundaries were 9.5–19.5, 19.5–29.5, and got a mid-point of 14.5 again, you forgot how to treat age last birthday.

d Since the data is discrete but rounded, the class boundaries are again 9.5–19.5, 19.5–29.5. The mid-point of the first class is thus $\frac{9.5+19.5}{2} = 14.5$ (000) people.

If you used the class limits, though you will have got the same answer, your method is strictly not correct. It would not work in the case of c, for example, and it is for such a reason that the class boundaries, and not the class limits, must be used.

The idea of multiplying the class mid-point by the class frequency is to get an estimate of the total value of the data in that class.

In the scenario, women's wages at Baby Gourmet were being compared with those outside. One set of figures that would probably be of interest relates to the wages of full-time female manual workers over the age of eighteen. These are given in table 24 below for the year in question (which was some time ago, as you can see from the figures!).

TABLE 24. GROSS WEEKLY WAGES OF WOMEN MANUAL WORKERS OVER 18 YEARS OF AGE

Gross wages per week (£)	Frequency
5 and under 15	20
15 ,, ,, 20	38
20 ,, ,, 30	36
30 ,, ,, 40	5
40 ,, ,, 60	1
Total 100	

Those earnings over £60 a week are so few as can be safely ignored, even taking into account the greater effect of such extremes.

Self-check

Calculate the mean of the figures in table 24.

The mean for these figures is calculated as follows:

Class mid-point	Frequency	Class mid-point × frequency
10.0	20	200
17.5	38	665
25.0	36	900
35.0	5	175
50.0	1	50
Total	100	Total 1990

Mean wage = £19.90. Note that this is not actually how the official statistics are calculated. This is done by taking total wages earned and dividing by the total number of workers.

The units for the number of wages, i.e. the frequency, were not given. In fact, the figures in that column were percentage relative frequencies. The mean is no different to what it would have been if actual numbers had been used. An example should make it clear why. Suppose the mean of the data in table 25 is calculated using the ordinary frequencies and then the percentage relative frequencies.

Self-check

Calculate the means in these two ways.

TABLE 25

| Price of goods (£) | Number of brands in this price range | |
	Actual number	Percentage
100 and over but under 200	3	30
200 and over but under 300	6	60
300 and over but under 400	1	10
	Total 10	Total 100

The mean, using the ordinary frequencies, is

$$£ \frac{3 \times 150 + 6 \times 250 + 1 \times 350}{10} = £ \frac{450 + 1500 + 350}{10}$$
$$= £ \frac{2300}{10} = £230.$$

Note that, because of the way the data is grouped, the class boundaries are 100–200, 200–300 and 300–400. The class mid-points are thus 150, 250 and 350 respectively. The mean, using the percentages, is

$$£ \frac{30 \times 150 + 60 \times 250 + 10 \times 350}{100} = £ \frac{4500 + 15,000 + 3500}{100}$$
$$= £ \frac{23,000}{100} = £230.$$

So all that happens is that the top and bottom of the fraction giving the mean are both multiplied by the same number (here 10, but not generally so, of course).

Self-check

Calculate the mean of the following data. What does it represent?

Production (units)	Number of days production was in this range
200–299	3
300–399	27
400–499	174
500–599	39
600–699	7
Total	250

The calculation is as follows:

Production (units)	Class mid-points	Frequency (days)	Class mid-points × frequency
200–299	249.5	3	748.5
300–399	349.5	27	9436.5
400–499	449.5	174	78,213.0
500–599	549.5	39	21,430.5
600–699	649.5	7	4546.5
		Total 250	Total 114,375.0

The mean is thus:

$$\frac{114,375.0}{250} = \frac{4 \times 114,375}{1000} = \frac{457,500}{1000} = 457.5.$$

This figure represents the average production per day. If you divided by the number of groups, you would have got $\frac{457,500}{5}$ = 91,500! This would obviously not have been in the range of the table. It must be wrong therefore.

Activity

Take your multiplication times from the previous chapters and calculate the mean in two different ways: (a) from the ungrouped frequency table; (b) from the grouped frequency table.

Were they the same? They do not have to be.

Self-check

Can you see why not?

It is because, as we saw earlier, the grouped frequency table *loses* the detail of the ungrouped one.

The calculations for the author's times are shown below. How different was your mean from his? (Do you think the author cheated and used easy numbers to multiply)?

(a)

Time	Frequency	Time × frequency
20	1	20
21	1	21
22	2	44
23	1	23
24	1	24
25	3	75
26	1	26
27	2	54
28	1	28
29	1	29
30	4	120
31	1	31
32	1	32
Total	20	527

Mean $= \frac{527}{20} = 26.35$.

(b)

Time	Class mid-point	Frequency	Class mid-point × frequency
20–24	22	6	132
25–29	27	8	216
30–34	32	6	192
		Total 20	Total 540

Mean $= \frac{540}{20} = 27.0$.

Note that they are *not* the same.

Review

1 What advantages do you think an average has over, say, a grouped frequency table when dealing with statistics?
2 Calculate the means for the following data. Comment on your results in each case, and say what they represent.
   a The monthly sales figures (£1000s) over a year of 121, 116, 104, 109, 110, 111, 96, 127, 101, 123, 119 and 107.

b The number of $\frac{1}{4}$ hours that Elsie Hall was late, from table 8 in Chapter 8.

c The operators times in table 12 in Chapter 8.

d The village populations in table 15 in Chapter 8.

ANSWERS

1 An average is just one figure. It summarizes the data in an effective way and communicates the essentials without confusing the reader with even the number of figures that appear in a grouped frequency table. In particular, it enables comparisons to be made between two sets of figures. With the grouped frequency tables this would be rather difficult.

One thing you should *not* have said is that it is more *accurate*. It is not that it is less accurate; its purpose is totally different. It does, however, contain less *detail* than a grouped frequency table which, in turn, contains less detail than an ungrouped one.

2 a The mean here is

$$\frac{121 + 116 + 104 + 109 + 110 + 111 + 96 + 127 + 101 + 123 + 119 + 107}{12}$$

$$= \frac{1344}{12} = 112 \text{ (£1000s) sales per month.}$$

This lies roughly in the middle of the range 96–127.

b

$\frac{1}{4}$ hrs lost	Frequency	$\frac{1}{4}$ hrs lost × frequency
1	5	5
2	4	8
3	2	6
4	1	4
5	1	5
Total 13		Total 28

Mean = 28/13 = 2.15 (to two decimal points) $\frac{1}{4}$ hrs lost *per day late*.

This is not the number of $\frac{1}{4}$ hours she was late on average overall, but only for those times *she was late at all*.

c Time for operation (seconds)	Class mid-point	Frequency	Class mid-point × frequency
360–379	369.5	3	1108.5
380–399	389.5	7	2726.5
400–419	409.5	15	6142.5
420–439	429.5	28	12,026.0
440–459	449.5	26	11,687.0
460–479	469.5	13	6103.5
480–499	489.5	6	2937.0
500–519	509.5	2	1019.0
	Total	100	43,750.0

Mean $= \frac{43,750}{100} = 437.5$ seconds.

Again, should you have divided by 8, you would have got an answer of $\frac{43,750}{8} = 5468.75$, which is way outside the range in the table. Remember to always divide by the total frequency.

The data is continuous, so the class boundaries are 359.5–379.5 and so on. Hence the mid-points are $\frac{359.5 + 379.5}{2} = \frac{739}{2} = 369.5$ and so on. This average represents the average time taken to perform the operation by the 100 operators. It is again roughly in the middle of the range.

2 d Mean $= \frac{555}{25} = 22.2$ (1000).

This figure gives the average population of towns in the area, in 1000s. Notice that here it is *not* in the middle of the range, but towards the beginning, where the bigger frequencies are.

The class boundaries here are .5–5.5, 5.5–10.5 and so on, as we saw earlier, since the discrete data is rounded. The class mid-points are thus 3, 8, etc. Note, though, that they

Population (1000s)	Class mid-points	Frequency	Class mid-points × frequency
1–5	3	10	30
6–10	8	5	40
11–20	15.5	5	77.5
21–30	25.5	1	25.5
31–50	40.5	0	0
51–70	60.5	0	0
71–100	85.5	3	256.5
101–150	125.5	1	125.5
	Total	25	555.0

don't just go up in 5s, since the class widths are not all the same. Indeed, the other ones are not whole numbers.

Once again you should have divided by the total frequency and not by the number of groups (8).

The mode – the figure in fashion

When we talk casually about the 'average man' (or average car, or whatever) we are certainly not thinking of the arithmetic mean. What we do mean is that he is the one we are most likely to meet, because there are more of him than of any other type of men. If you like, he is 'in the fashion', or *à la mode* as the French say. This common usage of the word 'average' has an equivalent in statistics. It is called the 'mode'. Basically, the mode is that value which occurs most often in the figures we are interested in; that is, the figure with highest frequency.

In an ungrouped frequency table this is easy to find unless there is a tie, i.e. more than one value with the same frequency. If this happens we simply have more than one mode. Actually, even in cases where there are 'local' peaks in the frequencies, these may still be referred to as modes. This point is returned to a little later.

Let us look at some examples of finding a mode. Consider first the ten different brands of tins of tomatoes used earlier:

Price	Number of brands
$10\frac{1}{2}$p	1
11 p	2
$11\frac{1}{2}$p	3
12 p	2
$12\frac{1}{2}$p	2

Self-check

What is the mode for these figures?

The mode, or 'modal value' as it is sometimes called, is the price with highest frequency, i.e. 3 in this case, giving a mode of $11\frac{1}{2}$p.

Self-check

Calculate the mode for the following figures, which are the result of a survey of 100 firms in a given industry:

Days lost through strikes in the year	Number of firms losing this number of days
0	76
1	7
2	4
3	2
4	1
5	5
6	3
7	1
8	0
9	0
10	1

The mode is 0. If you had 76, that was the *frequency* of the mode, *not* the mode itself.

If you thought that 0 couldn't be the mode, and so chose 1, you were mistaken. The mode is that value that occurs most often, whatever it is.

It is considerably more difficult to find the mode where grouped data is concerned. The first thing to do is to find the class in which the mode must lie. This is called the 'modal class'. It is the class having the highest frequency *per unit class width*.

Self-check

Why isn't it just the class with the highest frequency? Look at the table below, and see if this helps you to answer this question.

Wages per week (whole £s)	Number of employees
50–69	20
70–79	40
80–84	25
85–89	20
90–99	30
100–109	25
110–129	30

If we just pick the class with the highest frequency in the table, it is class 70–79. But this has a width of £10 (the wages are to the nearest *complete* pound). The 'frequency density' in this class is thus $\frac{40}{10} = 4$. But the 'frequency density' for class 80–84 is $\frac{25}{5} = 5$. That means the mode is not in class 70–79, since there is one other class with more frequencies in it *per pound wages in the class*.

The histogram for this data is shown in the self-check on page 263 in the last chapter.

Self-check

How can we find the modal class from that histogram: can you see?

The *heights* of rectangles in a histogram are, in fact, proportional to this 'frequency density', since their areas are proportional to

the frequencies in the classes. So, for example, the height of the
rectangle for class 70–79 is 40, which is ten times the 'frequency
density', and for class 80–84 it is 50, which is also ten times the
frequency density. So the modal class is the one with the tallest
rectangle in the histogram.

‖ *Self-check*

What is the modal class in table 24 (page 294)?

Here the modal class is that with class interval '15 and under 20'
and frequency 38. This can be seen clearly in the histogram for
this data shown below. This emphasizes the modal class pur-
posely, because its rectangle is *double* the frequency in height,
since it is only £5 wide.

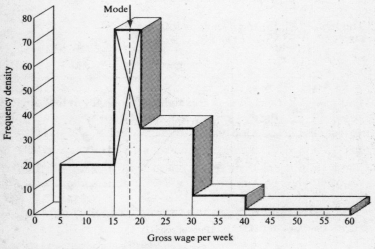

Figure 49. Histogram for table 24

Now once we have located the modal class, the mode itself lies
somewhere in that class interval. If the values allocated to that
class are distributed evenly about the class mid-point that would
be the mode. But if the heights of the two rectangles on either
side of the one for the modal class are unequal it implies this

assumption is probably invalid. There are probably more values on that side of the modal class nearest its 'tallest neighbour'. In the histogram for the wages data of table 24, this is the right-hand side. There is a reasonably straightforward method of finding the mode in such cases.

The top right-hand corner of the rectangle to the left of the modal class is joined by a straight line to the top right hand corner of the rectangle for the modal class itself. A similar line is drawn from the rectangle on the right. This is shown in figure 49. These two lines cross at the mode. That is, if a vertical line is drawn through the point where they cross, it will cut the horizontal axis at the modal value. For the wages data this is around £18.

Self-check

Find the mode for the data given in table 25.

The histogram for the data is as follows:

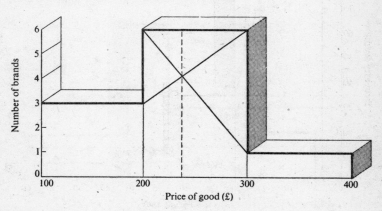

The mode is represented by the dotted line. Its value is about £235. Remember the mean was £230.

If you said the mode was £250, the mid-point, then you were forgetting that the frequencies within it would not be centred on the mid-point, probably because of the difference in the frequencies for the classes on either side. If you said it was 6, that is the frequency of the modal class and *not* the mode.

Self-check

The same data as in the last self-check question was classified differently and the following table produced:

Price of goods (£)	Number of brands
100 and over but under 225	4
225 and over but under 275	5
275 and over but under 400	1

Find the mode using this data.

The histogram for the data is as follows, using a standard class width of 50.

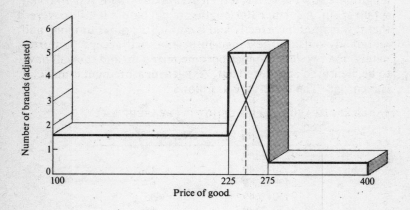

Area of rectangle for class 100–225 is 50 × 4 = 200.
Area of rectangle for class 225–275 is 50 × 5 = 250.
Area of rectangle for class 275–400 is 50 × 1 = 50.

So their heights are $\frac{200}{125} = 1.6$, $\frac{250}{50} = 5$ and $\frac{50}{125} = 0.4$, respectively.

Once again, the dotted line represents the mode. Its value is about £245 this time, though.

The difference between this and the answer to the self-check on page 305 is a result of the different method of grouping the data.

Did you remember to 'adjust' the heights of the rectangles and not to put them all equal in height to the frequencies? If you didn't, you would have had a mode about £235, which is *purely coincidentally* the same as the mode in the self-check on page 305. If you said the mode was 5, you chose the frequency of the modal class, which is incorrect.

The mode as such is seldom used in statistics. However, it is often useful to look at the histogram, or grouped frequency table, to find the modal class. This gives us some idea of the pattern of frequencies. Sometimes we can see more than one 'peak'. Look at the following, for example.

A machine cuts pipes into lengths. It is set for 25 cm and 100 lengths are cut. However, it then breaks down. It is repaired and set up again. A further 100 lengths are cut before it is discovered that it was reset incorrectly and is cutting the pipes too long and marginally outside the range inspection will accept. Unfortunately, the two lots of pipes become mixed up and they all have to be measured and sorted out. As each measurement is made, it is recorded. The results are as follows:

TABLE 26. MEASURED PIPE LENGTHS (NEAREST MM)

Pipe length	Number of pipes
2250–2349	3
2350–2449	15
2450–2549	67
2550–2649	35
2650–2749	64
2750–2849	13
2850–2949	3

Self-check

Draw the histogram for this data. Comment on and explain the result.

If we draw the histogram for this data it appears as below:

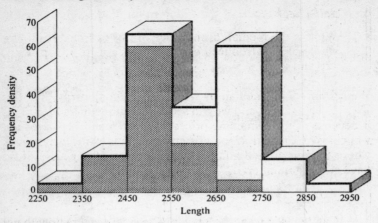

Figure 50. Histogram for table 26

There are two peaks, one at class interval 2450–2550 and the other at 2650–2750. This is the result of two different populations of tubes being mixed together to form one. The shaded portion of the histogram shows where those pipes within tolerance from the first run might lie. We then say there are two modes here, or that the distribution of frequencies about the classes is 'bimodal'. This is, in fact, the most common use of the mode in statistical work, to obtain an indication of when two (or more) populations of different characteristics are mixed together.

The median – the one in the middle

A common-sense interpretation of the word 'average' is 'in the middle'. We probably mean this when we say someone is 'of average intelligence' for example, though there may be over-tones of the mode about it. There is a statistical equivalent to this usage. It is called the 'median'. Basically, the median is that figure that divides the remaining ones into two equal groups such that all those in one group are less than the median and all those in the other are greater than it. In other words, it is the figure in the middle.

Self-check

What is the median brand price of tins of tomatoes in the wholesalers introduced earlier if they are $10\frac{1}{2}$p, 11p, $11\frac{1}{2}$p, 12p and $12\frac{1}{2}$p?

We can find their median by writing them in an array, like this $10\frac{1}{2}$, 11, $11\frac{1}{2}$, 12, $12\frac{1}{2}$ and we can see that the median is $11\frac{1}{2}$p. This is because of the remaining prices, two ($10\frac{1}{2}$p and 11p) are less, while two (12p and $12\frac{1}{2}$p) are greater. This will always work where there is an odd number of figures, but a snag arises if we have an even number.

Self-check

Can you see what the snag is? Can you suggest how to get over it?

There is then no middle figure. This means we have a choice of figures. If they are the same, as they may well be when large numbers are involved, there is no problem. If they are different, the usual procedure is to take a value mid-way between them (i.e. add them together and divide by 2).

Self-check

What is the median price of the six brands of tinned tomatoes which were priced $10\frac{1}{2}$p, 11p, $11\frac{1}{2}$p, 12p, $12\frac{1}{2}$p and 13p?

If we write these prices out in an array we get $10\frac{1}{2}$, 11, $11\frac{1}{2}$, 12, $12\frac{1}{2}$, 13, and there is no middle one. There are two middle prices $11\frac{1}{2}$p and 12p, so we take the median as $(11\frac{1}{2} + 12)/2 = 11.75$p.

Now you may have noticed that the mean and the median have been the same for the figures we have used so far. This is because they were symmetrical, i.e. they were evenly balanced. But now consider the prices involving the 20p tin.

Self-check

What is the median for the prices including the 20p tin, i.e.
for $10\frac{1}{2}$p, 11p, $11\frac{1}{2}$p, 12p and 20p?

The median here is also $11\frac{1}{2}$p. In other words, it is the same as for
the set of figures where the 20p was replaced by $12\frac{1}{2}$p. This is now
different from the mean, which was 13p. So, unlike the mean,
the median is totally unaffected by extremes.

But how do we calculate the median when frequencies are
given? It is actually easiest to use cumulative frequencies. For
example, if we take the ten prices of tomatoes, the cumulative
frequencies would be as follows:

PRICES OF TINS OF TOMATOES

Price (pence)	Number of brands	Cumulative number of brands
$10\frac{1}{2}$	1	1
11	2	3
$11\frac{1}{2}$	3	6
12	2	8
$12\frac{1}{2}$	2	10
Total 10		

Self-check

What is the median for the above table?

Here we are looking for the fifth and sixth values in order,
because there are ten in all, and, so these two are in the middle.
These are actually both $11\frac{1}{2}$p, so that is the median. If they had
been different here, too, the value mid-way between the two
would have been chosen.

Self-check

Calculate the median number of times employees were late
from the data in table 5 in Chapter 8.

The calculation is as follows:

Number of times late	Number of employees	Cumulative number of employees	
0	35	35	
1	14	49	←Median
2	6	55	is 36th
3	5	60	value,
4	3	63	i.e. 1.
5	2	65	
6	2	67	
7	1	68	
8	0	68	
9	1	69	
10	1	70	
11	0	70	
12	0	70	
13	1	71	
Total	71		

The median is the 36th item in order, since it is the middle one of the 71 items of data. Here that is a value of 1 time late, as shown, since the 36th item lies within the 14 that have that value. If you said the answer was 49 or 14 then you were using the frequencies and not the *values*.

If you got an answer of $6\frac{1}{2}$, you were using the values themselves and taking the halfway point between the first, 0, and the last, 13. This ignored all of the frequencies completely and wasn't correct.

Self-check

If we leave out Elsie Hall (the one who was thirteen times late) what would the median be then?

If the last item is completely left out, there are now only 70 of them. There is no one in the middle, so we must look for the 35th and the 36th ones and take a point halfway between them. In the table above, you can see that the 35th value is 0 but the

36th one is 1. So the median is halfway between 0 and 1 – that is, it is .5.

If you said that it would still be 1, you missed the fact that removing Elsie Hall reduced the total by 1, causing the median to change and involve the frequencies for the value of 0 times late.

If you said it was $\frac{35 + 49}{2} = 42$ or $\frac{35 + 14}{2} = 24.5$ then you were using the frequencies again and not the *values* as you should.

To find the median when the data is in the form of a grouped frequency table requires a different method. The one shown here is based on the use of the ogive. The way it operates is as follows. The halfway point of the cumulative frequencies is found on the vertical axis. In figure 51, opposite, which shows the ogive for the wages of table 24, this point is marked as A. Since the total frequency is 100 (%), the halfway mark is at 50 (%).

The next step is to draw a horizontal line from this point to meet the ogive. (Notice a smooth curve has been drawn.) This point is shown as B in the diagram. A vertical line drawn from there to the horizontal, wages, axis, meets it at a point corresponding to the median. This point is shown as C in the diagram. The value of the median for the wages data is, from the diagram, about £19.00.

Self-check

Find the median for the data given in table 12 (page 229).

The ogive for this data has been drawn already and is shown in figure 38 (page 275). From that graph, following the same procedure as outlined above, the median is about 435. You may have a slightly different answer, but it should not differ by much.

The median is not 50. It is a common mistake to say that the median *is* the halfway frequency, instead of the value of the variable *corresponding to* that frequency.

Activity

Take your multiplication times again. Find the mode and

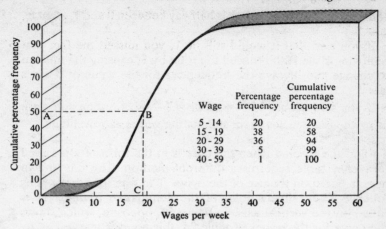

Wage	Percentage frequency	Cumulative percentage frequency
5 - 14	20	20
15 - 19	38	58
20 - 29	36	94
30 - 39	5	99
40 - 59	1	100

Figure 51. Ogive of data in table 24

the median of that data. Use the ungrouped frequency tables for this.

Now you have the mean, median and mode of your data, which of the three do you think most fairly reflects your performance on this task? If you were to be paid a bonus for exceeding your 'average' rate for this task, which average, mean, median or mode, would you want to be used?

Using the author's data on this task, the mode is 30 secs (there are 4 of this value) and the median is 26.5 secs (it lies between 26 and 27). This is shown at the top of page 314.

The value of the mean was 26.35 secs. In this case, the mean and the median are near to each other. The mode, however, is quite a lot different. If the author were to be paid a bonus for exceeding the average calculation time, he certainly wouldn't choose the mode!

Review

Find the mode and the median for the following data:

Making sense of the data collected

Time (secs)	Frequency	Cumulative frequency
20	1	1
21	1	2
22	2	4
23	1	5
24	1	6
25	3	9
26	1 ←Median is 26.5	10
27	2	12
28	1	13
29	1	14
30	4 ←Mode is 30	18
31	1	19
32	1	20

Total 20

a The number of $\frac{1}{4}$ hours that Elsie Hall was late, from table 8 (page 221).

b The number of minutes Elsie Hall was late, from table 11 (page 222) – the grouped frequency table. Use graphs. Did you have any difficulties with the mode? How did you resolve them?

c The number of minutes Elsie Hall was late, from table 10 (page 221) – the ungrouped frequency table.

Comment on the differences between the mode and the median in each case. Comment also on any differences between the answers to (b) and (c) and explain why they occur.

ANSWERS

a The table, together with cumulative frequencies, is shown at the top of page 315.

The number of hours lost having the highest frequency is 5, so this is the mode.

As there are 13 days on which Elsie was late, the median will correspond to the 6th in order. That is the median is 2, because the 6th day in order lies in that group of 4 values of 2, as shown.

¼hr lost		Frequency	Cumulative frequency	
1←	Mode →5		5	
2	is 1	4←	9	←Median
3		2	11	is 2
4		1	12	
5		1	13	

If you said the median was 3, i.e. the middle one of 1–5, you were forgetting to take into account the frequencies.

The difference between the mode and the median is because the frequencies start high and get lower. As the median has to be in the middle, it must be some distance away from the mode.

b The graphs required are the histogram (for the mode) and the ogive (for the median). These are shown below.

The mode is difficult to find in cases where not all of the class intervals are equal. Strictly speaking, unless the modal class and the classes on either side of it are equal in size, finding the mode in this way does not really work. However, it is used here to obtain an approximate result.

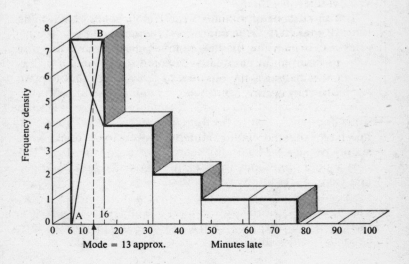

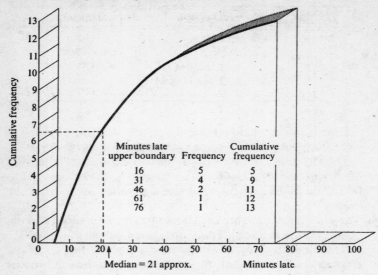

Minutes late upper boundary	Frequency	Cumulative frequency
16	5	5
31	4	9
46	2	11
61	1	12
76	1	13

Median = 21 approx.　　　　　Minutes late

As there is no rectangle to the left of the tallest one, the line AB from the left upwards, has to be drawn from the 'top' of a rectangle of *zero* height. The mode is approximately 12. Did you get this?

The median is approximately 21. Note that, because the times are taken *to the nearest whole minute* the upper boundaries are 16, 31, 46, 61 and 76 mins. Notice, too, that the *halfway* point in the cumulative frequency is 6.5 and *not* 7, as it was with the ungrouped frequency table. This is because we are plotting frequency against *upper bound*, and this shifts the values somewhat. If you used 7, remember in future to use the exact mid-point; that is, the total frequency divided by 2. You may have obtained slightly different answers to the ones given, simply because of slight differences in drawing the lines. But they should be reasonably near those given. Again the mode and median are different because of the higher frequencies at the beginning.

c The figures, together with the results, are shown opposite. Here there are two modes, 11 and 24. One of these is now equal to the median – 24.

Minutes late	Frequency	Cumulative frequency
10	1	1
11	2	3
12	1 Modes are	4
13	1 11 & 24	5
24	2	7 ←Median
27	1	8 is 24
28	1	9
39	1	10
43	1	11
50	1	12
69	1	13
Total	**13**	

If you said the modes were 2 and 2, you were again forgetting that you are supposed to use the *values*. The same applies
if you said the median was 7 (or 2).

The difference between these results and the results in **b** can
be explained by the fact that those in **b** were the result of
grouping the values together and so losing some of the detail.
The fact that there were two modes was lost, even.

11 | When an average on its own is not enough

How widely dispersed is the data?

Suppose you were told that the average takings of a shop per day last year were £1100. If you picked a figure for a day at random, what would you expect it to be? Near enough to £1100 presumably? But how near? Would you, for example, be surprised if it was only £800? Actually, an average by itself gives you no information which would guide you on whether to be surprised or not. It doesn't tell you how far away from £1100 the takings ever get. That is you have no indication as to the *dispersion* of these figures. In addition to the mean, then, we need another figure which is a measure of this dispersion.

One simple measure that we have met already is the range. This at least tells us that we can be very surprised indeed to see a figure outside of it. But it tells us little else. It is also drastically affected by extreme values. For example, suppose one day in the year the weather was so bad that the takings were only £50 or so. The next worse takings could be £300 or more. That one day would then increase the range by £250! What we really want to know is what happens inside the range.

Consider the two histograms in figures 52 (a) and (b).

They represent two 'frequency distributions', i.e. two different ways in which the frequencies are distributed among the classes (or values in ungrouped data). While they have the same mean and the same range they are obviously very different. In (a), the frequencies vary only a little and the histogram is fairly 'flat'. In (b) the frequencies are low at the ends but high in the middle and the histogram has a district peak. We need some statistic that can sum up the differences between such distributions.

One useful measure is, like the median, based on the fractions

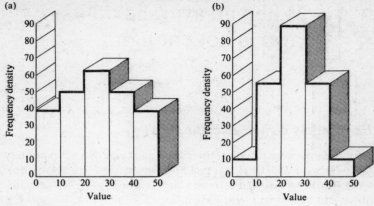

Figure 52

of the total frequency. Like the median, it too can be found from the ogive. Before seeing how this is done, though, we need to look more closely at the use of relative frequencies.

If relative cumulative frequencies are used in an ogive, then the *value of the variable* (on the horizontal axis) corresponding to any particular fraction (on the vertical axis) is called a 'fractile'. If percentage relative cumulative frequencies are employed, which is more common, the corresponding entity is called a 'percentile'. That is a percentile is the *value of the variable* corresponding to some percentage relative cumulative frequency. We can use the data on wages from table 24 of Chapter 10 to illustrate this. The ogive for this is shown in figure 53.

The median, which we have already calculated, corresponds to the second *quartile* or 50th *percentile*. This quartile is that fractile for a fraction of $\frac{1}{4}$. The second quartile is thus $\frac{1}{4} + \frac{1}{4} = \frac{1}{2}$ of the total frequency, or 50% of it.

Self-check

Can you see where the 80th percentile, or the 8th decile, is in figure 53. (The decile corresponds to the fraction $\frac{1}{10}$.)

To find the 80th percentile, we need to first find the point on the

320 Making sense of the data collected

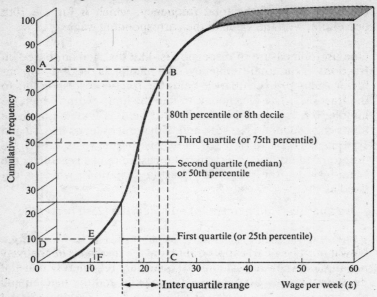

Figure 53

vertical axis corresponding to 80% of the total frequency. This is point A in the diagram. We then draw a horizontal line to meet the ogive. This is point B in the diagram. Finally, we draw a vertical line down to meet the horizontal axis, point C in the diagram. It meets this axis at the 80th percentile. In this case that is about £25 per week.

Self-check

Find the first decile, or 10th percentile, of the same data.

To find the 10th percentile, the starting point is the point 10% of the total frequency on the vertical axis. This is marked as D in the diagram. Following the same procedure as with the median, the point, F, on the diagram is reached. This corresponds to the 10th decile. From the graph, its value is about £10.50.

If you said that the answer was 10, then you were confusing

the percentage of the total frequency, which *is* for the 10th percentile, with the value of the corresponding wage.

One useful measure of dispersion is, like the median, based on fractions of the total frequency. The median is the 50th percentile or 2nd *quartile*, a quartile being the fractile corresponding to the fraction $\frac{1}{4}$. The idea here is to find the limits within which the middle 50% (i.e. $\frac{1}{2}$) of the items of data lie. It is evident that these limits correspond to the 75th and 25th percentile, or the 3rd and 1st quartile. The difference between these two is called the 'interquartile range'. The general measure in use is actually the 'semi-interquartile range' or 'quartile deviation', which is defined as

$$\frac{\text{3rd quartile (75th percentile)} - \text{1st quartile (25th percentile)}}{2}$$

Now it must be clearly appreciated that the median is *not* halfway in value between the 1st and 3rd quartiles. It is merely that $\frac{1}{4}$ of the data items lie between the 1st quartile and the median and also between the median and the 3rd quartile. This means that it would not have been correct to define the quartile deviation as the difference between the median and the first quartile, or, indeed, as the difference between the 3rd quartile and the median. It is, in fact, the arithmetic mean of these two. This point can better be appreciated by means of an example. Consider the data on women's wages in table 24.

Self-check

From the ogive for the data in table 24 already drawn, estimate the quartile deviation.

From figure 53 above, we can see that the 1st quartile is about £16.00 and the second about £23.00. The median was found previously to be £19.00. It can be seen that £23.00 − £19.00 = £4.00 is not equal to £19.00 − £16.00 = £3.00. However, the quartile deviation equals $\frac{£23.00 - £16.00}{2}$ = £3.50 and is, indeed the mean of these two.

Self-check

Find the semi-interquartile range from the data in table 15 of Chapter 8.

The ogive for this data appears in figure 40 of Chapter 9. From this, the semi-interquartile range can be estimated as $\frac{18-4}{2}$ = 7(000).

If you got an answer of $\frac{18.75-6.25}{2}$ = 6.25(000) then you used $\frac{3}{4}$ of the total frequency (i.e. $\frac{3 \times 25}{4}$ = 18.75) as the 75th percentile and $\frac{1}{4}$ of the total frequency (i.e. $\frac{1}{4}$ x 25 = 6.25) as the 25th percentile, which was wrong. These were the frequencies from which the 3rd and 1st percentiles were obtained.

How widely scattered is the data on average?

The measure of dispersion which is favoured in most statistical calculations is, however, the 'standard deviation'. This is the only one which can be utilized in further calculations, as will be discussed in later chapters. It is, however, rather more difficult to calculate than the others, but the general idea behind it will be described here.

An intuitive measure of dispersion is the average difference between the data values and the mean, or, as statisticians put it, the average 'deviation' from the mean. Unfortunately, precisely because the mean is the 'balance point', this value is zero: the negative deviations cancel out the positive ones exactly. For example, with the five tomato prices again, the mean of $10\frac{1}{2}$p, 11p, $11\frac{1}{2}$p, 12p and $12\frac{1}{2}$p is $11\frac{1}{2}$p. The deviations from the mean are thus $10\frac{1}{2}-11\frac{1}{2} = -1$p, $11-11\frac{1}{2} = -\frac{1}{2}$p, $11\frac{1}{2}-11\frac{1}{2} = 0$p, $12-11\frac{1}{2} = \frac{1}{2}$p and $12\frac{1}{2}-11\frac{1}{2} = 1$p, which add up to zero.

What we need to do is to remove the negative signs. This can be done by squaring the deviations. So for the above prices we obtain $(-1)^2 = 1$, $(-\frac{1}{2})^2 = \frac{1}{4}$, $0^2 = 0$ $(\frac{1}{2})^2 = \frac{1}{4}$ and $(1)^2 = 1$. Adding these up we no longer get zero, but $2\frac{1}{2}$. Dividing this by 5 we find that the mean of these squared deviations is $\frac{1}{2}$. However, the units here are 'pence squared', which is not very satisfactory. So we take the square root to obtain the standard deviation in pence. In this case it is $\sqrt{\frac{1}{2}} = .7\text{p}$ (to one decimal place). Note that, like the mean, the standard deviation can give answers which are not possible for a discrete variable. It is also strongly affected by extreme values. Take the set of prices including the 20p, for example.

Self-check

Calculate the standard deviation of the prices $10\frac{1}{2}\text{p}$, 11p, $11\frac{1}{2}\text{p}$, 12p and 20p, given earlier for the tins of tomatoes.

These prices were $10\frac{1}{2}\text{p}$, 11p, $11\frac{1}{2}\text{p}$, 12p and 20p. We saw earlier that they had a mean of 13p. The standard deviation here is thus

$$\sqrt{\frac{(10\frac{1}{2}-13)^2 + (11-13)^2 + (11\frac{1}{2}-13)^2 + (12-13)^2 + (20-13)^2}{5}}$$

$$= \sqrt{\frac{(-2\frac{1}{2})^2 + (-2)^2 + (-1\frac{1}{2})^2 + (-1)^2 + 7^2}{5}} = \sqrt{\frac{6\frac{1}{4} + 4 + 2\frac{1}{4} + 1 + 49}{5}}$$

$$= \sqrt{\frac{62\frac{1}{2}}{5}} = \sqrt{12.5} = 3.5 \text{ (to one decimal place)}.$$

Now this is considerably more than the .7 of above. The 20p price is responsible for this.

Self-check

What would be the standard deviation of the tomato prices if they were $9\frac{1}{2}\text{p}$, 11p, $11\frac{1}{2}\text{p}$, $12\frac{1}{2}\text{p}$ and 13p? Compare this with the first result above (.7p) in the initial example.

The mean of these prices is

$$\frac{9\frac{1}{2} + 11 + 11\frac{1}{2} + 12\frac{1}{2} + 13}{5} = \frac{57\frac{1}{2}}{5} = 11\frac{1}{2}\text{p}.$$

This is actually the same as that for the initial example. But the standard deviation here is

$$\sqrt{\frac{(9\frac{1}{2}-11\frac{1}{2})^2 + (11-11\frac{1}{2})^2 + (11\frac{1}{2}-11\frac{1}{2})^2 + (12\frac{1}{2}-11\frac{1}{2})^2 + (13-11\frac{1}{2})^2}{5}}$$

$$= \sqrt{\frac{(-2)^2 + (-\frac{1}{2})^2 + 0^2 + 1^2 + (1\frac{1}{2})^2}{5}}$$

$$= \sqrt{\frac{4 + \frac{1}{4} + 0 + 1 + \frac{9}{4}}{5}} = \sqrt{\frac{7\frac{1}{2}}{5}} = \sqrt{1.5}$$

= 1.22p (to two decimal places).

Note that this is somewhat larger than the .7p of the initial set of data. This is because there is a greater dispersion. Did you remember to subtract $11\frac{1}{2}$ from each item of data? And did you remember to take the square root at the end?

But suppose we have an ungrouped frequency table? How do we calculate the standard deviation in such cases?

We can calculate the standard deviation where there are frequencies as follows. First calculate the squared deviation from the mean *for each figure*. Then multiply each by its frequency. This is the same as simply adding it together that number of times. Add together all these results and proceed as before. For example, if we take the following ten prices for tins of tomatoes from earlier, 1 x $10\frac{1}{2}$p, 2 x 11p, 3 x $11\frac{1}{2}$p, 2 x 12p and 2 x $12\frac{1}{2}$p, then their mean, as we have already seen, is 11.6p and their standard deviation is

$$\sqrt{\frac{(10.5-11.6)^2 + 2 \times (11-11.6)^2 + 3 \times (11.5-11.6)^2 + 2 \times (12-11.6)^2 + 2 \times (12.5-11.6)^2}{10}}$$

$$= \sqrt{\frac{(-1.1)^2 + 2 \times (-.6)^2 + 3 \times (-.1)^2 + 2 \times (.4)^2 + 2 \times (.9)^2}{10}}$$

$$= \sqrt{\frac{1.21 + 2 \times .36 + 3 \times .01 + 2 \times .16 + 2 \times 81}{10}} = \sqrt{\frac{1.21 + .72 + .03 + .32 + 1.62}{10}}$$

$$= \sqrt{\frac{3.9}{10}}$$

$$= \sqrt{.39} = 0.6 \text{ (to one decimal place)}.$$

Self-check

What is the standard deviation of the tomato prices if they are as follows? Comment on the result in relation to the example above, given that the mean of these figures is 11.6p, as in the example.

Price	Frequency
$10\frac{1}{2}$	1
11	2
$11\frac{1}{2}$	10
12	6
$12\frac{1}{2}$	1
	—
Total	20

The mean here is 11.6, so the standard deviation is

$$\sqrt{\frac{1 \times (10.5 - 11.6)^2 + 2 \times (11 - 11.6)^2 + 10 \times (11.5 - 11.6)^2 + 6 \times (12 - 11.6)^2 + 1 \times (12.5 - 11.6)^2}{20}}$$

$$\sqrt{\frac{(-1.1)^2 + 2 \times (-.6)^2 + 10 \times (-.1)^2 + 6 \times (+.4)^2 + 1 \times (+.9)^2}{20}}$$

$$= \sqrt{\frac{1.21 + 2 \times .36 + 10 \times 01 + 6 \times .16 + .81}{20}} = \sqrt{\frac{1.21 + .72 + .1 + .96 + .81}{20}}$$

$$= \sqrt{\frac{3.80}{20}}$$

$$= \sqrt{.19} = .44\text{p (to two decimal places)}.$$

This is less than the standard deviation in the example, even though the actual values, and even the mean, is the same. The reason for this is that more values are concentrated in the centre than in the example. The frequency polygons (page 326) show this clearly.

If you forgot to multiply each of the separate values by their frequency, you will have got the wrong answer. You will have, in fact:

$$\sqrt{\frac{1.21 + .36 + .01 + .16 + .81}{20}} = \sqrt{\frac{2.55}{20}} = \sqrt{.1275} = .36\text{p (to two}$$
decimal places).

Or perhaps you even forgot to divide by the total frequency and got

$$\sqrt{\frac{2.55}{5}} = \sqrt{.51} = .71\text{p (to two decimal places)}.$$

Neither answer is correct. With grouped frequency tables, the class mid-points are used as they were for the mean. Otherwise the calculation is the same as above.

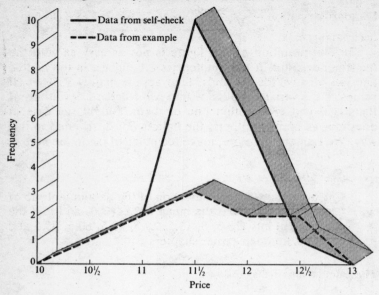

Frequency

Price

—— Data from self-check
- - - Data from example

Self-check

Calculate the standard deviation of the wages figures in table 24 of Chapter 10.

The standard deviation for these figures which, as we have seen, have a mean of £19.90, is calculated as follows:

Column 1 Class mid- point	Column 2 Class mid- point – mean	Column 3 Col. 2 squared	Column 4 (percentage) frequency	Column 5 Col. 3 × col. 4
10.0	−9.9	98.01	20	1960.20
17.5	−2.4	5.76	38	218.88
25.0	5.1	26.01	36	936.36
35.0	15.1	228.01	5	1140.05
50.0	30.1	906.01	1	906.01
			Total 100	Total 5161.50

Standard deviation = $\sqrt{\frac{5161.50}{100}}$ = $\sqrt{51.615}$ = £7.18 (to two decimal places).

The interpretation of this figure is not as easy as with the quartile deviation. If the frequencies are highest in the middle and tail off towards the ends, then approximately 95% of all values of the variable will lie within two standard deviations of the mean and 68% within one of them. But in the case in question, as in many others, the data is not distributed in this way. We cannot, therefore, make too much of the figure here.

Self-check

Calculate the standard deviation of the data in table 15 of Chapter 8, given that the mean is 22.2(000) and that the class mid-points are 3, 8, 15.5, 25.5, 40.5, 60.5, 85.5 and 125.5, as found in earlier chapters.

The calculations are as follows:

Column 1 Population (1000s)	Column 2 Population class mid-point	Column 3 Mid-point – mean (22.2)	Column 4 Frequency	Column 5 (Col. 3)²	Column 6 Col. 4 × Col. 5
1–5	3	−19.2	10	368.64	3686.40
6–10	8	−14.2	5	201.64	1008.20
11–20	15.5	−6.7	5	44.89	224.45
21–30	25.5	+3.3	1	10.89	10.89
31–50	40.5	+18.3	0	334.89	0
51–70	60.5	+38.3	0	1466.89	0
71–100	85.5	+63.3	3	4006.89	12,020.67
101–150	125.5	+103.3	1	10,670.89	10,670.89
			Total 25		Total 27,621.50

Standard deviation = $\sqrt{\frac{27,621.5}{25}}$ = $\sqrt{1104.86}$.

So the standard deviation = 33.24(000) (to two decimal places). Check that you didn't divide through by 8 instead of 25 and that you remembered to take the square root.

If you got an answer of zero, then you forgot to square the figures in column 3. Remember that the deviations about the mean will sum to zero.

Activity

Using the multiplication times, as in the ungrouped frequency table, find their standard deviation. Compare yours with the author's, which is calculated below. Which of the two shows greater variation?

The standard deviation for the author's times is found as follows:

Time	Time − mean (26.35)	(Time − mean)²	Frequency	Frequency × (time − mean)
20	−6.35	40.3225	1	40.3225
21	−5.35	28.6225	1	28.6225
22	−4.35	18.9225	2	37.8450
23	−3.35	11.2225	1	11.2225
24	−2.35	5.5225	1	5.5225
25	−1.35	1.8225	3	5.4675
26	− .35	0.1225	1	0.1225
27	+ .65	0.4225	2	0.8450
28	+1.65	2.7225	1	2.7225
29	+2.65	7.0225	1	7.0225
30	+3.65	13.3225	4	53.2900
31	+4.65	21.6225	1	21.6225
32	+5.65	31.9225	1	31.9225
			Total 20	Total 246.5500

So the standard deviation = $\sqrt{\frac{246.55}{20}} = \sqrt{12.3275}$

= 3.51 secs. (To two decimal places).

Now calculate the standard deviation of your times from the grouped frequency table. Is it different to the one calculated using ungrouped data? If so, why do you think that is?

The calculations of the standard deviation from the author's grouped data are shown below, using the mean of 27 found from this grouped data earlier.

Column 1 Time (secs)	Column 2 Class mid-point	Column 3 Mid-point – mean	Column 4 (Col. 3)^2	Column 5 Frequency	Column 6 Col. 4 x Col. 5
20–24	22	−5	25	6	150
25–29	27	0	0	8	0
30–34	32	+5	25	6	150
				Total 20	Total 300

Standard deviation $= \sqrt{\frac{300}{20}} = \sqrt{15} = 3.87$ (to two decimal places).

It is different to the one calculated with the ungrouped data. This is because a lot of the detail is lost when grouping occurs.

Note that the units for all these measures of dispersion mentioned are the same as those for the variable concerned, i.e. pounds in the case of the wages. When we want to compare two different sets of data we need a measure of dispersion independent of units. One which is often used is the 'coefficient of variation'. This is the standard deviation divided by the mean and is thus a unitless ratio. For example, the coefficient of variation for the women's wages of above is $\frac{£7.18}{£19.90} = .36$ (to two decimal places).

Review

1 Calculate the standard deviation for the data in table 5, Chapter 8 on the lateness record of the Baby Gourmet plant.

2 Calculate the range, the semi-interquartile range and the standard deviation of the operation times in table 12, Chapter 8. What is the coefficient of variation for that data? What do each of these mean in terms of the given data?

ANSWERS

1 The mean of this data was calculated in the previous chapter as 1.6 (to one decimal place) and this value will be used here.

Column 1 Times late	Column 2 Times late − mean	Column 3 (Col. 2)^2	Column 4 Frequency	Column 5 Col. 3 × Col. 4
0	−1.6	2.56	35	89.60
1	− .6	.36	14	5.04
2	.4	.16	6	.96
3	1.4	1.96	5	9.80
4	2.4	5.76	3	17.28
5	3.4	11.56	2	23.12
6	4.4	19.36	2	38.72
7	5.4	29.16	1	29.16
8	6.4	40.96	0	0
9	7.4	54.76	1	54.76
10	8.4	70.56	1	70.56
11	9.4	88.36	0	0
12	10.4	108.16	0	0
13	11.4	129.96	1	129.96
			Total 71	Total 468.96

So the standard deviation = $\sqrt{\frac{468.96}{71}} = \sqrt{6.61}$
= 2.57 (to two decimal places).
The mean of this data was calculated in a previous chapter as
437.5 secs, and this is the value that will be used here.

The semi-interquartile range can be obtained from the ogive. This is shown in figure 54. It is plotted from the following data.

Upper class boundary	Frequency	Cumulative frequency
379.5	3	3
399.5	7	10
419.5	15	25
439.5	28	53
459.5	26	79
479.5	13	92
499.5	6	98
519.5	2	100
	Total 100	

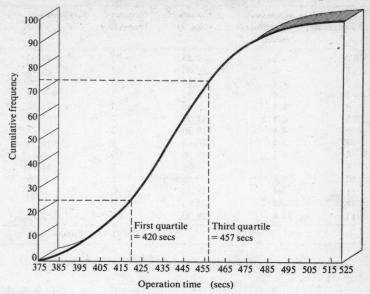

Figure 54. Ogive for machine operation times from table 12 (Chapter 8)

The result is that the 1st quartile is 420 secs and the second is 457 secs, or thereabouts. Actually, from the table we know that the first quartile is 419.5, but we cannot really read with that accuracy from a graph.

The semi-interquartile range is thus $\frac{457 - 420}{2} = \frac{37}{2} = 18.5$ secs. For this data this means that the middle 50% of the data occupies a span of times of 18.5 secs.

If we compare this with the range, which is $519.5 - 379.5 = 140$ secs, then we see that 50% of the data lies in only 18.5 secs out of those 140 secs.

Did you remember to read off the *values* corresponding to the 25th and 75th percentiles, rather than take the 25 and 75 themselves.

The standard deviation can be calculated as follows:

Column 1 Mid-point of class	Column 2 Mid-point – mean	Column 3 (Col. 2)^2	Column 4 Frequency	Column 5 Col. 3 × Col. 4
369.5	−68	4624	3	13,872
389.5	−48	2304	7	16,128
409.5	−28	784	15	11,760
429.5	− 8	64	28	1792
449.5	12	144	26	3744
469.5	32	1024	13	13,312
489.5	52	2704	6	16,224
509.5	72	5184	2	10,368
			Total 100	Total 87,200

Standard deviation = $\sqrt{\frac{87,200}{100}}$ = $\sqrt{872}$ = 29.5 seconds (to one decimal place).

Since the distribution of the frequencies in this case is reasonably symmetric, this means that about $\frac{2}{3}$ of the data lies within 29.5 secs of the mean, i.e. between 437.5 − 29.5 and 437.5 + 29.5 secs, or 408 − 467 secs.

The coefficient of variation is $\frac{29.5}{437.5}$ = .07 (to two decimal places). This means that, in relation to its magnitude, this data varies very little.

Is the data distributed symmetrically?

Another question that needs to be asked about a set of data is, Is the data symmetrically distributed? Consider the histograms in figure 55(a), (b) and (c). Now each of these could represent data with the same mean and standard deviation. But they are obviously very different. In the first case we have a 'symmetric distribution', while in the other two we have what is called a 'skewed distribution'. The second histogram shows positive skew – that is, the data is concentrated more towards the left, while the third shows negative skew – that is, the data is concentrated more towards the right. The data on women's wages is positively skewed, for example. So, too, is the data on timekeeping for the Baby Gourmet plant.

What then can we use as a measure of skewness? Well,

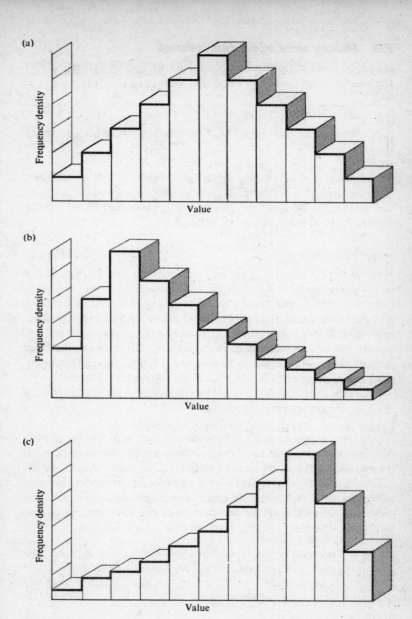

Figure 55

consider where the median would be in the three histograms above.

Self-check

Where, roughly, would the medians be in the histograms in figure 55?

In the first, it would be in the middle, because the frequencies are distributed symmetrically. In the second, it would be to the left of middle because the frequencies are higher there. In the third it would, similarly, be to the right.

Self-check

Where, roughly, would the means be in the three histograms?

On the other hand, the means, being more affected by extremes, would tend to remain nearer the middle. If you were to cut out the shape of the histogram in cardboard, the point where you would have to put a pin in to balance it would be on the mean. The mode, incidentally will always be at the peak, wherever that is. All three measures of central tendency coincide in the case of a perfectly symmetric distribution.

The above suggests that mean-median might indicate the degree of skewness and, indeed, it does. However, for the same reasons as applied to the coefficient of variation, we want to remove the units. We do this by dividing by the standard deviation. We also multiply by 3, for reasons which we won't go into here. The result is called the 'Pearson coefficient of skewness'. It is thus given by $\frac{3 \times (\text{mean} - \text{median})}{\text{standard deviation}}$.

Note that when this is negative, the distribution is negatively skewed and when positive, positively skewed. Values of .3 and below can be regarded as relatively low skew while if they are above .6 or so they are strongly skewed.

Self-check

What is the coefficient of skewness for the women's wages data?

The coefficient of skewness for the women's wage is thus
$\frac{3 \times (£19.90 - £19.00)}{£7.18} = 0.38$ (to two decimal places).

Self-check

The mean times late at Baby Gourmet was 1.6, the median number of times late was 1 and the standard deviation was just calculated as 2.57. What is the coefficient of skewness? What does this indicate about the frequency distribution in question?

The coefficient is $\frac{3 \times (1.6 - 1)}{2.57} = \frac{3 \times .6}{2.57} = \frac{1.8}{2.57}$
$= .7$ (to one decimal place).

This shows that the data is positively skewed, and fairly strongly so.

Making comparisons

The statistical measures introduced in this chapter between them characterize a distribution. One of the uses to which they can be put is the comparison of one distribution with another, or with single items of data. The first is treated in Volume 2. We can now look at the second. For example, the £16.70 at Baby Gourmet compared with the wages of women manual workers in general.

In the scenario on page 286, Jenny Wright initially compared her women's earnings with the figure of £42 from the papers. The very first question to ask here is, Was the correct distribution used? In this case it wasn't. The £42 was from a distribution of wages which was

- for men workers only;
- for manual and non-manual;
- for workers in all industries;

- for those over twenty-one only;
- inclusive of overtime and bonus payments.

You can only compare like with like here if any meaning is to be attached to the results. A better set of data to have chosen would have been women's pay in the food industry, and this is just what was used in the end.

But here, too, care must be taken. All the other problems of using secondary data could arise. Since these are government figures, the only one likely to give trouble in practice is that of the currency of the data. In the case of wages, the published statistics are generally at least two months out of date. Apart from these difficulties, however, there are more connected with the actual measures used. The official figures on average wages, for example, use the mean. Now this has the advantage that it is

- the only measure of central tendency that can be used in further calculations, e.g. averages of averages;
- commonly used when arithmetical calculations are involved, so people know it e.g. in batting averages in cricket;
- the 'balance point' of the distribution, making use of every value.

But its disadvantages are that it is

- very much affected by extreme values; e.g. very high wages for just a few people will push up the mean wage;
- likely to give 'impossible' results when discrete variables are concerned;
- not too easily understood where large numbers of figures are involved.

In the scenario, then, care must be taken when comparing the standard wage for women at Baby Gourmet with a mean wage, principally because of the point about extreme values affecting it. This is important in cases, such as this, where the distribution is skewed.

Perhaps the median would have been a better measure to use. It does, after all, have the advantage that it is

- easily understood;

- completely unaffected by extreme values, so that these do not even need to be known;
- usually the actual value of one of the items of data.

But, apart from the fact that, for wages, it is not readily available in the published figures, the median has other general disadvantages. It is

- not useful for further calculations;
- not based on all the values.

The median wage may well be a fairer statistic to compare wages at Baby Gourmet with, therefore, if we want to ignore the extreme wages. On the other hand it does ignore much of the data.

What about using the mode? This has the advantages that it is

- easily understood, and, in fact, the most obvious measure;
- usually the actual value of one of the items of data;
- completely unaffected by extreme values (unless they form the mode, of course) so these don't actually even need to be known.

But it does also have disadvantages. It is
- not based on all the values;
- not useful for further calculations.

This measure shares the advantages and disadvantages of the median with respect to extreme values. It is also the most easily comprehensible measure for the women at Baby Gourmet. Unfortunately, in a skewed distribution like that for wages, it is also likely to be the lowest, or highest, of these measures, depending on whether the skew is positive or negative. So it would be the one that would show the Baby Gourmet wage in the best light.

If we now look at the figures for the wages, we get the following:

Standard wages at Baby Gourmet for women manual workers per week £16.70

Mean wage of all women manual workers over eighteen per week £19.90

Median wage of all women manual workers over eighteen per week £19.00

Modal wage of all women manual workers over eighteen per week £18.00

We see that the women at Baby Gourmet come off badly on all measures, but that the mode is nearest their wage. What significance can we place on these differences, however? In making any such comparison we must, of course, take into account how widely dispersed the figures are. Consider the median of £19.00. Is £16.70 very much different from this? Here, of course, the quartile deviation would be used. This measure has similar advantages and disadvantages to the median. Its advantages are that it is

● completely unaffected by extreme values (outside 50% round the median, of course);
● easily understood.

And it has the disadvantages that it is

● not based on all the values;
● not all that informative about how the values are distributed overall.

In this case, with a positively skewed distribution of wages, it could be considered a considerable advantage that it is not influenced by the extreme values.

The difference between the Baby Gourmet wage of £16.70 per week and the median of the wage distribution it is being compared with, £19.00, is £2.30. This is well within the £3.50 quartile deviation. On these figures it doesn't look as though the women at Baby Gourmet are terribly badly done by. On the other hand, it could well be argued that, since one per cent of women earn over £40 per week, in comparison with these they aren't doing too well. Here the lack of effect of extreme values on the quartile deviation would actually be regarded as the disadvantage that this measure does not utilize all the available data. Also, the quartile deviation does not tell us what happens inside, or outside, that 50% of the values. Is £16.70 inside 25% of the values round the median, for example? There is no way of knowing from the quartile deviation alone. The standard deviation normally tells us more about the way in which the values are distributed. This measure has the advantages that it is

- based on every value of the distribution;
- statistically very sound and used in further calculations (see Volume 2);
- tells us a great deal about the way the values are distributed *if the distribution is symmetrical*.

But it has the disadvantages that it is

- very much affected by extreme values;
- difficult to understand;
- only really useful in practice when the distribution is fairly symmetrical.

While it looks, at first sight, as though this measure should prove very useful in our wages case, it really isn't very. Firstly, the wages distribution is skewed so we cannot use its full power. For example, it is unlikely that 68% of the figures lie within one standard deviation of the mean. Secondly, it is based on the mean which, as we have seen, has certain drawbacks in the case of a skewed distribution. The difference between the Baby Gourmet wage of £16.70 and the mean of the wages distribution with which it is being compared, £19.90, is £3.20. This is well within the standard deviation of £7.18. We cannot place a great deal of importance on this, however.

As for the range, it really would not have been very useful at all in the case of the wages, even if it could have been accurately determined. Though this measure does have one big advantage in that it is

- very simple

it does have the great disadvantages that it is

- totally dependent on the extreme values;
- totally uninformative as to how the values are distributed inside it;
- impossible to calculate if the extreme values are unknown.

It can be seen, then, that the problems involved in comparing the Baby Gourmet wage with another wage distribution are not simple. The fact that wage distributions tend to be positively skewed is a major difficulty. There are several bases for comparison, all of which have advantages and disadvantages. Which one is chosen depends very much on what you are trying to get out of the figures. This is one of the things that makes wage negotiations very difficult. The key is to be informed about the various statistical considerations involved so as to be able to fully appreciate these problems.

Review

The salary figures, including commission, for the sales representatives of a large firm are as below. Calculate the coefficient of skewness and comment on your result. One of the salesmen earns £18,000. How does this compare with the salaries earned by salesmen there generally? What measures should such a comparison be made on?

Salary over the year (£1000 gross)	Percentage of salesmen earning this salary
10 and under 12	5
12 and under 14	15
14 and under 16	20
16 and under 18	25
18 and under 20	30
20 and under 22	5

To calculate the coefficient of skewness, the median and the mean and standard deviation are required. The last two can be calculated as shown below:

Column 1 Salary mid-point	Column 2 Frequency	Column 3 Col. 1 × Col. 2	Column 4 Mid-point − mean	Column 5 (Col. 4)^2	Column 6 Col. 2 × Col. 5
11	5	55	−5.5	30.25	151.25
13	15	195	−3.5	12.25	183.75
15	20	300	−1.5	2.25	45.00
17	25	425	.5	.25	6.25
19	30	570	2.5	6.25	187.50
21	5	105	4.5	20.25	101.25
	Total 100	Total 1650			Total 675.00

Mean $= \frac{1650}{100} = 16.5$ (£000).

Did you remember to multiply the mid points by the corresponding frequencies? And divide by the total frequency?

Standard deviation $= \sqrt{\frac{675}{100}} = \sqrt{6.75} = 2.6$ (£000) (to one decimal place).

Did you remember to multiply the squares in column 5 by the frequency? And divide by the total frequency? The median may be estimated from the ogive. The data for plotting this is shown below:

Upper-class boundary	Frequency	Cumulative frequency
12	5	5
14	15	20
16	20	40
18	25	65
20	30	95
22	5	100
	Total 100	

The ogive itself is shown in figure 56. From this the median is 16.8 (000). You may have a slightly different answer because of differences in the graph.

Using these figures, the coefficient of skewness is

$$\frac{3 \times (16.5 - 16.8)}{2.6} = \frac{3 \times (-.3)}{2.6} = \frac{-.9}{2.6} = -.35 \text{ (to two decimal places)}.$$

So the data is very slightly negatively skewed. That is, there are more salesmen earning large salaries than small ones.

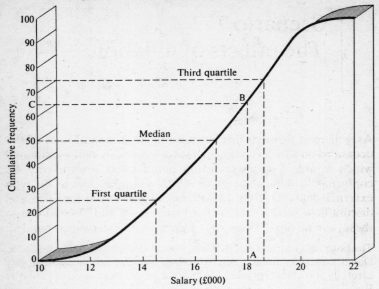

Figure 56

The salesman who earns £18,000 is above the median, which was £16,800 and also the mean, which was £16,500. But he is below the mode, which lies somewhere between £18,000 and £20,000 (the modal class).

Probably one of the best measures to use here would be the quartile deviation. From the ogive, the first quartile is £14,500 and the third is £18,600. The quartile deviation is thus $\frac{18,600 - 14,500}{2}$ = £2050. The salesman lies towards the upper end of the range, i.e. just less than £18,600. We can see his position on the ogive, in fact, by working back from the salary to the cumulative frequency. The lines AB and BC show just this. It is also clear from the table that, since £18,000 is a class boundary, 65% of the salesmen earn less than he does.

Scenario 7
The effects of inflation

As you read through this scenario make a mental note of the occasions on which changes in a set of figures are being examined which would, if they weren't all summarized in some way, be confusing to deal with. Note which examples are to do with external data. Chapter 12 will refer back to the scenario and discuss how some of the sets of data in it, and fluctuations in these, can be dealt with so as to make them more meaningful.

The board of Gourmet Foods were getting very worried about inflation. David Lowe, the finance director, was given the task of looking very carefully at costs and pricing. Much of the actual hard work was done by Ray Barnes, the cost accountant for the company, and his assistants.

As part of the exercise, Ray visited the Baby Gourmet plant to talk to the head chef, Karl Rogan. In particular, he wanted to discuss with him the purchase of ingredients and the use of gas and electricity. So Len Brown, the head of purchasing, became involved as well. They discussed the rise in price of these ingredients and ways of cutting costs by changing the proportions of the ingredients, substituting less costly ones and so on. They also examined various ways of saving energy.

As a first step, they decided to work out just what the average rise in the overall price of the ingredients and of energy had been over the previous year. This would then, they hoped, give them some idea of the magnitude of the problem. They could compare this with government statistics on wholesale prices in the food industry. Ray performed some statistical calculations which showed that prices had risen, over all ingredients, by about twenty-five per cent over the year. Energy prices had risen dramatically too.

In his calculations he had to take into account that different amounts of each ingredient were used and that the price increases for each of them varied. For energy, a similar problem existed with gas and electricity. Also, because of changing prices, the proportions of the various ingredients had been changed over the year. The statistical technique that Ray used took all of these things into account.

They also looked at the government statistics on the movement of retail prices, to get some idea of what the housewife was facing. It was obvious that the price of Baby Gourmet food was going to have to be raised. It was important, though, that such a rise should not be too much more than the rise in food prices generally. It was for this reason that the government statistics were consulted.

The scenario indicates the need for statistics which give the clearest picture possible of movements in prices. The same is true of other variables, such as production. When looking at movements, or differences, in some figures from time to time, firm to firm, nation to nation and so on, the actual values themselves are of very little consequence. In the scenario, for instance, the interest was really in the proportion of the change in the price of the ingredients.

In particular, when two different sets of figures are to be compared, it is often necessary to look at the basic percentage changes in both. This is what would be done in the scenario with the retail price figures and the possible changes in the price of Baby Gourmet food. The rise in the latter should not be too much more than the rise in food prices.

Many government statistics are presented in this way. Rather than give details of the prices of various goods in the shops, for instance, the government publish statistics which show how the price of the average family's shopping changes over a time.

This is given in what is basically the form of a percentage. Of course, it is not just prices that are treated this way. As mentioned above, we may look at volumes, of production and so on, and of values, e.g. the Gross National Product.

Since such figures usually involve several factors all fluctuating differently, some averaging process needs to be used which gives the overall picture. The following chapter describes what this process is and how the results are presented.

After having studied this chapter, you should be in a position to calculate changes in sets of figures, such as those in the scenario, and to use the results of such calculations by others effectively.

12 | Bringing out the changes clearly

Comparing 'now' with 'then'

In the scenario we saw how Gourmet Foods management were concerned with inflation and how the raw figures themselves were difficult to assimilate. Look at the series of figures in table 27, for the price per unit of one of the ingredients of Baby Gourmet food over a number of years:

TABLE 27. THE RISING COST OF AN INGREDIENT

Column 1 Year	Column 2 Cost (to Gourmet Foods) per unit (£)	Column 3 Difference over previous year	Column 4 Percentage increase over previous year*	Column 5 Figure as percentage of previous year*	column 6 Figure as percentage of that for 1977*	Column 7 Figure as percentage of that for 1979*
1977	150				100.00	75.76
1978	165	15	10.00	110.00	110.00	83.33
1979	198	33	20.00	120.00	132.00	100.00
1980	250	52	26.26	126.26	166.67	126.26
1981	265	15	6.00	106.00	176.67	133.84

*To nearest .01%.

Though it is evident that the price is rising, it is not clear quite by how much. We could take the differences and display these, as in table 27 (column 3). This shows that the increase from 1977 to 1978 was equal to that from 1980 to 1981.

Self-check

Does this mean that the inflation from 1980 to 1981 was as bad as that from 1977 to 1978?

Well, going on the differences it does. But it would seem that an increase of 15 on 250 is not really as bad as one of 15 on 150. The differences do not show this, but the *percentage* increases do. These also appear in table 27 (column 4). The two increases above can now be seen to be 10% and 6% respectively. This fits in more with our ideas of which one is worst.

This kind of discussion leads on to the idea of expressing each year's figure in terms of a percentage of the previous year. Thus, in the figures given, the 1978 one is 110% of the 1977 one.

Self-check

What are the corresponding percentages for the other years?

These are again shown in table 27 (column 5). Such figures are called a 'chain index'. Each one in the series is expressed in terms of a percentage of the previous one.

Self-check

Calculate the chain index for the following figures:

Year	Sales (units)
1975	320
1976	336
1977	420
1978	462
1979	693

The chain index is as below:

Year	Sales (units)	Chain index
1975	320	
1976	336	$\frac{336}{320} \times 100 = 105$
1977	420	$\frac{420}{336} \times 100 = 125$
1978	462	$\frac{462}{420} \times 100 = 110$
1979	693	$\frac{693}{462} \times 100 = 150$

While a chain index gives an idea of change from year to year, an alternative method is often used which produces an index expressing all figures as a percentage of that for a given year, called the 'base year'. This is called a 'fixed base index'.

Self-check

Express the figures in column 2 of table 27 as percentages of the figure for 1977.

These percentages are shown in table 27 too (column 6). Note that the index for 1977 is 100, as 150 is 100% of 150. Index numbers of this type give you an idea of change in the variable concerned relative to what it was in some given year. Long-term comparisons then become easier than with the chain index. You can see this from table 27.

Self-check

Calculate index numbers with 1974 as base year, for the following figures:

Year	Income from investments, etc. as percentage of total UK personal income (to one decimal place)
1974	10.0
1975	9.0
1976	9.5
1977	10.1
1978	9.6

Source: *UK in Figures*, 1975–79 edition.

The index numbers are as follows overleaf:

348   *Making sense of the data collected*

Year	Figure	Index (1974 = 100)
1974	10.0	$\frac{10.0}{10.0} \times 100 = 100$
1975	9.0	$\frac{9.0}{10.0} \times 100 = 90$
1976	9.5	$\frac{9.5}{10.0} \times 100 = 95$
1977	10.1	$\frac{10.1}{10.1} \times 100 = 101$
1978	9.6	$\frac{9.6}{10.0} \times 100 = 96$

Self-check

Calculate the percentage increases from year to year in the index numbers in column 6 of table 27. What do you notice about the results?

The results are the same as the percentages in column 4. That is, a chain index can be as easily derived from one with a given base year by calculating the percentage that each index number is of the preceding one.

Self-check

Can we calculate the index numbers of column 6 directly from the chain index of column 5 in a similar way to that in the previous self-check?

We certainly can't do it directly. If we divide any chain index number, say for 1980, by that for the base year, here 1977, we don't arrive at the figure in column 6. Hence

$$\frac{126.26}{110.00}$$

is *not* equal to 166.67; it is in fact 1.15 (to two decimal places). A rather more long-winded method would be required to actually arrive at the required result. For this, and for other reasons to be covered later, a chain index is not often used.

It shouldn't be thought that only the first figure in a series can be used as a base, though this is most often the case. We could use any year. For example, we could use 1979 as base year for the figures of table 27.

Self-check

If we did, what index numbers would we get?

Column 7 of table 27 shows what result we would obtain. Note that the year 1979 now has an index number of 100, and that those for the years before are now less than 100. For example, for 1977 we have $\frac{150}{198} \times 100 = 75.76$ (to two decimal places).

Self-check

Calculate an index for the data in the self-check on page 347, but this time with 1976 as the base year.

The index numbers are as follows:

Year	Figure	Index (1976 = 100)
1974	10.0	$\frac{10.0}{9.5} \times 100 = 105.3*$
1975	9.0	$\frac{9.0}{9.5} \times 100 = 94.7*$
1976	9.5	$\frac{9.5}{9.5} \times 100 = 100$
1977	10.1	$\frac{10.1}{9.5} \times 100 = 106.3*$
1978	9.6	$\frac{9.6}{9.5} \times 100 = 101.1*$

* To one decimal place.

This time you should have made the figure for 1976 equal to 100 and expressed all the other figures as percentages of it.

Note that we do not refer to index numbers in terms of percentages, but rather in terms of 'percentage points'. Thus if an index number goes from 120 to 150, we say that it has risen 30 points, *not*, by 30 per cent. It has, in fact, risen by $\frac{30}{120} \times 100 = 25\%$.

Self-check

Look at the index numbers below and answer the following questions:

a What was the percentage price rise from 1979 to 1980?

   b How many percentage points did the index rise from 1980 to 1981?

   c During which period did the price of this product rise fastest?

THE PRICE OF A CERTAIN PRODUCT

Year	Price index (1978 = 100)
1978	100
1979	120
1980	140
1981	160

(Note the phrase '1978 = 100' is just another way of saying that 1978 is the base year.)

ANSWERS

a It was $\frac{140 - 120}{120} \times 100 = \frac{20}{120} \times 100 = 16\frac{2}{3}\%$.

If you said it was 20%, then you were using the percentage points rise and not the percentage rise itself. 140 is *not* 20% more than 120 but, interpreted as an index, 140 *is* 20 *percentage points* higher than 120.

b It rose $160 - 140 = 20$ points. If you said $14\frac{2}{7}\%$ then you found the percentage increase of 160 on 140 and *not* the increase in percentage points.

c The fastest price rise occurred from 1978 to 1979, when it rose by $\frac{120 - 100}{100} \times 100 = 20\%$. If you said that it rose at a constant rate, then you were confusing the rise of 20 percentage points each year with the yearly percentage rises, which were not all 20%. We have already seen that the percentage rise from 1979 to 1980 was $16\frac{2}{3}\%$. From 1980 to 1981 it was $\frac{160 - 140}{140} \times 100 = \frac{20}{140} \times 100 = 14\frac{2}{7}\%$. So the 20% is the fastest growth.

It should be noted that index numbers need not vary just over time, though they do mostly. For example, they can be used to compare figures from different countries, firms, etc. One of them is chosen as a base and so has index 100. The figures for all the other countries, firms, or whatever, are expressed as a percentage of the one for the base country, firm, etc. For example, suppose there are three firms A, B and C, with gross profits of 100,000, 140,000 and 170,000 respectively. An index can be made with, say firm A as 100. The index numbers would then be

for A $\frac{100,000}{100,000} \times 100 = 100$

for B $\frac{140,000}{100,000} \times 100 = 140$

for C $\frac{170,000}{100,000} \times 100 = 170.$

Even when they do vary over time, of course, they need not be for yearly figures; they could be for monthly or quarterly ones, or any other convenient period. Yearly indexes over time are used in this chapter merely out of convenience. Everything that is said about them can be extended to cover these other areas. When calculating index numbers we will be involved a great deal of the time in the ratio of one of a set of figures to another, e.g. a price for a commodity in one year over that for another year. Such ratios involving one single factor (here a commodity) are called 'relatives'. So, for instance, the ratio of two prices for the same commodity at two different times is called a 'price relative'. If we were dealing with quantities, we would have a 'quantity relative' and so on. The term 'relative' is also used when the ratio is multiplied by 100 to give a percentage. But, most of the time, there is not just one factor involved, but many.

What happens when there is a combination of factors?

Table 27 is fairly straightforward for one ingredient. But the other ingredients would also have changed price, and *not necessarily all by the same amount.* How, then, are we to construct an index which represents, in one figure, how the cost of the baby food has changed, taking into account *all* ingredients? Let's look at a simplified case.

Suppose the baby food contains two ingredients, A and B, that their prices in 1980 are £100 and £300 per unit respectively, and that in 1981 they are £120 and £330 per unit respectively.

How can we construct an index of the total price of raw materials based on these figures?

Self-check

To start off, what are the price relatives for each ingredient separately, with 1980 as base?

Well, for ingredient A we have $\frac{120}{100} \times 100 = 120$
and for B $\frac{330}{300} \times 100 = 110$.

Now, somehow or other, we have got to average these. A straight average of the two gives $\frac{120 + 110}{2} = \frac{230}{2} = 115$.

On the surface, then, it would appear that a suitable value for an 'all ingredients' index would be 115.

Self-check

But what is wrong with the reasoning if we then take this as an index for the overall price of ingredients?

To see exactly what is wrong, suppose the product required 25 units of A and 75 units of B per unit of manufacture. The *cost* of the raw materials per unit of production is then

$25 \times 100 + 75 \times 300 = 25,000$ for 1980
and
$25 \times 120 + 75 \times 330 = 27,750$ for 1981.

The 1981 cost of raw materials is thus $\frac{27,750}{25,000} \times 100\% = 111\%$ of the 1980 cost.

Now the index of *prices* ought to show the same attention to the relative importance of each ingredient. Indeed, assuming the relative importance remains *unchanged* from 1980 to 1981, the price index ought to *equal* this value. In fact, in this case, the above method is a perfectly good one for using to calculate the price index we are looking for, if the quantities remain constant. The case where they do not is covered later in this chapter.

An index calculated in this way is called 'aggregative', since it shows what happens when a number of different factors act together. It may be distinguished from a 'simple' index, which is what we have been discussing up till now. It is found by multiplying every quantity by its corresponding price for each year, and then expressing the later one as a percentage of the other.

> *Self-check*
>
> A company specializing in one particular product has two factories. In 1980 the labour costs per unit of production were 350 in one, while in the other they were 300. In 1981 these rose to 400 and 350 respectively. If, in both years, the first factory produced 2000 units and the second 1000, construct an aggregative index number showing overall costs per unit of production. How would you interpret your result?

The index number is

$$100 \times \frac{(2000 \times 400 + 1000 \times 350)}{(2000 \times 350 + 1000 \times 300)} \quad \text{(for year 1981)}$$

$$= 100 \times \frac{(800,000 + 350,000)}{700,000 + 300,000} = \frac{115,000,000}{1,000,000} = 115.$$

This means that overall, *and allowing for the different production* figures in each factory, labour costs in the company rose by 15% from 1980 to 1981.

The reason the simple average of 115 for the Baby Gourmet ingredients did not come out the same as the 111 can now be seen. It gave equal importance, or *weight*, to each ingredient. But since more of one was used in making the baby food, its price was more important. Averaging like this, so as to give more weight to some figures than to others, is a very important activity in statistics and is looked at in more detail in the next section.

Giving more weight to some figures than to others

Consider what appears to be a simple problem. One group of 100 workers is found to have an average wage of £70 in one particular week, and another group of 200, one of £100.

> *Self-check*
>
> What is the average wage for the two groups combined?

As with the ingredient prices, it cannot just be the simple average. This would give $\frac{70 + 100}{2} = \frac{170}{2} = £85$ per week – that is, one exactly half way in between. But surely since there are more earning the higher wage it ought to be nearer to that. In fact we can attack the problem as follows. The *total* weekly wages earned by the first group was

$$£100 \times 70 = £7000;$$

while by the second group it was

$$£200 \times 100 = £20,000.$$

The total wages together were thus £7000 + £20,000 = £27,000.

Since this total was earned by 300 men, their average wage for the week was $£\frac{27,000}{300} = £90$ a week.

If we write the whole process out in one expression we get the average wage is given by $\frac{100 \times 70 + 200 \times 100}{100 + 200}$

Such averages are called 'weighted averages' and the *200* and *300* are called the 'weights'. Note that each figure to be averaged is multiplied by its weight, the results are then all added together and this number divided by the *total of the weights*.

Let's look at a different example of a weighted average. Suppose a company sells four different products and that the percentage profits on each are 30%, 25%, 35% and 10%.

Self-check

What is the average profit that the company makes (over the three products)?

On the face of it, it is $\frac{30 + 25 + 35 + 10}{4} = \frac{100}{4} = 25\%$.

Now while this is the average of the profits on the products, it is *not* the average profit made by the company. Again, we must take into account how much of each product is sold. But we must be very careful exactly what we do use as weights. It is no use, for example, employing the volume (i.e. quantity) of sales.

Self-check

Why not?

Well, to exaggerate things somewhat, suppose one product sold in hundreds of thousands at 5p each, and the rest in tens at hundreds of thousands of pounds each. We would give enormous weight to the first and virtually none to the rest, if we did as suggested above. But it may well be that the 5p product is the one with the 10% profit. Let's take some actual figures to see clearly what would happen. We'll assume that the products' prices and sales are as below.

Product	A	B	C	D
Price/unit (£)	100,000	200,000	500,000	0.05
Sales (units)	10	20	20	399,950
Profit per unit (%)	30	25	35	10

Self-check

What is the average profit weighted by sales in units?

It is

$$\frac{10 \times 30 + 20 \times 25 + 20 \times 35 + 10 \times 399,950}{10 + 20 + 20 + 399,950} \%$$

$$= \frac{300 + 500 + 700 + 3,999,500}{400,000} \%$$

$$= \frac{4,001,000}{400,000} \% = \frac{40.01}{4} \% = 10.0025\%$$

which is as near 10% as makes no odds. That is, we might just as well have ignored products A, B and C.

Self-check

What, then, should we use as weights?

Since profit is accounted in terms of value, we should really use *value* of sales as weights. These figures can be obtained for each product by multiplying the price per unit by the number of units sold. They work out to

£100,000 × 10 = £1,000,000 for A
£200,000 × 20 = £4,000,000 for B

£500,000 × 20 = £10,000,000 for C
and £0.05 × 399,950 = £19,997.50 for D.

> ## Self-check
>
> What, then, is the average profit weighted by value of sales?

It is

$$\frac{1,000,000 \times 30 + 4,000,000 \times 25 + 10,000,000 \times 35 + 19997.50 \times 10}{1,000,000 + 4,000,000 + 10,000,000 + 19997.50} \%$$

$$= \frac{30,000,000 + 100,000,000 + 350,000,000 + 19,975}{15,019,997.50} \%$$

$$= \frac{480,199.975}{15,019,997.50} \% = 31.97\% \text{ (to two decimal places).}$$

That is, we may as well have ignored product D! (In effect, we did by approximating.)

> ## Self-check
>
> A company exports 25% of its produce (by value). Its profit on home sales is 30% and on sales abroad 20%. What is its average profit?

We need to find the weighted average, using values of sales at home and abroad as weights. The answer is thus:

$$\frac{25 \times 20 + 75 \times 30}{100} \% = \frac{500 + 2250}{100} \% = \frac{2750}{100} \% = 27.5\%.$$

If your answer was $\frac{30 + 20}{2} = 25\%$ then you did not take into account that 75% of sales were exports and so would have a bigger effect than home sales.

Let's go back to the problem of the Baby Gourmet ingredients. Instead of the aggregative index, let's calculate the weighted average for the price relatives of each separate ingredient, A and B.

> ## Self-check
>
> What weights should be used?

We cannot simply use the amount of each ingredient, as this ignores the cost factor. That is to say, even if we used a lot of a particular ingredient and its price had gone up a great deal, if that price itself was very low compared to that for other ingredients, it wouldn't matter too much. This suggests, then, that we ought to use the relative costs of ingredients as their weights. But is it the costs for 1981 or those for the base year (1980) that we are interested in? This is, in fact, rather a tricky point. It is, actually, those for the base year, just because it *is* the base year. That is, we are expressing the index in terms of percentage of that year.

Self-check

Calculate the index using base year costs as weights.

First of all we have to calculate the weights, i.e. the costs for 1980. These are

$25 \times £100 = £2500$ for ingredient A

and $75 \times £300 = £22,500$ for ingredient B.

The weighted average is then

$$\frac{2500 \times \frac{120 \times 100}{100} + 22,500 \times \frac{330 \times 100}{300}}{2500 + 22,500}$$

(NB $\frac{120 \times 100}{100}$ and $\frac{330 \times 100}{300}$ are the price relatives.)

$$= \frac{2500 \times 120 + 22,500 \times 110}{25,000} = \frac{300,000 + 2,475,000}{25,000}$$

$$= \frac{2,775,000}{25,000} = 111.$$

You will see that this agrees with the result obtained earlier by the aggregative method.

One point that should be made concerns the units for the ingredients. Note that it has not been assumed that they were the same in both cases. They could have been 100 *kg* for A, say, and 1000 *litres* for B. As long as prices are given in terms of the *same unit*, a price per unit multiplied by any number of units will result in an amount of money (the value of that many units).

Self-check

Use the weighted average method to recalculate the index for the self-check on page 353.

The weights are

$2000 \times 350 = 700,000$

for the first factory and

$1000 \times 300 = 300,000$

for the second. These are the *total* labour costs of production for each factory for 1980. The weighted average is thus

$$\frac{700,000 \times \frac{400}{350} \times 100 + 300,000 \times \frac{350}{300} \times 100}{700,000 + 300,000}$$

$$= \frac{80,000,000 + 35,000,000}{1,000,000} = \frac{115,000,000}{1,000,000} = 115.$$

This agrees with the result in the self-check on page 353.

Review

1 The following figures show the percentage of local and central government total expenditure that went on education for the years 1974–78.

Year	Percentage of total (to two decimal places)
1974	12.50
1975	13.73
1976	12.07
1977	12.60
1978	12.18

(Source: *UK in Figures* 1975–79.)

a Calculate a chain index for these figures.
b Calculate a simple fixed base index, with 1974 = 100, for the same figures.
c Calculate a simple fixed base index for the same figures with 1978 = 100.

d Between which years did % expenditure (i) increase most, (ii) decrease most? Which index is best to get these answers from?

2 Look at the index numbers below for the crude death rates per 1000 population in various countries in 1968:

Country	Index (UK = 100) (to one decimal place)
USA	79.8
Japan	56.3
W. Germany	100.0
France	94.6
UK	100.0
Poland	68.1

(Source: *Facts in Focus*, Penguin, 1972)

a By what percentage did the West German death rate exceed that of Japan?

b Which of these countries had the lowest death rate?

c Which country's death rate was nearest to that of Poland?

3 A company has stocks of a particular component bought at three separate prices. 2000 were bought at 5p, 1500 at 4.5p and 500 at 4p. What was the average *cost per unit* of this stock?

4 A particular family spends every holiday in the same rented cottage. The rent went up by 30% one year and, at the same time, fares to the cottage increased by 16%. In the year before the rises, the expenditure on fares was £50 and on the rent £175. Calculate a weighted average index for the basic price of the holiday after the rises, compared to the year before. Interpret your result.

ANSWERS

1 The answers to **a**, **b** and **c** are shown in the table overleaf. To find the highest and lowest increases *from year to year*, the chain index is best. If you said the base year one, remember that it is expressed as a percentage of the figure for the base

Year	Percentage expenditure	Chain index	Index (1974 = 100)	Index (1978 = 100)
1974	12.50		$\frac{12.50}{12.50} \times 100 = 100$	$\frac{12.50}{12.18} \times 100 = 102.6^*$
1975	13.73	$\frac{13.73}{12.50} \times 100 = 109.8^*$	$\frac{13.73}{12.50} \times 100 = 109.8^*$	$\frac{13.73}{12.18} \times 100 = 112.7^*$
1976	12.07	$\frac{12.07}{13.73} \times 100 = 87.9^*$	$\frac{12.07}{12.50} \times 100 = 96.6^*$	$\frac{12.07}{12.18} \times 100 = 99.1^*$
1977	12.60	$\frac{12.60}{12.07} \times 100 = 104.4^*$	$\frac{12.60}{12.50} \times 100 = 100.8^*$	$\frac{12.60}{12.18} \times 100 = 103.4^*$
1978	12.18	$\frac{12.18}{12.60} \times 100 = 96.7^*$	$\frac{12.18}{12.50} \times 100 = 97.4^*$	$\frac{12.18}{12.18} \times 100 = 100$

*To one decimal place.

year, so it is not straightforward to get percentage increases from year to year from this type of index.

The highest increase was, then, from 1974 to 1975, during which time percentage expenditure rose by nearly 10%. The greatest decrease was from 1975 to 1976, during which time percentage expenditure fell by just over 12%.

If your answers were 1975 to 1976 and 1976 to 1977 you were misreading the table. The chain index for example, shows how the percentage *from* 1975 *to* 1976, and not from 1976 to 1977.

2 a West Germany's death rate as a percentage of that of Japan was $\frac{100}{56.3} \times 100 = 177.6$ (to one decimal place) If you said 100 − 56.3 = 43.7%, then you were confusing *percentage points* with percentages.

b Japan. It had the lowest index and so lowest rate.

c The USA. It had an index of 79.8 − 68.1 = 11.7 points different from Poland. If you said Japan, this was very nearly, but not quite as near as the USA. The difference there is 68.1 − 56.3 = 11.8 points.

3 The average cost is the weighted average, where the different quantities are the weights. It is thus

$$\frac{2000 \times 5p + 1500 \times 4.5p + 500 \times 4p}{2000 + 1500 + 500} = \frac{10,000p + 6750p + 2000p}{4000}$$

$$= \tfrac{18,750p}{4000} \quad = 4.6875p.$$

If you said it was $\frac{5p + 4.5p + 4p}{3} = \frac{13.5p}{3} = 4.5p$ then you were forgetting that as there were different levels of stock of each price, these levels had to be taken into account.

4 The 30% and 16% rises would have different impacts on the total expenditure according to how much expenditure was affected by each. We need a weighted average, then, with these expenditures weight, we get

$$\frac{175 + 30 + 50 \times 16}{175 + 50} = \frac{6050}{225} = 26.9 \text{ (to one decimal place)}.$$

This result means that the holiday price, taking into account fares and rent, rose by 26.9%

A change in emphasis

So far we have largely looked at cases where the index could be relatively easily determined because of a basic stability from year to year; for example, in quantities purchased (for a price index). But in many cases this cannot be assumed. In the scenario, for example, changing prices led to alterations in the proportions of the ingredients of the baby food. Since these were used in the index of prices, we must look at the implications for its calculations.

Suppose then that, because of rising prices, the proportions of ingredients C and D used in Baby Gourmet food are changed between 1980 and 1981, as follows (the changes were within the leeway allowed by the recipe):

Ingredient	C	D
Price 1980	10	8
(£/unit) 1981	12	15
Quantity used (units per unit of production) 1980	2	3
1981	3	2

|| *Self-check*

|| Why would the change in the proportions of C and D used
|| benefit Baby Gourmet?

If the same quantities of C and D were used in 1981 as had been
used in 1980, the cost of these ingredients would have been

$$2 \times £12 + 3 \times £15 = £24 + £45 = £69.$$

With the new proportions, however, it was

$$3 \times £12 + 2 \times £15 = £36 + £30 = £66$$

thus saving £3 per unit of production. The cost in 1980 was

$$2 \times £10 + 3 \times £8 = £20 + £24 = £44.$$

|| *Self-check*

|| What was the percentage increase in *costs* from 1980 to
|| 1981 (with *changed* proportions)?

It was given by $\frac{66}{44} \times 100 = 150$ (i.e. a 50% increase).

However, in this case we cannot argue that this is the same as
the index of *prices*. This point is, perhaps, slightly obscure, but it
is quite vital. When we are calculating a *price index*, what we are
actually doing is finding a weighted average of a set of *price*
relatives. Similarly, if we are calculating a *quantity* or *value*
index, the weighted average is of *quantity* or *value* relatives,
respectively. Mathematically speaking, this can only be done if
the quantity (in the case of a price index) or its equivalent (in the
case of others) is held constant.

Although it is difficult to explain non-mathematically, an idea
of the reasons behind the difficulty can be given by using the
Baby Gourmet illustration.

When we are looking at prices of ingredients we are looking at
them in terms of units of the ingredient. When we look at costs,
we are looking at these in terms of the unit of production. As
long as the quantities of the ingredients that go into the unit of
production are constant, there is a fixed relationship between
the unit of production and the units of ingredients. When com-

paring one year with another, therefore, this fixed relationship is
the same in both cases and so cancels out. Thus a comparison of
costs is equivalent to a comparison of prices. This is what we saw
in the section beginning on page 351: 'What happens when there
is a combination of factors?' If the quantities of ingredients used
varies, however, this fixed relationship no longer holds and so
does *not* cancel out when costs for different years are compared
and this is *not* equivalent to comparing prices.

If we want to use a comparison of costs as a basis for calculating
the *price* index, we have to choose the *same quantities* for both
years. Thus with the baby food, we have to *either* assume in our
calculations that the quantities in 1980 were the same as in 1981
or vice versa. There are thus *two different possible price indexes*,
one assuming 1981, or *current* year, quantities and one assuming
1980, or *base* year, ones. These are called the 'Paasche index'
and the 'Laspeyres index' respectively. Both are calculated as
was the aggregative index earlier, by forming a ratio.

Self-check

Calculate the Paasche and the Laspeyres *price* index for
1981 for ingredients C and D of above, with 1980 = 100.

The Paasche index uses the 1981 quantities and so is

$$100 \times \frac{3 \times 12 + 2 \times 15}{3 \times 10 + 2 \times 8} \quad \begin{array}{l}\text{(1981 quantities; 1981 prices)}\\\text{(1981 quantities; 1980 prices)}\end{array}$$

$= 100 \times \frac{36 + 30}{30 + 16} = 100 \times \frac{66}{46} = 143.5$ (to one decimal place).

The Laspeyres index, using 1980 quantities, gives

$$100 \times \frac{2 \times 12 + 3 \times 15}{2 \times 10 + 3 \times 8} \quad \begin{array}{l}\text{(1980 quantities; 1981 prices)}\\\text{(1980 quantities; 1980 prices)}\end{array}$$

$= 100 \times \frac{24 + 45}{20 + 24} = 100 \times \frac{69}{44} = 156.8$ (to one decimal place).

So the Paasche is less than the percentage increase in costs and
the Laspeyres more. Note that this is not always the case. The
next section explains this further.

If we wanted a *quantity* index to be obtained from a comparison of costs, a similar argument would show that we need to choose the *same prices* for both years. As with the price index, choice of the current year prices gives the Paasche and of the base year prices, the Laspeyres index.

|| *Self-check*

|| Calculate the Paasche and the Laspeyres *quantity* index for 1981 for the ingredients C and D of above, with 1980 = 100.

The Paasche index uses the 1981 prices and so is

$$100 \times \frac{(3 \times 12 + 2 \times 15)}{(2 \times 12 + 3 \times 15)} \quad \begin{array}{l}\text{(1981 quantities, 1981 prices)*}\\ \text{(1980 quantities; 1981 prices)}\end{array}$$

$$= 100 \times \frac{(36 + 30)}{(24 \times 45)} = 100 \times \frac{66}{69} = 95.7 \text{ (to one decimal place)}.$$

The Laspeyres index uses the 1980 prices and so is

$$100 \times \frac{(3 \times 10 + 2 \times 8)}{(2 \times 10 + 3 \times 8)} \quad \begin{array}{l}\text{(1981 quantities; 1980 prices)}\\ \text{(1980 quantities; 1980 prices)}\end{array}$$

$$= 100 \times \frac{(30 + 16)}{(20 + 24)} = 100 \times \frac{46}{44} = 104.5 \text{ (to one decimal place)}.$$

To summarize then, we have:

- cost comparison 1981 with 1980 $\dfrac{\text{(1981 quantities; 1981 prices)}}{\text{(1980 quantities; 1980 prices)}}$

- Paasche price index (1980 = 100) $\dfrac{\text{(1981 quantities; 1981 prices)}}{\text{(1981 quantities; 1980 prices)}}$

- Laspeyres price index (1980 = 100) $\dfrac{\text{(1980 quantities, 1981 prices)}}{\text{1980 quantities; 1980 prices)}}$

- Paasche quantity index (1980 = 100) $\dfrac{\text{(1981 quantities; 1981 prices)}}{\text{(1980 quantities; 1981 prices)}}$

- Laspeyres quantity index (1980 = 100) $\dfrac{\text{(1981 quantities; 1980 prices)}}{\text{(1980 quantities; 1980 prices)}}$

– where 1980 is the base year and 1981 the current year. For

*Compare this with the Paasche *price* index on page 363.

different years, just substitute the base year for 1980 and the current year for 1981.

> ### Self-check
>
> The price of gas per therm in 1975 was 9.5p and in 1976 was 12.2p. The corresponding figures per unit of electricity were 1.975p and 2.225p. Suppose the 'average' family used 500 therms of gas and 1600 units of electricity in 1975 and that the corresponding figures for 1976 were 550 therms and 1600 units. Calculate aggregative price and quantity indexes for gas and electricity for 1976 with 1975 as base,
>
> **a** on the Paasche index basis;
> **b** on the Laspeyres index basis.
>
> Interpret your results (briefly).

ANSWERS

a The Paasche price index used 1976 quantities and so is

$$100 \times \frac{(550 \times 12.2 + 1500 \times 2.225)}{(550 \times 9.5 + 1500 \times 1.975)} = 100 \times \frac{(6710 + 3337.5)}{(5225 + 2962.5)}$$

$$= 100 \times \frac{10,047.5}{8187.5} = \frac{1,004,750}{8187.5} = 122.7 \text{ (to one decimal place)}$$

b The Laspeyres price index uses 1975 quantities and so is

$$100 \times \frac{(500 \times 12.2 + 1600 \times 2.225)}{(500 \times 9.5 + 1600 \times 1.975)} = 100 \times \frac{(6100 + 3560)}{(4750 + 3160)}$$

$$= 100 \times \frac{9660}{7910} = \frac{966,000}{7910} = 122.1 \text{ (to one decimal place)}.$$

The quantity indexes are

Paasche: $100 \times \dfrac{(550 \times 12.2 + 1500 \times 2.225)}{(500 \times 12.2 + 1600 \times 2.225)} = 100 \times \dfrac{(6710 + 3337.5)}{(6100 + 3560)}$

$$= 100 \times \frac{10,047.5}{9660} = \frac{1,004,750}{9660} = 104.0 \text{ (to one decimal place)}.$$

Laspeyres: $100 \times \dfrac{(550 \times 9.5 + 1500 \times 1.975)}{(500 \times 9.5 + 1600 \times 1.975)} = 100 \times \dfrac{(5225 + 2962.5)}{(4750 + 3160)}$

$$= 100 \times \frac{8187.5}{7910} = \frac{818,750}{7910} = 103.5 \text{ (to one decimal place)}.$$

If you got the indexes mixed up, check with the list on page 364. You should not have calculated the relative cost: that figure is not equal to any of the index numbers.

The results tell us that energy consumption and price both rose, but the former more than the latter. If the pattern of consumption had remained the same, the price index would have shown a 22.1% rise. If prices had remained constant, the quantity would have shown a 3.5% increase. These were the Laspeyres indexes. The Paasche ones show that the increases were on the assumption of present consumption or prices holding in the past.

An alternative method of calculation

The above method of calculating indexes is not the only one. It also rather obscures the fact that the Paasche and Laspeyres indexes are both a form of weighted average. We can calculate these indexes as weighted averages directly. In the case of both the price and the quantity indexes, the weights used are the expenditures on each of the items in the index. That is, they correspond to a quantity multiplied by a price. But there is a difference between the Paasche and the Laspeyres indexes. The Laspeyres is the straightforward one. The weights there are just the expenditures during the base year on the various items in the index. The Paasche index, on the other hand, although it uses expenditure as weights, mixes the quantities and prices from the different years.

The calculations which follow illustrate the use of these weights. In the calculation of a price index, they are used to weight the price relatives. In the calculation of a quantity index they are used to weight the quantity relatives.

If we look at the Paasche and Laspeyres price indexes in terms of *weighted averages of price relatives*, we see that different weights are used in each case. For both we use some estimates of *expenditure* per item *in the base year* as weights, but with the Paasche the quantities *for the year to be indexed* (the *current* year) are used in the calculation of the expenditure, rather than those of the base year itself, as in the Laspeyres. The prices used, however, are the base ones.

Self-check

Calculate the Paasche and Laspeyres price indexes for ingredients C and D, as weighted average price relatives, with 1980 = 100.

The Paasche price index has weights of
$3 \times 10 = 30$ for ingredient C (1981 quantity; 1980 prices)
and $2 \times 8 = 16$ for ingredient D (1981 quantity; 1980 prices).
   The price relatives are
$100 \times \frac{12}{10} = 100 \times 1.2 = 120$ for C
and $100 \times \frac{15}{8} = 100 \times 1.875 = 187.5$ for D.
   The Paasche price index is thus

$$\frac{30 \times 120 + 16 \times 187.5}{30 + 16} = \frac{3600 + 3000}{46}$$

$$= \frac{6600}{46} = 143.5 \text{ (to one decimal place).}$$

The Laspeyres price index uses the same price relatives but has weights of

$2 \times 10 = 20$ for C (1980 quantity; 1980 price)

and $3 \times 8 = 24$ for D (1980 quantity; 1980 price).

This index is thus

$$\frac{20 \times 120 + 24 \times 187.5}{20 + 24} = \frac{2400 + 4500}{44}$$

$$= \frac{6900}{44} = 156.8 \text{ (to one decimal place).}$$

   These calculations agree with the aggregative method shown earlier.

The same reasoning applies to the quantity indexes, if calculated in terms of quantity relatives. For both, we use some estimate of expenditure per ·tem *in the base year* as weights, but taking the current year price for the Paasche index and base year prices for the Laspeyres, the quantities in both cases being those of the base year.

368   *Making sense of the data collected*

Self-check

Calculate the Paasche and Laspeyres quantity indexes, for ingredients C and D, as weighted average quantity relatives, with 1980 = 100.

The quantity relatives are

$100 \times \frac{3}{2} = \frac{300}{2} = 150$ for C

and $100 \times \frac{2}{3} = \frac{200}{3} = 66.7$ for D (to one decimal place).

The Paasche quantity index has weights of
$2 \times 12 = 24$ for ingredient C (1980 quantity; 1981 price)
and $3 \times 15 = 45$ for ingredient D (1980 quantity; 1981 price).

The Paasche quantity index is thus

$$\frac{24 \times 150 + 45 \times 66.7}{24 + 45} = \frac{3600 + 3000}{69} = \frac{6600}{69}$$
$= 95.7$ (to one decimal place).

The Laspeyres quantity index has weights

$2 \times 10 = 20$ for ingredient C (1980 quantity; 1980 prices)
and $3 \times 8 = 24$ for ingredient D (1980 quantity; 1980 prices).

The Laspeyres quantity index is thus

$$\frac{20 \times 150 + 24 \times 66.7}{20 + 24} = \frac{3000 + 1600}{44} = \frac{4600}{44}$$
$= 104.5$ (to one decimal place).

Again, these agree with the result obtained earlier.

Self-check

Use the data in the self-check on page 365 to calculate the Paasche and Laspeyres price and quantity indexes by the weighted price/quantity relatives method. Suppose that the only data you had was the price for the two years and the *expenditure* for the base year only. Would you be able to calculate any of the four indexes? If so, which one(s)?

For the Paasche price index the weights are

550 × 9.5 = 5225 for gas
and 1500 × 1.975 = 2962.5 for electricity.

The price relatives are
$100 \times \frac{12.2}{9.5} = 128.4$ (to one decimal place) for gas
and $100 \times \frac{2.225}{1.975} = 112.7$ (to one decimal place) for electricity.

The Paasche price index is thus
$$\frac{5225 \times 128.4 + 2962.5 \times 112.7}{5225 + 2962.5} = \frac{670,890 + 333,873.75}{8187.5}$$
$$= \frac{1,004,763.75}{8187.5}$$

= 122.7 (to one decimal place).

The Laspeyres price index uses the same price relatives, but with weights:

500 × 9.5 = 4750 for gas
and 1600 × 1.975 = 3160 for electricity.

The Laspeyres price index is thus
$$\frac{4750 \times 128.4 + 3160 \times 112.7}{4750 + 3160} = \frac{609,900 + 356,132}{7910} = \frac{966,032}{7910}$$
= 122.1.

Similarly, the quantity index can be calculated as follows. The quantity relatives are

$100 \times \frac{550}{500} = 110$ for gas
and $100 \times \frac{1500}{1600} = 93.75$ for electricity.

The weights for the Paasche quantity index are

500 × 12.2 = 6100 for gas
and 1600 × 2.225 = 3560 for electricity.

The Paasche quantity index is thus
$$\frac{6100 \times 110 + 3560 \times 93.75}{6100 + 3560} = \frac{671,000 + 333,750}{9660} = \frac{1,004,750}{9660} =$$
104.0 (to one decimal place).

The weights for the Laspeyres quantity index are
500 × 9.5 = 4750 for gas
and 1600 × 1.975 = 3160 for electricity.

The Laspeyres quantity index is thus

$$\frac{4750 \times 110 + 3160 \times 93.75}{4750 + 3160} = \frac{522,500 + 296,250}{7910} = \frac{818,750}{7910} =$$

103.5 (to one decimal place).

Thus these indexes are, as they mathematically must be, the same as the aggregative ones. If only the data as listed was available, then no quantity index could be calculated, since the current year quantities would not be given, and neither could they be calculated. The Paasche price index could not be calculated since that too needs current year weights. The Laspeyres price index could be calculated, though, as it doesn't.

Which method is best?

We have thus two choices of index number in general, the Paasche and the Laspeyres.

|| *Self-check*
|| When do these give the same answers?

They will give the same answers in general only when the quantities (for a price index) or prices (for a quantity index) are the same for the two periods being compared. Each of these may be calculated in one of two ways, as an aggregative index or as a weighted-average price relative index. Which one do we choose and how do we calculate it?

Let us start with 'Which one?' Neither are totally satisfactory in any realistic situation. The Paasche index makes life more difficult in that up-to-date knowledge is required both of prices *and* quantities in order to calculate it. This is often somewhat difficult to come by. For example, in order to calculate a Paasche index of retail prices, family spending patterns would have to be known for the year for which the index is required. (Family spending is used with weighting this index, as explained in the next section.) It is difficult to get such up-to-date information on spending. But if it can be calculated, this index gives the current picture more accurately than the Laspeyres one. On the other hand, of course, with the weights continually changing, when a long time separates current and base years, the weights may have changed considerably and thus a distorted picture is obtained.

The Laspeyres index suffers from the opposite faults in many respects. After a time, the weights from the base year become unrepresentative. In the Baby Gourmet ingredients, for example, the recipe may have been considerably modified. Some ingredients may even have been left out and new ones put in! It does, on the other hand, give a better basis for comparison as the weights remain constant. It has one big advantage: it is easier to construct. The weights need to be calculated only once.

Arithmetically, as we have seen, the two give different answers. But one is not necessarily always more than the other. In fact it can be shown that if the quantities *increase* then the Laspeyres price index is *less* than the Paasche, and vice versa. On the whole, the Laspeyres index overestimates and the Paasche underestimates rise, and vice versa for falls. Which one is calculated will then usually depend on the purpose for which it is to be used. Further discussion on this point will be found in the examples of the next section.

As to the method of calculating either, this will depend on what data is available. The aggregative method is generally the simplest, but it does need a knowledge of the quantities (for prices indexes) or whatever (for others). Often all that is available is the expenditure. In the previous examples of weighted price (or quantity) relatives, we have constructed the expenditure from the price and quantity. In practice, if we knew both we would actually use the aggregative method. But sometimes a cost is known, whereas the quantity is not, and would have to be calculated, so weighted price relatives are used. Again, this is discussed further in the context of the examples of the next section.

While index numbers have their uses, too much reliance should never be placed on them. Care should always be taken to establish what kind of index and what base year are being employed. Frequently, an index which has existed for some time has been revised, e.g. new weights used. Strictly, then, values before the revision cannot be compared with those after. On the other hand, if it is not revised, it becomes an unreliable indication of what is happening.

The cost of living and other examples

In the scenario, the price of Baby Gourmet food was compared with the 'cost of living', as measured by the government's retail price index. This index is compiled by the Central Statistical Office in conjunction with other government agencies. It measures changes in the average level of prices of commodities and services purchased by an average British household. The present series uses 15 January 1974 = 100. The index is a cross between the Laspeyres and the Paasche, and it is calculated by the weighted-mean price relatives method. The weights are obtained through a yearly Family Expenditure Survey. The sampling method for this was explained in Chapter 5. Since, however, it takes a good deal of time to obtain and process these results, they cannot be used in the year for which they are collected, but only for the next one. Thus, in fact, the weights used represent neither the base nor the current year, but the previous year. This is why it was earlier described as a cross between the Paasche and Laspeyres.

Figures for the index are actually published each month, for example in the *Department of Employment Gazette*.* The prices of selected goods are examined, and the index worked out. The goods are divided into eleven categories and separate indexes worked out for each one. Within each category a number of different types of item are *sampled* and, again, an index is compiled for each type within the category. For example, within the category 'food' there are several types including 'fish', 'meat and bacon' and 'milk, cheese and eggs'. For each type, a range of representative items are sampled, for example, the prices of eggs of various sizes will be examined, using various kinds of retail outlet.

The eleven categories are shown below, together with the weights that were given to each, from the Family Expenditure Surveys of 1976 and 1979 applied in 1977 and 1980.

This index does not cover income tax, national insurance, pensions, life insurance, betting, clubs, professional fees, or the like. It is of great importance because certain things, such as

*See Appendix on page 413.

	Category	Weight (1977)	Weight (1980)
I	Food	247	214
II	Alcoholic drink	83	82
III	Tobacco	46	40
IV	Housing	112	124
V	Fuel and light	58	59
VI	Durable household goods	63	69
VII	Clothing and footwear	82	84
VIII	Transport and vehicles	139	151
IX	Miscellaneous goods	71	74
X	Services	54	62
XI	Eating out	45	41
	Total	1000	1000

'granny bonds' savings, civil service pensions and some wages, are linked to it. Union negotiators almost always take it into account in wage bargaining. It is important, therefore, to see that it is not really a 'cost of living' index at all. Apart from the fact that a number of expenses are excluded, it is a *price* index anyway, and not a cost one. There is also some sampling error involved. It would be unrealistic to examine the price changes of *every* possible item in every shop, so a sample is taken. Furthermore, the weights are derived from samples. As we have seen earlier, this then leads to a certain amount of error.

Further information about this index is contained in *Method of Construction and Calculation of the Index of Retail Prices* (No. 6 in the series 'Studies in Official Statistics'), published by HMSO.

The government publish other retail price indexes. In July 1968, pensioner indexes were introduced, one for single-person and one for two-person households. These at present exclude housing costs from the list of items taken into consideration. Apart from this, these indexes are calculated in the same way as the general index of retail prices.

Because the retail price index shows changes in indirect taxation but *not* in direct taxation or national insurance, a further index was introduced in 1979, but calculated also for years prior to then. This is the tax and price index, which is, in effect, a weighted average of the changes in prices and the changes in direct taxes and national insurance, using the average net income and the average direct taxes as weights. The data on income and taxes is derived from a sample survey of tax records.

The index of retail prices is not the only index published by the government. The index of industrial production is also produced by the Central Statistical Office in conjunction with other government agencies. It measures changes in the volume of UK industrial production of consumer and capital goods, both for home and export. It excludes agriculture, trading, transport, finance and service industries, public and private, *except* gas, electricity and water. The present series uses 1975 = 100. The index is a base-weighted, i.e. Laspeyres, one, and is calculated by the weighted-mean quantity relatives method. The weights were obtained from the 1975 Census of Production.

Figures for the index are actually published each month, for example in the *Monthly Digest of Statistics*.* A number of different individual production series are combined to give this index. These are grouped together at various levels, to give intermediate indexes. The broadest grouping is according to the Standard Industrial Classification. Within each order, a number of separate industries are represented. For example, within the order 'bricks, pottery, glass cement, etc.' there are several industries including 'Bricks, fireclay and refractory goods' and 'Abrasives and building materials, etc. not elsewhere specified'. This system was discussed earlier in Chapter 6.

The 1975 weights for broad groupings of industries as determined by the Census of Production then are given below, together with the equivalent ones from the 1970 census.

Further information about this index is contained in *The Measurement of Changes in Production*, (No. 25 in the series 'Studies in Official Statistics'), published by HMSO.

Other indexes produced by the government include a wholesale price index, as mentioned in the scenario, indexes of wage rates and average earnings, an agricultural price index, a construction costs index, indexes for the volume and value of imports and exports, and many more.

*See Appendix on page 413.

Order(s)*	Weight (1970)	Weight (1975)
II Mining and quarrying	37	41
III Food, drink and tobacco	84	77
IV & V Chemicals, coal, etc.	65	66
VI Metal manufacture	57	47
VII to XII Engineering and allied industries	319	298
XIII to XV Textiles, leather and clothing	76	67
XVI to XIX Other manufacturing	144	142
XX Construction	146	182
XXI Gas, electricity and water	72	80
Total	1000	1000

*Order I, 'Agriculture, forestry and fishing', is excluded from the index, as are orders XXIII to XXVII, the service and distribution industries.

Review

1 A small motor manufacturer makes two models of cars. In January 1974, model A was priced at £3000 and model B at £4000. 30 model A and 20 model B cars were produced that month. In August 1977, the corresponding prices were £5500 for model A and £7500 for model B. Production had fallen to 25 for the former and 15 for the latter. Construct, using the aggregative method **a** a Pasche index of production and **b** a Laspeyres index of production for August 1977, with January 1974 = 100. Comment on your result. Has production fallen? If so by what percentage.

2 A wholesaler deals in both white and brown flour. In January 1976, he sold £300 worth of white and £50 worth of brown while in October 1980 he sold £240 worth of white and £60 worth of brown. In the meantime the price of white flour had risen by 75% and of brown 85%. Calculate, using the weighted-mean price relatives method, a flour price index, with January 1976 = 100, for October 1980, using the data for this wholesaler, and **a** with base year 'expenditure' as weights; **b** with current

376 Making sense of the data collected

year 'expenditure' as weights. Which of these, *if any*, are (i) the Laspeyres index, (ii) the Paasche index?

3 In 1976 a sample survey was carried out into how much people spent on records a month. Separate estimates were obtained for singles and LPs. Record prices were thereafter sampled at monthly intervals. What type of record price index would be suitable? What drawbacks do you think it would have? What method of calculation would be used?

4 The retail price index and the index of average earnings in the manufacturing industries for a number of years are shown below. How did earnings compare with prices over the period?

Year	Index of retail prices (Jan. 1974 = 100)	Index of average earnings (Jan. 1970 = 100)
1974	108.5	177.1
1975	134.8	223.7
1976	157.1	260.9

5 If the *1975* weights for the index of industrial production are as given in the text, would a 20% increase in the gas, electricity and water index have more or less effect on the overall index than a 10% increase in that for construction (assuming the others remained constant)?

ANSWERS

1 Since it is an index of production, we are concerned with quantities. The Paasche index is

$$100 \times \frac{(5500 \times 25 + 7500 \times 15) \text{ (Aug. 77 quantities and prices)}}{(5500 \times 30 + 7500 \times 20) \text{ (Jan. 74 quantities and Aug. 77 prices)}}$$

$$= 100 \times \frac{(137,500 + 112,500)}{(165,000 + 150,000)} = 100 \times \frac{250,000}{315,000}$$

= 79.37 (to two decimal places).

The Laspeyres index is

$$100 \times \frac{(3000 \times 25 + 4000 \times 15) \text{ (Aug. 77 quantities, Jan. 74 prices)}}{(3000 \times 30 + 4000 \times 20) \text{ (Jan. 74 quantities and prices)}}$$

$$= 100 \times \frac{(75,000 + 60,000)}{(90,000 + 80,000)} = 100 \times \frac{135,000}{170,000}$$

$= 79.41$ (to two decimal places).

Did you get them the wrong way round or did you calculate the *price* index by mistake? Check with the list on page 00 to make sure you see where the above formulae came from.

The two answers are very close, so a reasonable picture of the situation is obtained from either. Production has fallen *to* about 79% of the Jan. 1974 figure, i.e. *by* about 31%. If you said production had fallen by 79% you were forgetting that an index number shows what percentage of the base year is the current year figure.

2 The first thing to do is to calculate the price relatives. These are 175 and 185. If you said 75 and 85 you were forgetting that the price relatives show the ratio of the prices. 75% and 85% are the *increases*.

a The Laspeyres index is found by using base year 'expenditure' as weights, and is

$$\frac{300 \times 175 + 50 \times 185}{300 + 50} = \frac{52,500 + 9250}{350} = \frac{61,750}{350}$$

$= 176.4$ (to one decimal place).

b The weighted average here is

$$\frac{240 \times 175 + 60 \times 185}{240 + 60} = \frac{42,000 + 11,100}{300} = \frac{53,100}{300} = 177.$$

The first one is the Laspeyres index since it uses the base year expenditure as weights. The second one, however, is *not* the Paasche, as that would have current year quantities but *base year prices* to make up the weights. If you got this wrong, look up the appropriate section again.

3 Because expenditure was sampled only in 1976, it would not be possible to use a Paasche index as that needs *current* quantities. So a Laspeyres index would be suitable here. Because the sample found expenditure, it would be simplest to keep these as weights and so use a weighted average price index. The price relatives could be calculated from the monthly figures and the base year figures.

4 The first thing to notice is that a different base year is used in each set of figures. You must be very careful, then, in compar-

ing the two. Although earnings rose 46.6 *points* from 1974 to 1975, the *percentage* increase was only

$$\frac{46.6}{177.1} \times 100 = 26.3\% \text{ (to one decimal place).}$$

The percentage increase in prices over that period was

$$\frac{(134.8 - 108.5)}{108.5} \times 100 = \frac{26.3}{108.5} \times 100 = 24.2\% \text{ (to one decimal place).}$$

So although earnings were slightly ahead of prices, they were not vastly so. If you said they were, you were mixing up percentage points with percentage rises.

Similarly, from 1975 to 1976 earnings rose by

$$\frac{(260.9 - 223.7)}{223.7} \times 100 = \frac{37.2}{223.7} \times 100 = 16.6\% \text{ (to one decimal place),}$$

while prices rose by

$$\frac{(157.1 - 134.8)}{134.8} \times 100 = \frac{22.3}{134.8} \times 100 = 16.5\% \text{ (to one decimal place).}$$

The difference here is even less than in 1974–75. So earnings were marginally ahead of prices over the period in question.

5 A 20% increase in the gas, electricity and water index, which has a weight of 80, would alter the overall index by an amount proportional to $20 \times 80 = 1600$.

A 10% increase in that for construction would alter it by an amount proportional to $10 \times 182 = 1820$, since its weight is 182.

The 10% change in the index for construction would thus have more effect.

If you just compared 20% with 10% and said that the first must have a greater effect, then you were forgetting that these changes would be weighted.

Scenario 8
Machine breakdowns

As you read through the following scenario make a mental note of anything that happens in it that cannot be accurately predicted – that is, that happens by chance. The chapter which follows deals with chance and will refer back to the scenario to illustrate some of the concepts introduced. But look out, too, for any clues to the kind of information that can be gathered about the working of chance that will enable us to say something more about it.

Rex Johnson, from production administration, constantly reported difficulties with production scheduling because of machine breakdowns. Extra overtime was having to be worked to meet targets. This, of course, meant that the production budgets were not being adhered to. Rex told Martin Grey, the plant manager, that the situation could really only be remedied by better maintenance or new machinery. As regards the new machinery, Rex received the reply that the board was reluctant to undertake any new investment at present. But the idea of improving maintenance stuck in Martin's mind.

It was the machine that put the baby food in the jars that was the cause of most of the trouble. There had been quite a sharp increase in breakdowns over the previous year. When Martin had asked John McNab, the chief maintenance engineer, if a major overhaul might solve the problem, he had replied that it would be almost as expensive as buying a new machine. Apparently the problem lay in the fact that many parts of it were worn. Thus, the only thing that would do any good would be to replace all of these, which would be very costly.

When Martin had then asked John if it wasn't expensive anyway, since those parts were replaced when breakdowns occurred, he had said that they weren't. The majority of breakdowns involved readjustments rather than replacements. And it was this remark, together with Rex's that had set Martin off thinking.

Before he could be sure his idea was correct, however, he needed some data to back it up. He asked Rex if he would get this for him.

What he wanted was a table showing the number of times breakdowns of various lengths had occurred with that machine over the past few months. In addition, he required to know how long it took a maintenance engineer to respond to a call, on average.

Martin's idea was quite simple. From what John had said, he had gathered that most breakdowns required only a short time to correct, but there were a great many of them. The figures he had asked for should confirm this and give him some idea of the actual times involved. He would then see what improvement could be gained from decreasing the time taken for an engineer to arrive.

What Martin would have to do would be to work out the cost of the time lost by having machines and workers idle. This would presumably reflect the fact that overtime was having to be worked to make up the loss. This cost could then be compared with the costs of various methods of shortening the time waiting for service. Where the former exceeded the latter, it would be worthwhile carrying out those improvements.

The figures obtained showed that it would actually be worthwhile employing a maintenance engineer to deal solely with the machine for putting the food into the jars, when other benefits of doing this were taken into account. For example, it would be possible to reduce overtime worked by other maintenance engineers if such a step were taken. So Martin decided that this is exactly what he would do.

We saw in Chapter 4 how chance played a part in the selection of random samples. In this scenario we can see how chance operates to produce machine breakdowns at various different times. These breakdowns do not occur regularly, but, nevertheless, something can be said about how often they happen 'on average'.

Chapter 13 investigates exactly what is meant by chance and looks at such figures as the average above that tell us something, at least, about how it operates. It is found that, in many cases, patterns may be seen in the effects of chance if observed a great many times.

A study of such statistical patterns is vital to 'inferential statistics', which is concerned with drawing inferences out of the data collected. If we can detect some pattern behind things then this allows us to 'fill in the missing parts', as it were. That is to say, if there is incomplete data, knowing the pattern that it must fit enables us to estimate what the rest of the data would look like.

After studying this chapter you should understand what is

meant by chance and be able to calculate the chances of various
events occurring.

13 | The effects of chance

Chance and uncertainty

Chapter 3 introduced the idea of randomness, an equal chance for all. In the first part of this chapter, we are going to look at exactly what we mean by chance. Let us first of all, then, consider the two extremes of complete impossibility, when there is no chance at all, and complete certainty, when there is every possible chance. These are actually rarer occurrences than most people think. That the sun will rise tomorrow is not a foregone conclusion, for example. It is extremely likely, thank goodness, but, nevertheless, not absolutely 100 per cent certain. Mathematics provides us with a great many certainties, 2 plus 2 will always equal 4, for instance. The reverse of certainty, in this sense, is impossibility. It is thus impossible for 2 plus 2 to be other than 4.

But outside of mathematics, the most we can usually say about any occurrence is that it has a greater, or lesser chance of happening than some other. For example, we can compare the chances of a company making a profit with those of it making a loss. What this means is that we face a great many uncertainties in real life. To a large extent it is the role of science to reduce this uncertainty. Thus, primitive astronomy was aimed at producing a calendar so that the time of the year could be determined accurately, for planting crops and so on. Today meteorology aims at predicting the weather. In business, economics is supposed to take some of the guesswork out of such things as the relationship between supply and demand or between the money supply and inflation. Very often, indeed, one of the main criteria for defining a science is the degree to which it reduces uncertainty. But when we have no other science to inform us, we can turn to the science of statistics, for this deals with uncertainty itself.

Activity

Take a 10p coin. Guess what the result is going to be when you toss it. Now toss it.

Were you right? If you were, it was by sheer chance you will agree. The point is that you weren't certain that it would be what you guessed.

Self-check

Were you certain that it would be either a head or a tail?

You ought to have been. These were the only two things it could have been.

Something like tossing a coin, which can have many different but unpredictable outcomes, only one of which can occur at once, is called a trial. This is the starting point for a discussion of chance. In this case, of course, there are only two outcomes, head or tail. But suppose we were to throw an ordinary die (the singular of dice)?

Self-check

What would be the possible outcomes?

They are that the result is 1, 2, 3, 4, 5 or 6.

This has little to do with business, of course. It is, however, convenient to use such examples because of their simplicity. Ones from business tend to be very complicated. One example from business, though, is the launching of a new share issue. This is a trial (in more ways than one!). The possible outcomes are a multitude. Some of these will mean that it is oversubscribed, while others will mean that it is undersubscribed.

Self-check

What are all the *possible* outcomes of the following trials?

a Tossing a coin once.

    b Making a profit/loss.
    c Counting those present at a committee meeting, if it has
       ten members who could attend.
    d Tossing two coins (A and B) together.

ANSWERS

a Heads or tails.
b Innumerable; but they all boil down to three: making a profit;
   making a loss; and breaking even.
c Any attendance between 0 and 10, i.e. eleven possibilities.
d The possible outcomes are:
   a head on coin A and a tail on coin B;
   a head on coin A and a head on coin B;
   a tail on coin A and a tail on coin B;
   a tail on coin A and a head on coin B.
   Note that a head on one coin and a tail on the other *can* be
   distinguished from the other way round, and so are different
   outcomes.

In statistics, we are interested in the chances of each possible
outcome of a trial occurring. For example, we want to be able to
say just how likely it is that we will throw a six on the die, or a
head on the coin. There are two basic approaches to this problem. The first is to use our experience of other occurrences of
that or similar trials. This is called the 'empirical' approach. The
second is to examine the nature of the trial in question. This is
called the '*a priori*' approach, which could be adopted even if the
trial had never before occurred.
   To illustrate the first one, let's look at a couple of examples.
Suppose one employee has been absent from work a great deal
over a period and another not at all.

   Self-check

   If you were asked to say which one was more likely to be
   absent tomorrow, what would be your response?

Based on our experience, we would undoubtedly say that the
former was more likely to be absent tomorrow than the latter.

Of course, this doesn't mean that the one with the bad attendance record *will* be absent tomorrow, any more than the other *won't*. What it does indicate is that we would be more suprised at one outcome than another. Again, look at the scenario. The Baby Gourmet works manager would be more surprised to see the sterilizing machine break down than the machine that puts food into the jars, as the latter was notoriously more unreliable. These are examples of experience guiding our expectations.

Now let's look at the *a priori* approach and some cases where we can use information about the trials themselves to guide us. Consider, for example, a ten-sided die. This is just like an ordinary die except that it has four more sides numbered 7 to 10. Now you have probably never seen such a die, but if you were asked to bet money on the outcome of (the trial of), rolling that die, you would almost certainly have a clear picture in your mind as to what would happen. You would expect the numbers to come at random, i.e., no one more than any other. If every other roll resulted in a 6, for example, you would rightly be extremely suspicious. Your expectations would be based on the assumption that each outcome of the throwing of an unbiased die is equally likely.

Calculating the chances using past experience

Suppose we do have the experience of a number of occurences of a trial, or of ones sufficiently similar. Just what is it about this experience that we can use as a basis of our expectations of the outcome of a further occurrence of that trial?

> *Activity*
>
> Take your coin and toss it fifty times, recording the results. Count how many heads and tails there are.

What were your results? When the author did this, they were 23 heads and 27 tails.

> ## Self-check
>
> How would you use these results to help you estimate the chances of getting a head or a tail on the next toss?

You could use the proportion of heads to tails as a guide. The more heads there were in the fifty, the more would be the chances of getting a head on the next toss. Actually, it is usual to take the *relative frequency* as an indicator of the chances for the future. In the case of the numbers above, this would be $\frac{23}{50}$ for heads and $\frac{27}{50}$ for tails. That is, we use the expression:

$$\frac{\text{number of occurrences of the particular outcome in the past}}{\text{number of times the trial has occurred with any outcome}}$$

to estimate the chance of that outcome occurring again.

> ## Self-check
>
> What were the relative frequencies of heads and tails in your data? Were they different to the author's? If so, what are the implications for this method of estimating chances?

The fact that yours and the author's data can be different shows that chances obtained in this way can vary. This point will be returned to later.

> ## Self-check
>
> Now take the case of the absentee in the last section. How would we estimate the chances of someone being absent from work by using his attendance record?

We would use the number of days missed as a guide. Actually we would use the *relative* frequency of absence, i.e.

number of days absent/number of working days.

If, for example, that employee had missed work on 13 out of the 65 working days last quarter, this fraction would be $\frac{13}{65} = \frac{1}{5}$.

|| *Self-check*

What would be the relative frequency of *attendance*?

By the same token, the relative frequency of attendance is $\frac{65 - 13}{65} = \frac{52}{65} = \frac{4}{5}$. We can say that, on past evidence, the chances of that employee being absent tomorrow are 1 in 5, and of he or she being present 4 in 5.

Now there are one or two points to be noted here.

|| *Self-check*

Do you think there are limits to the values that these relative frequencies have? If so what are they?

First, each relative frequency must lie between 0 and 1. For example, a person can't attend on more than the total number of working days (giving a relative frequency of 1) or on less than zero of them (giving a relative frequency of 0).

|| *Self-check*

So what does a relative frequency of 1 or 0 mean?

A relative frequency of 1 means that the particular outcome has always occurred in the past. Note that this does *not* mean that it will continue to do so. A relative frequency of 0 means that the particular outcome has never occurred in the past. Again, this does *not* mean that it won't in future.

|| *Self-check*

For *any* trial what must the sum of the relative frequencies for all the different outcomes be? Sum up the relative frequencies from your coin-tossing activity to see.

The sum of the relative frequencies for all the different outcomes of *any* trial must be 1. This is because the sum of the frequencies for each outcome must add up to the total number of times the trial took place. So, for the absentee, the sum of the relative frequencies of attendance and of non-attendance is $\frac{4}{5}$ + $\frac{1}{5}$ = 1.

As another example, consider the situation in the scenario. Suppose that we use the number of days last quarter when the machine did not break down as a basis for calculating the chances of it breaking down tomorrow. If there had been no day when the machine had broken down, the relative frequency for 'breakdown' would be zero. but this would not guarantee no breakdown tomorrow. Similarly, if there had been no day when the machine did not breakdown, the relative frequency for 'breakdown' would be 1. But, again, this wouldn't mean the machine would necessarily break down tomorrow. If there were only five days in the period when a breakdown did occur, then the relative frequency for 'breakdown' would be $\frac{5}{65} = \frac{1}{13}$. This means that the relative frequency for 'no breakdown' would be $\frac{65 - 5}{65} = \frac{60}{65} = \frac{12}{13}$. The sum of these two is $\frac{1}{13} + \frac{12}{13} = 1$. Hence the chances of a breakdown occurring tomorrow are 1 in 13, or, equivalently, of one not occurring 12 in 13.

One of the major problems of using this relative frequency approach is that they will, of necessity, change each time the event occurs. So, for example, suppose the above machine does break down on the 66th day after having only broken down on five days out of the previous 65 working days. The relative frequency of breakdowns is now $\frac{6}{66} = \frac{1}{11}$ and of no breakdowns $\frac{60}{66} = \frac{10}{11}$. In particular, of course, some outcome that has never occurred before may suddenly do so, changing its relative frequency from nothing to something. Or some outcome that has always occurred before may abruptly cease to do so, reducing its relative frequency from 1 to less than 1. This shows why the author's coin-tossing results and yours can differ.

Self-check

The attendance records of nine members of a committee over its last ten meetings are 10, 9, 6, 7, 8, 10, 8, 9 and 4. What would you estimate would be the chances of each of them turning up at the next meeting of the committee? Who is most likely to be absent?

It is not correct here to add up the attendances: there are actually nine different sets of ten trials involved. One set for each member. In each case the possible outcomes are attendances at a meeting or not. The chances of each turning up at the next meeting are based on the relative frequency of their attendance to date and are then

$10/10 = 1, 9/10 = .9, \quad 6/10 = .6, \quad 7/10 = .7, \quad 8/10 = .8$
$10/10 = 1, 8/10 = .8, \quad 9/10 = .9 \quad$ and $4/10 = .4.$

The one most likely to be absent is thus the last one, as that has the smallest chance. Don't forget that these chances say how likely the members are to attend; the smaller the chance, the less likely they are to attend, i.e. the more likely they are to be absent. If you picked either the first or the sixth, then you forgot to take this into account.

Review

You buy a car from a particular manufacturer and it breaks down after three days. Would you then say that all cars built by that manufacturer would break down just after you bought them (i.e. that the chance of a breakdown soon after purchase is 1 in 1)? Suppose you have nine friends, all of whom bought the same type of car as you, and that none of theirs broke down. On the basis of your and their results alone, what would you say were the chances of another one of your friends buying the same type of car and finding that it broke down just after he bought it? Suppose he does buy one, and it does not break down. Would you revise your idea of what the chances are of anyone buying one of these cars and having it break down very quickly? How do you explain the discrepancy between this figure and your previous estimate?

You certainly should not leap to that conclusion, though your frustration may tempt you to! However, it is true that, in the light of the lack of any other evidence, you can't really say what the chances are of a new car of that make breaking down shortly after purchase. The situation is a little better if you have nine friends with similar cars, though still far from ideal. If none of theirs break down, then your best estimate of the chances of a new one of these cars soon breaking down must be based on the relative frequency of breakdowns with the new cars. As you have ten examples, with only one breaking down, this estimate is 1/10. If you said 9/10 you got it the wrong way round; you found the chances of *not* getting a breakdown.

Now if another friend buys one of these cars, and it doesn't break down, you are in a position to revise your estimate of the chances. Because now only one out of the eleven broke down, the chances change to 1/11 of such a new car breaking down shortly after being purchased. This change is a result of *further information* becoming available. It is not 'a bad thing' that these figures differ; it is an inevitable consequence of using relative frequencies as a basis for an estimate of the chances. The more 'trials' that have occurred, the 'better' the estimate.

In the long run

The *a priori* situation, where the *nature* of trials can be used as a basis for predicting outcomes, is somewhat different. Do you remember the ten-sided die introduced earlier? What replaces relative frequencies *based on experience* when we consider its nature? What we, in fact, do is to *imagine* a series of repetitions of the trial, i.e. of throws of the die. We then calculate what the relative frequencies of each of the outcomes *would be* in this series. Now it is important to see that we use relative frequencies that would occur *in the long run*, i.e. if the series were very long. This concept is very important in statistics. The idea is that, while there may be local fluctuations (e.g. some premium bond may win its owner a prize in two successive draws), in the long run definite patterns emerge (e.g. every bond will win a prize). Of course, 'in the long run' in this case is rather too long term for it to ever actually occur. It would need very many years with the bond numbers unchanging for the pattern to unfold. In practice, many bonds would have been disposed of and others bought during that time, even if the scheme as a whole actually lasted that long.

Self-check

If you were to go on tossing your coin for a very long time, what do you think the relative frequency of heads and of tails would be? If the author were to do the same, would he get the same result?

If we assume that it is unbiased, then both would have an equal chance of occurring. So, over a long period, there should be as many heads as tails. The relative frequency of both should be $\frac{1}{2}$. The author should get the same result. *Thus, there is no real discrepancy in the long run.*

Let's return to the ten-sided die again. If we assume it is unbiased, then each possible outcome, i.e. each number, has an equal change of occurring. So to turn this into a figure, we imagine a long sequence of throws of the die in which each number occurs an equal number of times. Because there are ten possible numbers, this means that a tenth of the sequences will be 1's, a tenth 2's and so on. Thus the relative frequency for each number must 1/10 and the chances of any particular one coming up are 1 in 10.

Notice that, because we have relative frequencies again, we still get (a) each of them lying between 0 and 1 and (b) the total adding up to 1. However, the meaning to be attached to the relative frequency of 0 or of 1 is *now different*.

Self-check

What does it mean here if the *long run* relative frequency is **a** 0 and **b** 1?

Here, if it is 0, it really does mean that that outcome is impossible, since we have considered all *possible* ones, not just those that have occurred previously. Similarly, if it is 1, we have a 100-per-cent certain outcome. For example, if we had a ten-sided die with all faces numbered 1, the relative frequency of 2's in the long run would be 0, while the relative frequency of 1's would be 1.

Relative frequencies arrived at in this way are called 'probabilities'. So the probability of an outcome of a trial is a number between 0 and 1 inclusive. It indicates the chances of that outcome resulting from one trial. A zero probability indicates an impossible outcome, while one of 1 indicates 100-per-cent certainty for an outcome. The sum of the probabilities of all possible outcomes of a trial must be 1, as they are relative frequencies and so must sum to 1, as pointed out earlier.

Activity

We saw in the self-check on page 383 what the four possible outcomes of tossing two coins were. Take two coins and toss them together fifty times. Record your results in terms of the frequency of each outcome and draw a histogram for them. What is your empirical estimate of the chances of getting each of the possible outcomes? Don't forget to distinguish between 'a head on A and a tail on B' and 'a tail on A and a head on B'.

When the author performed this experiment, he obtained the following frequencies:

Coin A	Coin B	
head	head	= 10
head	tail	= 13
tail	head	= 12
tail	tail	= 15

The relative frequencies are, then:

Coin A	Coin B	
head	head	$\frac{10}{50} = .20$
head	tail	$\frac{13}{50} = .26$
tail	head	$\frac{12}{50} = .24$
tail	tail	$\frac{15}{50} = .30$

The histogram for these frequencies is shown in figure 57.

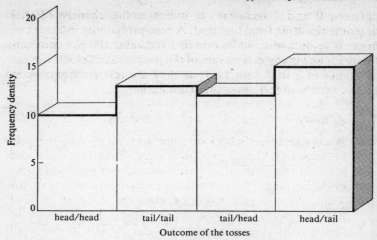

Figure 57. Histogram for author's tosses of two coins

Self-check

Does the fact that there is a head (or tail) on one coin affect what appears on the other?

No it doesn't. The outcomes of the two tosses can be regarded as separate trials, each *independent* of the other.

The concept of independence is an important one in statistics. If two trials are independent, then neither can influence the other. The process of random sampling can be regarded as a sequence of trials which select the sample items, one by one. Where the sampling is with replacement, these trials are independent. But where it is without replacement, the trials are not independent. The second item selected cannot have also been the first, and so on.

Self-check

In which of the following cases are the events described independent and in which are they not?

a A = 'a driver is drunk'; B = 'the same driver has an accident'.

b A = 'a man has larger than average feet'; B = 'the same man is above average intelligence'.

c A = 'a firm X goes bankrupt'; B = 'firm Y, which is owed money by X, goes bankrupt'.

d A = 'a man wins the pools one week'; B = 'the same man wins the pools the next week'.

e A = 'an unbiased coin is tossed fifteen times and all fifteen tosses result in heads'; B = 'the next toss of the same coin results in a tail'.

ANSWERS

a These events are not independent. If you said they were, you are asserting that a drunken person is no more likely to have an accident than one who is not. Do you really believe this?

b These events are independent. If you said they were not, then you were implying that big feet and high intelligence go together. You must have big feet. Do you think that, in an adult, these two factors are connected?

c They are certainly not independent. The fact that firm X went bankrupt cannot but affect the chances of firm Y going bankrupt too.

d These are, believe it or not, independent. If you thought that the fact that he won one week would affect his chances of winning again the next week, look at it again. Whether or not the man wins depends solely on the results of the matches played. In what conceivable way could the man winning the pools affect the results of the football matches?

e They are independent. This always seems to fool people, so if you said that they were dependent, you would not be alone. Some people argue that, since all fifteen tosses to date have been heads, the next one is very likely to be a head too. Others argue that, since all the fifteen tosses to date have been heads, it is about time for a change so the next one is more likely to be a tail. Which group did you side with? The true answer is that neither is right. If the coin is tossed again, how can what has gone on before influence the outcome?

The concept of independence should not be confused with that of causation. The two are very different. For example, in the text it was pointed out that sampling without replacement does not give independent selections. But it would be nonsense to claim that the selection of a particular item at one stage *caused* the selection of some other item at a later stage. Of course, where one event does cause another, the two cannot be independent. But this does not imply that one causes the other *because* they are dependent. This whole topic is taken up in Volume 2.

Looking at each toss of the two coins as a single trial again, can we now see how *a priori* relative frequencies for the possible outcomes can be derived? Well, as the two-coin outcomes can be regarded as having two independent *random* components, there is no reason to suppose that they are anything other than random themselves. That is, a head on A and tail on B is just as likely a combination as a tail on A and a tail on B or a head on A and a head on B or a tail on A and a head on B. The *a priori* relative frequencies, and so the probabilities, for these are thus all .25 or ¼. That is, each one of the four occurs one quarter of the time in the long run.

This now ties in with the coin-tossing experiment you did earlier, as follows. If you were to go on tossing your coins for a great deal longer than you would have the stamina for, you would eventually end up with relative frequencies of ¼ for each of the four possible outcomes. Fifty tosses are scarcely sufficient. The frequencies you get will vary from these if only this number of tosses are performed.

As another example, let's go back to dice again, but this time two six-sided ones. The possible outcomes of one throw of these dice are as below, in table 28. Also indicated in this table are the equivalent numbers thrown, i.e. the sums of the numbers on the two dice.

Now if we regard the dice as unbiased, the numbers thrown *on each die* are random, hence so are the *pairs of numbers*. That is, 3 on the first die and 2 on the second is just as likely as 1 on the first die and 5 on the second. But notice that 2 on the first die and 3 on the second is a *different* outcome to, and is clearly distinguishable from, 3 on the first and 2 on the second. In any very

TABLE 28. RESULTS OF TOSSING TWO SIX-SIDED DICE

First die	second die	number thrown
1	1	2
1	2	3
1	3	4
1	4	5
1	5	6
1	6	7
2	1	3
2	2	4
2	3	5
2	4	6
2	5	7
2	6	8
3	1	4
3	2	5
3	3	6
3	4	7
3	5	8
3	6	9
4	1	5
4	2	6
4	3	7
4	4	8
4	5	9
4	6	10
5	1	6
5	2	7
5	3	8
5	4	9
5	5	10
5	6	11
6	1	7
6	2	8
6	3	9
6	4	10
6	5	11
6	6	12

long run of throws, each of these thirty-six possible outcomes should occur an equal number of times, i.e. the relative frequency of each of them should be 1/36. So the *probability* of any one of the outcomes occurring is 1/36th.

Self-check

What are the probabilities of the following events occurring? A playing card is picked at random from a pack and it is

a a heart.
b a black card.
c an ace.

ANSWERS

a If the card is picked at random, then there is no reason to suppose that it will be any one in particular of the four suits. If cards were picked at random a large number of times, *and replaced* each time, each of the four suits would occur an equal number of times. That is, each would occur ¼ of the time. The probability of getting a heart is thus ¼.

b As there are an equal number of black and red cards, there is no reason to suppose that any one colour will be picked more than the other. In a long run of selections, then, we would expect to get as many black cards as white ones. That is, we would get half and half. The relative frequency for each would then be ½, and this would be the required probability.

c As there are as many aces as there are twos or threes or whatever, there is no reason to suppose that, in a large number of selections, aces or twos or any other value of card would occur more times than any other. So, since there are thirteen different values, aces will occur in 1/13 of the times, and so this is the required probability.

Activity

Now let's look at the fifty tosses of two coins again. Using the data you have already, classify it in another way. Record what the frequencies were for **a** two heads, **b** two tails, or **c** one head and one tail (*either* way round). Now draw another histogram. What is your *empirical estimate* of the chances of getting a different result on each coin?

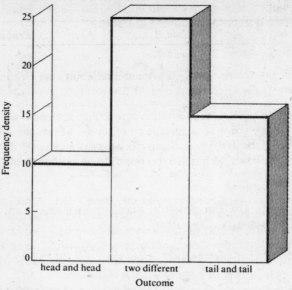

Figure 58. Histogram for author's data on tossing two coins

With the author's data, the histogram is as shown in figure 58. The frequencies are

a two heads 10   relative frequency 10/50 = .2
b two tails 15   relative frequency 15/50 = .3
c one head and one tail 25   relative frequency 25/50 = .5

These figures for the relative frequencies are also the estimates of the chances of getting each of these outcomes. So the estimate for the chances of getting a different result on each coin is, on the author's data, .5 or ½. How different was your result, if at all?

Now we can find the *probability* of getting a different result on each coin as follows. We have already found the 'long-run relative frequencies' for the four different outcomes of tossing two coins. The 'long-run relative frequency' for a different result on each coin is the sum of those for 'a head on A and a tail on B' and for 'a tail on A and a head on B', as shown below.

OUTCOME

Coin A	Coin B		Probability	
head	head		.25	
head	tail	} A and B different	.25	} .5
tail	head		.25	
tail	tail		.25	

Let's go back to the two dice again. Suppose now we redefine what we are going to regard as an outcome of this same trial, i.e. of tossing the two dice. Suppose we are interested in the total number thrown. What are the possible outcomes then?

|| *Self-check*

|| What are the possible outcomes for the total number thrown on the two dice?

Well, we can obtain 2, 3, 4, 5, 6, 7, 8, 9, 10, 11 or 12.

|| *Self-check*

|| Are these outcomes equally likely?

They are not. To see this we need to imagine the very long series of throws again. We have seen how, in the long run, each pair of numbers thrown will occur an equal number of times in this series. Now the total number thrown can be made up in different ways, e.g. a 3 can be a 1 and a 2 or a 2 and a 1, but not always in the same number of different ways, e.g. a 2 can only be made up in one way, but there are six different ways of making up a 7. This means that the relative frequencies of each total thrown cannot be equal.

To see what they actually are we need to discover in how many ways each total thrown can occur. To do this we can draw up a table.

|| *Self-check*

|| The table below shows the various totals which can be thrown. Complete the blank column which gives the number of ways in which this total can be obtained.

THROWING TWO SIX-SIDED DICE

Total thrown	Number of different ways it can occur
2	
3	
4	
5	
6	
7	
8	
9	
10	
11	
12	

The results you should have appear in table 29, below. Figure 59 shows the data in the form of a histogram.

TABLE 29. THROWING TWO SIX-SIDED DICE

Total thrown	Number of different ways it can occur
2	1
3	2
4	3
5	4
6	5
7	6
8	5
9	4
10	3
11	2
12	1

Note that this gives a symmetric frequency distribution. Now, consider a throw of 10. This can be arrived at in three different ways, a 4 and a 6, a 5 and a 5, or a 6 and a 4. The long-run relative frequency of each is $\frac{1}{36}$, i.e. 1 in 36 throws in that sequence will result in a 4 and 6, for example. So 3 in 36 throws in that sequence, i.e. those where there is a 4 and a 6 a 5 and a 5 or a 6 and a 4, will result in a throw of 10. Thus the relative frequency,

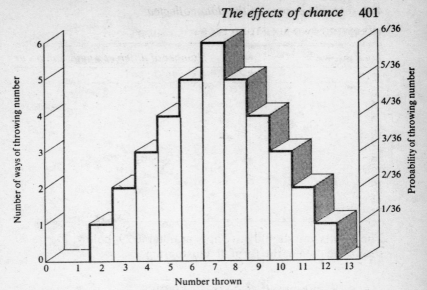

Figure 59. Number of different ways of making up the total number thrown on two dice

and so the probability, of a throw of 10 is $\frac{2}{36} = \frac{1}{12}$. Similarly, the probability of a 2 is $\frac{1}{36}$, of a 3 $\frac{2}{36} = \frac{1}{18}$ and so on.

Self-check

Add another column to the table showing the probabilities for each total thrown.

The resulting column would appear as in table 30 overleaf.

Because the probability is directly proportional to (it is one thirty-sixth of) the number of different ways of making up the total thrown, it can be shown as the same histogram as in figure 59. The probability scale is shown on the right.

When the probabilities are shown against the values of the variable we have what is called a 'probability distribution', in just the same way as we have frequency distributions.

TABLE 30. THROWING TWO SIX-SIDED DICE

Total thrown	Number of different ways it can occur	Probability
2	1	$\frac{1}{36}$
3	2	$\frac{2}{36} = \frac{1}{18}$
4	3	$\frac{3}{36} = \frac{1}{12}$
5	4	$\frac{4}{36} = \frac{1}{9}$
6	5	$\frac{5}{36}$
7	6	$\frac{6}{36} = \frac{1}{6}$
8	5	$\frac{5}{56}$
9	4	$\frac{4}{36} = \frac{1}{9}$
10	3	$\frac{3}{36} = \frac{1}{12}$
11	2	$\frac{2}{36} = \frac{1}{18}$
12	1	$\frac{1}{36}$

Self-check

Two coins are tossed together. What are the probabilities of **a** both results being the same, and **b** the two results being different?

The starting point should once again be the detailed outcomes. These were, if you remember:

Coin A	Coin B	Long-run relative frequency
head	head	$\frac{1}{4}$
head	tail	$\frac{1}{4}$
tail	head	$\frac{1}{4}$
tail	tail	$\frac{1}{4}$

If you didn't get this, look back in the text to where it was explained. Basically, since heads and tails are equally likely, there is nothing to distinguish the different combinations of results from the point of view of relative frequency.

If the results are the same, then they must either be two heads or two tails. But one in four outcomes are two tails (in the long run) and one in four are two heads, so one in two outcomes will be either two heads or two tails. That is, the long-run relative frequency of both results being the same is $\frac{1}{2}$, and this is also the probability.

The probability of the two results being different can be obtained in two different ways. The simplest one is to say that if they aren't different, then they must be the same. And we already know the probability of this. As the two between them cover all possibilities, their probabilities must add up to one; i.e. it is a certainty that one of the two must happen, either both results are the same, or they are different. So the probability of getting two different results is $1 - \frac{1}{2} = \frac{1}{2}$. Did you spot this way?

The other way is to go through the same process as was gone through with the first part. This was done in the text, so it won't be repeated here. The result is the same, the probability of getting two different results on each coin is $\frac{1}{2}$.

From what has been said above, it can be seen that if you got two answers which did not add up to 1, then at least one of them must be wrong.

Using patterns

Now probability defined as in the previous section is known as '*a priori* probability', since we need no experience of previous outcomes to calculate it. When, as in the section before that, we use past history, the relative frequencies so obtained cannot be said to be probabilities, since, for one thing, relative frequencies of 0 and 1 do not correspond to total impossibility and complete certainty. What we can do, however, is to use them as estimates of the probabilities of the outcomes; estimates that have to be revised each time the event occurs. Failing any better values, they can be used to predict outcomes.

This procedure is not very satisfactory, though, because of such things as the difficulties with the values of 0 and 1. And this is why we use *a priori* probabilities whenever we can. But to get them we need to find some patterns. In the last section, these patterns were relatively simple; that is, all detailed outcomes occurred with equal frequency and under perfect conditions (e.g. a totally unbiased die). In practice, of course, conditions are rarely perfect, so *a priori* probability is more conceptual than practical. The nearest we get to *a priori* probabilities in practice is with games of chance and this is why they loom so large in all discussions of probability.

Now statisticians do not need to devise patterns specifically for one *particular* set of outcomes, but only for *classes* of outcomes. That is to say, they can find patterns which apply to a wide number of outcomes of a similar nature. Think of the dice again. The pattern generated by a succession of throws of a six-sided die has a great deal in common with that generated with a ten-sided one, or indeed by one with any number of sides including two, i.e. a coin. In each case, every side should come up an equal number of times in the long run. So one *type* of pattern is applicable to all dice. Such a pattern would also cover instances where similar characteristics held, i.e. where a finite number of different outcomes have equal chances of occurring. When actually using this pattern we would need to know only the number of different possible outcomes.

Self-check

Suppose a group of workers want someone to complain to the management about some aspect of their work, but none of them wants to do it. They decide to put all their names on pieces of paper, put these into a hat, jumble them up and pick one at random. From a probability point of view, is this any different to getting a die with the same number of sides as there are men and rolling it?

No, it isn't. If each man were to have a different side of the die allocated to him, his chances of being chosen would be no different to if the 'names in the hat' method had been used. So we can apply the same pattern to the names in the hat as we did to the die.

Self-check

But what else do you now need to know before you can go
ahead and calculate these chances?

You need to know the number of men involved, i.e. the number
of different possible outcomes. A number such as this, which
allows us to apply the general pattern to a particular problem, is
called a 'parameter'.

Self-check

Can you see what the general rule is for calculating the
probability of one of a number of equally likely outcomes
occurring? Think of the results we got for the tossing of a
two-sided coin, a six-sided die and so on.

The general rule is that, since the total probability must add up
to 1 (that is, it is a certainty that one of the possible outcomes
must occur), and each of the separate probabilities must be
equal, then the probability of each outcome must be

1/the number of possible outcomes.

This result can now be applied to any situation in which there are
a number of equally likely outcomes.

Self-check

If, in the self-check on page 404, there were twenty
workers and they all put their names into a hat as described,
what would the probability be that George Smith, one of
the men, is selected?

Since there are twenty names, and no one is more likely to come
up than any other, George has a chance of 1 in 20 of being the
one. This is an application of the rule stated just a short while
ago.

But we have seen patterns other than just the equally likely
outcomes. Look back and you will see that the two-coin and two

dice problems involved probability distributions where not all the probabilities were equal. There is a histogram showing the distribution of the probabilities of getting various totals on the two dice in figure 59. Not all the rectangles in this are the same height.

The patterns we have been discussing can most easily be represented in terms of diagrams like the histogram. When we talk about the *type* of pattern, we mean the basic *shape* this diagram takes. The parameters tell us the *exact* shape, i.e. exactly how high each rectangle in the histogram is. But even without the parameters we would be able to draw the outline shape from a knowledge of what type of pattern was applicable in the case in question. Now statisticians have worked out standard methods of determining probabilities from the different probability distributions once their parameters are known. These generally involve the use of tables of values. For a few events, such as the throwing of a die, the required parameters may be obtained from a study of the nature of that event. This results, in effect, in the *a priori* probabilities of above. But, in practice, they need in most cases to be derived from past experiences, i.e. empirically. The parameters in such cases generally include the mean of the data collected and very often the standard deviation too.

So, instead of working out the empirical probabilities, what we do is to decide what probability distribution is appropriate in a given instance and obtain the parameters empirically. From a knowledge of the probability distribution, the actual probabilities themselves can then be calculated. This point is taken up in Volume 2.

Activity

Take three coins and toss them. Record your result in a table like that shown below. Repeat this operation thirty-two times. (Note: you need not distinguish between, for example, 'a head on A and B and a tail on C' and 'a head on A and C and a tail on B'.)

When the author did this he got the results as shown in the brackets. The histogram for these is shown in figure 60.

TABLE FOR RECORDING THE RESULTS OF THE COIN-TOSSING
EXPERIMENT

Outcome	Tally	Frequency
Three heads		(5)
Two heads and a tail		(14)
Two tails and a head		(10)
Three tails		(3)
		author's results

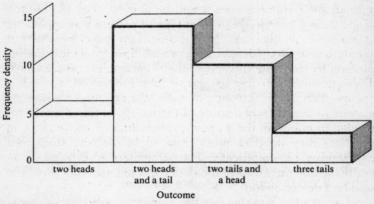

Figure 60. Results of tossing three coins 32 times.

Now use your results to estimate the probability of throwing 'two heads', 'two heads and a tail', etc.

Using the author's results, these probabilities, which are estimated from the relative frequencies, are:

Three heads 5/32 = .15625
Two heads and a tail 14/32 = .4375
Two tails and a head 10/32 = .3125
Three tails 3/32 = .09375

Review

1 Construct an *a priori* probability distribution for the following outcomes of tossing three coins:

- all three heads
- two heads and one tail
- two tails and one head
- all three tails

   If you tossed three unbiased coins thirty-two times, and the distribution of outcomes was 'perfect', i.e. it agreed with these probabilities, what would be the frequencies of these different outcomes? How does this square with the results of the activity of tossing three coins?

2 There are more than £1,000,000,000 worth of premium bonds held, but assume that this is the exact figure. A man holds £5 worth of them. What are his chances of winning the major prize in some given month? (Hint: treat each bond separately at first.) Does it make any difference whether the bonds are in a block, i.e. have successive serial numbers, or not?

ANSWERS

1 The best way to start to answer this question is to list the exact outcomes in as great a detail as possible. That is to say, to list what appears on each coin. Let's call the coins A, B, and C. The detailed outcomes possible are then:

	Coin A	Coin B	Coin C
1	H	H	H
2	H	H	T
3	H	T	H
4	H	T	T
5	T	H	H
6	T	H	T
7	T	T	H
8	T	T	T

There is no reason to suppose that, over a long period of time, any one of these outcomes would occur more than any other. So the relative frequency for each of them in the long run would be $\frac{1}{8}$, as there are eight of them.

   Now there is only one way of getting three tails. But there

are three ways of getting two heads and one tail. i.e. 2, 3 and 5 of above. There are also three ways of getting two tails and one head, i.e. 4, 6 and 7 of above. In exactly the same way as the two-sided die, the relative frequencies in the long run, and so the probabilities, are therefore:

Outcome	Probability
all three heads	$\frac{1}{8}$
two heads and one tail	$\frac{3}{8}$
two tails and one head	$\frac{3}{8}$
two tails	$\frac{1}{8}$

So this is the required probability distribution.

If thirty two tosses of three coins were performed, and the results came out 'perfect', then the relative frequencies would be the same as the probabilities, and so would be:

Outcome	Relative frequency	Frequency
all three heads	4/32 $= \frac{1}{8}$	4
two heads and one tail	12/32 $= \frac{3}{8}$	12
two tails and one head	12/32 $= \frac{3}{8}$	12
three tails	4/32 $= \frac{1}{8}$	4

The reason that this result is not always obtained in practice is that these are long-term frequencies, and so would only generally occur after a vast number of throws.

2 From the rule given earlier, if we imagine the premium bond draw to be like rolling a 1,000,000,000-sided die, the probability of any one particular premium bond coming up is $\frac{1}{1,000,000,000}$! Now if we look at the number of ways in which the man can win, this is like looking at the number of different ways we could throw a particular number on three dice. He can win in five different ways, because he has five different premium bonds.

If you said he could win in thirty two different ways, then

you were thinking that more than one of the bonds could simultaneously win prizes. But there is only one major prize and so only one bond can win. He has five of them, so there are five ways. If there are these five different ways in which he could win, and the probability of each of them is $\frac{1}{1,000,000,000}$, then he must stand five times as much chance of winning as this. That is, the probability of that man winning the major prize is $\frac{5}{1,000,000,000} = .000000005$! Or, if you want to look at a different way, we can write down the winning outcomes and their probability as follows, and interpret them as relative frequencies:

Outcome	Probability	Relative frequency	Total relative frequency
Premium bond A wins	$\frac{1}{1,000,000,000}$	$\frac{1}{1,000,000,000}$	
Premium bond B wins	$\frac{1}{1,000,000,000}$	$\frac{1}{1,000,000,000}$	
Premium bond C wins	$\frac{1}{1,000,000,000}$	$\frac{1}{1,000,000,000}$	$\frac{5}{1,000,000,000}$
Premium bond D wins	$\frac{1}{1,000,000,000}$	$\frac{1}{1,000,000,000}$	
Premium bond E wins	$\frac{1}{1,000,000,000}$	$\frac{1}{1,000,000,000}$	

The relative frequencies show the long-run (very long-run) occurrences of wins by that man with each of his bonds. That is, if there were enough draws, eventually he would win once in every 1,000,000,000 draws! With each bond! If each bond wins once, then the man himself wins five times, giving the total relative frequency, and so probability, of 5 in 1,000,000,000 times. If you said that the man's overall chance of winning was 1 in 1,000,000,000, then you were forgetting that having more than one bond increases his chance of winning.

Now nothing has been said about which numbers the bonds have on them. The probability calculated was completely independent of these. It could not make any difference, then, whether the numbers were in a block or otherwise. Some people wrongly argue that having the bonds in a block gives

ERNIE a bigger 'area' to 'aim at', as it were, so increasing the chances of 'hitting it'. But you could equally well argue, again wrongly, that by spreading the numbers about, you cover a wider range and so stand a better chance of being in the region that ERNIE picks. Did you take up one of these positions?

Appendix:
Where to find
statistical data

The purpose of this appendix is very briefly to outline the major sources of statistical data and to give some information about how to use them.

We are very fortunate in the UK to have very good statistics produced by the government. But there are also other sources of data, like the trade associations. These are also touched on here, though obviously no exhaustive list of them can be given.

The Central Statistical Office of the government publish two excellent free booklets on government statistics. The first is *Government Statistics: A Brief Guide to Sources*, which is exactly what it says it is. The second is *Profit from Facts*, which is a guide to the kinds of use a business can find for government statistics. You are strongly recommended to read both of these pamphlets.

Using statistics

As was stated in the first chapter, a business has a variety of statistical needs. Many of these will be satisfied by internal data. Sometimes a market research bureau or other similar organization will be required to get specialist data from outside the firm. But, increasingly, the government is supplying data, in its various publications, which saves a business the task of collecting it. Other data is available from non-government sources. Such data can be divided roughly into two categories:

- *general* – figures on the national economy and on financial matters, such as the exchange rate, stocks and shares prices and so on;
- *specific* – figures which apply specifically to the area in which the company operates, e.g. the food industry, in the case of Gourmet Foods Ltd.

Of course, different types and sizes of firm will have different requirements. In general, the larger the firm the greater its requirement for statistics. British Petroleum, for instance, needs an enormous range of statistics to operate.

Self-check

Can you list some of the statistics you think BP would need?

Prices of oils and other raw materials would obviously be one type. It would also require figures on shipping. Being international it would need exchange rates. Being so large it would be very interested in the state of the British economy. There are many more but these give the idea.

Smaller firms will use statistics for estimating the market. For example, Gourmet Foods will be interested in figures on births for its Baby Gourmet range. Such firms can also get an idea of how the industry in general is faring, so as to compare their own performance with this data. Firms which import and/or export will use figures for imports and exports for comparisons too. There are many more reasons why statistics of this type are required. We can summarize all of these as follows. Statistics may be used in

- *marketing* – to check market sizes
    to see trends in market shares
    to check prices
    to check on competitive imports
    to check on competitive exports
    to find retail outlets
    to discover expenditure patterns
- *purchasing* – to check on the price of materials
    to check on available materials
- *personnel* – to check on employment patterns
    to check on hours worked and wages paid
- *finance* – to check on financial ratios in the industry in general, and so on.

Government statistics

The source of most of the external statistics described in the previous section is the government. The various government departments, like Trade, Industry, Environment, Employment, and the Treasury, all produce statistics relevant to their own interests. Each have their own statistical divisions. In addition, the Business Statistics Office and the Office of Population Censuses and Surveys specialize in the collection of business data, such as sales, stocks, and demographic data, i.e. population, births, deaths, marriages, respectively. All the above operations are coordinated by the Central Statistical Office to form the Government Statistical Service.

While the service exists primarily to serve government needs, it has, of recent years, been developing a service for business over and above that function. The government is in a unique position to help business because of its possession of the machinery for gathering data and the expertise to process it. Ultimately, of course, the value of the service will depend on the quality of data fed to it. Here businesses can help by cooperating with government surveys. Many businesses, especially small ones, have complained about the chore of filling in government forms, and the Statistical Service is attempting to improve communications in this area. But it is ultimately to the good of business as a whole if firms do cooperate fully in such exercises.

There are several government publications which will help you to understand how to use government statistics. *Statistical News* is published quarterly under the guidance of the Central Statistical Office and contains news of developments in government statistics. The *Guide to Official Statistics* is a comprehensive guide to government statistics, including one-off reports, articles, etc. Both of these are charged for. There are, however, three very good free booklets:

Facts from your Figures outlines the necessity for official statistics and gives some idea of how they are compiled.
Profit from Facts illustrates, with case studies, how government statistics may be (and have been) used by business.
Government Statistics: A Brief Guide to Sources lists major government sources of statistics.

Major government sources of statistics

There are one or two major sources of statistics with which the reader should be familiar:

British Business (previously *Trade and Industry*), weekly news from the Departments of Industry and Trade, contains more detailed figures than any other standard government publication. It contains general business news, reports from abroad, reports from Parliament, EEC news, details of new products and patents and of new publications, and a summary of economic indicators. It also contains a special statistical section. What actually appears each week varies, but over the year statistics might be provided on the following, for example:

balance of payments
acquisitions and mergers
liquidity
rate of return on capital
computer services

consumer's expenditure
production by industry
cinema admissions
food consumption
foreign trade
gross domestic product
house prices
industrial production

overseas investment
clothing – orders and deliveries

vehicle production
imports
pension funds investment
expenditure on research and
  development
retail sales
royalties
shipping
manufacturers and distributors
  stocks

capital expenditure
insolvencies
new registrations
structure of company financing
output and employment in the
  construction industry
earnings and wages by industry
sales and orders by industry
film industry overseas earnings
footwear – deliveries and stocks
furniture – deliveries and orders
hire purchase business
mortgages
insurance companies,
  investments and assets
industry's investment intentions
production and deliveries of man-
  made fibres
exports by industry
official reserves
regional development grants
retail prices

retail stocks
financial assistance to industry
consumption and stocks of steel
payments and earnings abroad by
  the television industry

textiles – sales and stocks   tourism
unemployment   wholesale prices

Employment Gazette, monthly news from the Department of Employment, contains articles and statistics on matters of interest to the department. There are special features every month, many of which contain further statistics to those published on a regular basis. There is also regular news concerning major events in labour and employment, such as public sector wage settlements. Regular statistics include:

employment –	the working population
	numbers in selected occupations
	regional figures
	accidents at work
	trade union membership
output –	output per head
	wages and salaries per unit of output for selected industries
unemployment–	regional unemployment
	unemployment by age group
	unemployment by selected industries
	vacancies
earnings–	average earnings by industrial classification
	average hours worked by industrial classification
	basic wage rates
	overtime by region
	short time by region
labour costs	
prices	
expenditure (by families)	
stoppage of work–	stoppages by industrial classification
	causes of stoppages
	length of stoppages
	days lost per 1000 workers by industry

Monthly Digest of Statistics, monthly digest of government statistics by the Central Statistical Office, contains many tables of statistics, relating to the past few years, on:

national income and expenditure   textile and other manufactures
population and vital statistics   construction

labour
social services
justice and crime
agriculture and food
production, output and costs
energy
chemicals
metals, engineering and vehicles

transport
retailing and catering
overseas finance
home finance
tax and price index
entertainment
weather

Every January there is a supplement giving definitions of items and units employed in the *Monthly Digest*. This should be consulted before using the data in the digest.

Annual Abstract of Statistics, a yearly abstract of government statistics by the Central Statistical Office, contains many tables of statistics, relating to a number of previous years, on:

area and climate
population and vital statistics
social conditions
justice and crime
education
labour
defence
production
agriculture, fisheries and food

transport and communications
distributive trades and services
external trade
balance of payments
national income and expenditure
personal income, expenditure and
    wealth
home finance
banking, insurance
prices

Economic Trends, monthly economic statistics from the Central Statistical Office, contains tables and charts for all the main economic indicators over the previous five or so years, together with the latest information on these. There are also charts showing cycles in the British economy and some specific economic indicators, over a period of twenty years. There are articles on various aspects of the economy too. This publication is particularly recommended for its diagrams and illustrations. Statistics are given on, amongst other subjects:

gross domestic product
personal incomes
consumer expenditure
retail sales
investment by manufacturing
    industry

prices
visible trade
balance of payments
exchange rates
money stock
domestic credit

investment intentions
stock changes
energy consumption
output and orders
employment and unemployment
wages

government receipts and
   expenditure
public sector finance
industrial funding
bank lending
interest rates

There is also an annual supplement which provides data on key economic indicators over longer periods of time: about a half go back twenty-five years.

Social Trends, a yearly compendium of social statistics by the Central Statistical Office, contains information basically about how people live. In format it is very much like *Economic Trends*. There are one or two articles on some points of social interest and a wealth of figures and diagrams. It contains statistics, going back various differing periods of time, on:

population
households and families
social groups
education
employment
income and wealth
resources and expenditure

health and public safety
housing
environment, transport and
   communications
leisure
participation
law enforcement

Financial Statistics, a monthly guide to financial statistics by the Central Statistical Office in collaboration with the Treasury, certain government departments and the Bank of England; contains statistics on:

local authority borrowing
banking
hire purchase
unit trusts
insurance

building societies
interest and mortgage rates
the balance of payments
exchange rates
company finance

Regional Statistics, an annual examination of regional differences by the Central Statistical Office, contains regional statistics on:

agriculture and forestry
education
employment
energy

population
production, distribution and
   investment
savings and household expenditure

health	social characteristics
housing and environment	social services
personal incomes	transport

In addition to all the above there is the *Blue Book* on national income and expenditure and the *Pink Book* on the UK balance of payments, both published yearly and compiled by the Central Statistical Office.

All of the above have to be purchased but there are two free items which are very useful. The Treasury publish a monthly *Economic Progress Report*, which contains articles on economic topics and government policy, particularly regarding budgets. It also gives recent values of the key economic indicators. There is also a free yearly booklet available from the Government Statistical Service, called *The United Kingdom in Figures*, which gives some basic data on the British economy.

Lastly, but by no means least, the Business Statistics Office issues Business Monitors. There is a wide range of these indeed and it is not possible to list them all here. They include:

MM1	Monthly data on road vehicles and new registrations.
MA3	Annual analysis of the accounts of listed and unlisted companies.
MQ5	Quarterly analysis of insurance companies' and private pension funds' investment.
MQ7	Quarterly analysis of acquisitions and mergers of companies.
MA8	Annual analysis of the nationality of vessels involved in trading with the UK by sea.
MQ10	Quarterly analysis of overseas trades by industry.
PM series	Monthly analysis of trade figures for various industries.
PQ series	As above, but quarterly.
PA series	As above, but annually.

Just as an example, *PQ 239.2* is a quarterly Business Monitor on British wines, cider and perry. It contains details of sales, exports and imports of such wines, production figures and consumers' expenditure.

Summary of government statistics

Table 31 gives a brief summary of some of the most useful government statistics and their sources under several major headings:

TABLE 31. SOURCES OF GOVERNMENT STATISTICS

Information	*Collectors of data*	*Publication*
POPULATION AND VITAL STATISTICS		
Census of population	• Office of Population Censuses and Surveys (OPCS)	• *Census Reports, England and Wales,* (1911, 1921, 1931, 1951, 1961, 1966 (sample census). 1971 and 1981)
	• General Register Office (Scotland) (GROS)	• *Census Reports* (1951, 1961, 1966 (sample census), 1971 and 1981)
	• General Register Office (Northern Ireland) (GRONI)	• *Census Reports* (1951, 1961, 1966, 1971 and 1981)
Deaths, causes of death, marriages, births, electors, general population	• OPCS • GROS • GRONI	• *Annual Reports*
Population, births, deaths, marriages, infectious diseases, population estimates, migration	• OPCS • GROS • GRONI	• *Population Trends* (Q) • *Quarterly returns* • *Quarterly returns*
Family statistics, deaths, morbidity, population estimates and projections, migration, local authority vital statistics	• OPCS	• *Monitor Series* (M) *Series FM* (Family Statistics) *Series DH* (Deaths) *Series MB* (Morbidity)

Table 31 continued

Information	Collectors of data	Publication
Family statistics, deaths, morbidity, populaton estimates and projections, migration, local authority vital statistics	• OPCS	*Series MN* (Migration) *Series VS* (Local authority vital statistics) Series PP (Population projections and estimates)

SOCIAL CONDITIONS

Information	Collectors of data	Publication
Social services	• Central Statistical Office (CSO)	• *Civil Appropriation Accounts* (A)
Public health	• OPCS	• *Population Trends* (Q)
	• GROS	• *Quarterly Returns*
	• GRONI	• *Quarterly Returns*
Housing	• Department of the Environment	• *Housing and Construction Statistics (Q)*
Crime	• Home Office	• *Criminal Statistics,* England and Wales
	• Home Office: Scottish Office	• *Criminal Statistics,* Scotland (A)
Education	• Department of Education and Science	• *Statistics of Education,* Volumes 1–6 (A)

WORK

Information	Collectors of data	Publication
Detailed analysis of work force by age, sex and industry	• Department of Employment	• *British Labour Statistics: Yearbook* (A)

Table 31 continued

Information	Collectors of data	Publication
Analysis of incomes by range, source, sex, marital status, family size, region and county	● Department of Employment	● *Survey of Personal Incomes* (A)
Wage rates and hours of work	● Department of Employment	● *Time Rates of Wages and Hours of Work* (Y) ● *Changes in Rates of Wages and Hours of Work* (M)
Employment, unemployment, unfilled vacancies, overtime, short-time working, stoppages, trade union membership, etc.	● Department of Employment	● *Employment Gazette* (M)
Earnings from employment by occupation, region, etc.	● Department of Employment	● *New Earnings Survey* (Y)
Industrial accidents, injuries, and diseases	● Health and Safety Executive	● *Health and Safety Statistics* (A)

PRODUCTION AND SALES

Information	Collectors of data	Publication
Industrial production	● Departments of Trade and Industry	● *British Business* (formerly *Trade and Industry*)
Census of production: total purchases, total sales, stock, work in progress, capital expenditure, employment, wages and salaries	● Business Statistics Office	● *Report on the Census of Production* (in *Business Monitor PA* Series)

Table 31 continued

Information	Collectors of data	Publication
Sales by industry	● Business Statistics Office	● *Quarterly statistics of Manufacturers' Sales* (Q) (in *Business Monitor PQ* series) ● *Monthly Statistics* (M) (in *Business Monitor PM* series)
Census of distribution	● Department of Industry	● *Report on the Census of Distribution* (last one published 1974 for 1971 figures)
Sales in various kinds of shop	● Business Statistics Office	● *Retail Trade* (M) (*Business Monitor SDM 28*)
Types and number of businesses, turnover, gross margin, employees	● Business Statistics Office	● *Annual Statistics on Retail Trades* (*Business Monitor SDA 25*)

THE ECONOMY

Information	Collectors of data	Publication
Overseas trade	● Department of Trade	● *Overseas Trade Statistics of the UK* (M)
Overseas trade by industry	● Business Statistics Office	● *Overseas Trade Analysed in Terms of Industries* (M) (*Business Monitor M10*)
Government expenditure	● CSO	● *National Appropriation Accounts* (A)
National income and expenditure	● CSO	● The *Blue Book* (A)
Balance of payments	● CSO	● The *Pink Book* (A)

Table 31 continued

Information	Collectors of data	Publication
PRICES		
Retail prices	● Department of Employment	● *Employment Gazette* (M)
Wholesale prices	● Departments of Trade and Industry	● *British Business* (W) (formerly *Trade and Industry*)
Import and export prices	● Departments of Trade and Industry	● *British Business* (W)
Agricultural prices	● Ministry of Agriculture, Fisheries and Food	● *Agricultural Statistics* (A)

Note:
1. The above is only a very small selection from the statistics provided by the government. For further details consult the *Guide to Official Statistics* (HMSO).
2. A = annual; Q = quarterly; M = monthly; W = weekly.

Other sources of statistical information

In addition to government sources, there are, of course, many others. Some of the more useful ones are:

Financial Times (daily) contains share prices and measures of their overall level – the Financial Times Share Indexes – as well as articles and information on business.

Nationalized Industries Reports and Accounts (annually) (plus a monthly publication by the British Steel Corporation) for each industry, contain data on output, stocks, capacity and so on.

The Bank's Reviews (quarterly – except for Lloyd's), from the major banks, contain articles and statistics: Barclay's also publish a quarterly *International Review*.

Bank of England Quarterly Bulletin (quarterly) contains reports on financial and economic matters, special articles and technical notes as well as a statistical annexe, containing figures on, amongst other subjects:

deposits etc. of British and overseas banks
government debt

money stock
reserves
exchange rates UK and overseas
flow of funds
interest rates

Other sources of information include the Confederation of British Industry – on investment intentions each month, for example; the Building Societies Association – on interest rates, deposits, house prices, for example; and other trade associations such as the Society of Motor Manufacturers and the British Radio Equipment Manufacturers Association.

The contents of
Using Statistics in Business 2

Now that you have read this book, you are ready to move on to Volume 2. To give you an idea of the ground covered by it, here is the contents list of the second volume.

Part 1: Drawing conclusions
1 Some naturally occurring patterns
2 What can we learn by looking at only a proportion of the available data?
3 Making estimates and testing significance
4 Determining the relationship between two sets of data
5 Determining the trend

Part 2: Informing others
6 Presenting the information visually
7 Lies, damned lies and statistics
8 Gathering data and making a case

Appendix: Standard normal tables
Index

Index

absolute error 185 ff
  in differences 204 ff
  in products 199 ff
  in quotients 203 ff
  in sums 196 ff
abstraction of data 45, 67 ff
accounting 23
aggregative index 352
approximate figures 179 ff
approximations 179 ff
a priori approach to chance
  384, 390 ff
a priori probability 403 ff
arithmetic mean 289 ff
  of ungrouped data 289 ff
  of grouped data 292 ff
  advantages and disadvantages of
    336
array 212
attribute sampling 132
attribute variable 153, 169
averages 289 ff

base (in index numbers) 347
bias 153 ff
bivariate data 251
budgetary control 24
business statistics 20, 24

census 89
chain index 346
chance 382 ff
check digits 162
class 226
  modal 303
  open-ended 242
class boundary 226

  upper 226
  lower 226
class interval 237
class limit 226
  upper 226
  lower 226
class mid-point 292
class width 237
classification of data 47, 58, 170 ff
cluster sampling 122 ff, 141 ff
coefficient of skewness 334
coefficient of variation 329
constant 152
  non-numeric (attribute) 153
  numeric 153
continuous variable 179 ff
cumulative frequency 218
cumulative totals 217

data collection 42, 43
  employing others to do 57
  methods 44 ff
  reducing costs of 161 ff
data processing 22, 23
decile 319
descriptive statistics 20, 21
discrete variable 181 ff
dispersion 318
domain of a variable 152

economic indicators 28
empirical approach to chance 384,
  385 ff
empirical probability 385 ff
equal interval sampling 106
error 59, 154, 184
  absolute 185 ff

bias 153 ff
cumulative 187
random 157 ff
relative 192 ff
rounding 188
sampling 157
ways of reducing 161 ff
external statistics 28
extrapolation 247 ff

final stage sampling 126
final stage sampling units 126
first stage sampling 126
fixed base index 347
form design 49, 81
fractile 319
frequency 213
cumulative 218
relative 276, 386, 390
frequency density 263
frequency distribution 310
frequency polygon 252 ff
frequency table 213 ff
ungrouped 220
grouped 222 ff

graph 247 ff
'greater (more) than' cumulative
frequency graph 254 ff, 272 ff
grouped frequency 222 ff

histogram 261 ff

independence 393, 395
index numbers 345 ff
choice between 370
index of industrial production 374
inferential statistics 20
inspection 45, 66 ff
internal statistics 26
interpolation 247 ff
inter-quartile range 321
interviews 44, 72 ff
by telephone 73

Laspeyres index 363 ff
advantages and disadvantages of
370 ff

'less than' cumulative frequency
graph 254 ff, 272 ff

market research 24, 28, 57
mathematical limits 233
mathematics 22, 23
median 308 ff
advantages and disadvantages of
336
of grouped data 312 ff
of ungrouped data 308 ff
misusing statistics 31
mode 301 ff
advantages and disadvantages of
337
of grouped data 303 ff
of ungrouped data 30 ff
multi-stage sampling 126 ff, 139 ff

null hypothesis 32

observation 45, 63 ff
direct 63
indirect 64
obstacles to collecting reliable
information 53
ogive 254 ff
discrete data 254 ff
continuous data 272 ff
open-ended class 242

Paasche index 363 ff
advantages and disadvantages of
370 ff
panels 132
parameters 405
percentile 319
pilot survey 59
population 92
precision 188
price relative 351, 366
primary data 173 ff
primary sampling units 126
probability 391
a priori 403 ff
empirical 385 ff
probability distribution 401

quantity relative 351
quartile 319, 321
quartile deviation 321
    advantages and disadvantages of
      333
questionnaires 44, 75 ff
    design of 78 ff
quota sampling 118 ff, 142 ff

random error 157 ff
random sample 94
range 237, 318
    advantages of, disadvantages of
      339
raw data 211
recording (of information collected)
    47
relative error 192 ff
    in differences 204 ff
    in products 200 ff
    in quotients 203 ff
    in sums 197 ff
relative frequency 276, 386, 390
response rate (to questionnaires) 76
retail price index 372 ff
rounding 186 ff
rounding error 188
rule of evens 230

sales forecasting 25
samples 55, 89
    non-random 112
    random 94
    simple random 96, 135 ff
sample survey 55
sampling 89 ff
    area 127
    attribute 132
    cluster 122 ff, 141 ff
    equal interval 106
    example of 133 ff
    methods 144 ff
    multi-stage 126 ff, 139 ff
    quota 118 ff, 142 ff
    reasons for 91
    stratified random 133 ff, 138 ff
    systematic 106

without replacement 96, 393
    with replacement 96, 393
sampling error 157
sampling frame 102
secondary data 173 ff
secondary sampling units 126
secondary statistics 173
second stage sampling 126
semi-inter-quartile range 321
simple index 352
simple random sample 96, 135 ff
skewness 332 ff, 337
    coefficient of 334
standard deviation 322 ff
    advantages and disadvantages of
      339
    of grouped data 325 ff
    of ungrouped data 322 ff
Standard Industrial Classification
    (SIC) 170
statistics 20, 21, 22
    how they can help management 25
    secondary 173
stratified random sampling 113 ff,
    138 ff
subjectivity 168 ff
    reduction of 169
systematic sampling 106

tally marks 49, 216
trials 383
    independent 393
true value (of a variable) 154

univariate data 251

variable 152
    continuous 179 ff
    discrete 181 ff
    non-numeric (attribute) 153, 169
    numeric 153
    true value of 154
vital statistics 20

weighted average 353 ff, 366
weights 353

Reference, language and information

☐	**A Guide to Insurance**	Margaret Allen	£1.95p
☐	**The Story of Language**	C. L. Barber	£1.95p
☐	**North-South**	Brandt Commission	£2.50p
☐	**Manifesto**	Francis Cripps et al	£1.95p
☐	**Save It! The Energy Consumer's Handbook**	Gary Hammond, Kevin Newport and Carol Russell	£1.25p
☐	**Mathematics for the Million**	L. Hogben	£1.95p
☐	**Militant Islam**	Godfrey Jansen	£1.50p
☐	**The State of the World Atlas**	Michael Kidron and Ronald Segal	£6.95p
☐	**Practical Statistics**	R. Langley	£1.95p
☐	**A Guide to Speaking in Public**	Robert Seton Lawrence	£1.25p
☐	**How to Study**	H. Maddox	£1.50p
☐	**Dictionary of Life Sciences**	E. A. Martin	£1.95p
☐	**Your Guide to the Law**	ed. Michael Molyneux	£3.50p
☐	**Common Security**	Palme Commission	£1.95p
☐	**The Modern Crossword Dictionary**	Norman Pulsford	£2.25p
☐	**English Proverbs Explained**	James Reeves	£1.75p
☐	**Pan Spelling Dictionary**	Ronald Ridout	£1.50p
☐	**A Guide to Saving and Investment**	James Rowlatt	£2.50p
☐	**Career Choice**	Audrey Segal	£2.95p
☐	**Logic and its Limits**	Patrick Shaw	£2.95p
☐	**Names for Boys and Girls**	L. Sleigh and C. Johnson	£1.50p
☐	**Straight and Crooked Thinking**	R. H. Thouless	£1.50p
☐	**The Best English**	G. H. Vallins	80p
☐	**Money Matters**	Harriet Wilson	£1.25p
☐	**Dictionary of Earth Sciences**		£1.95p
☐	**Dictionary of Economics and Commerce**		£1.50p
☐	**Dictionary of Philosophy**		£2.50p
☐	**Dictionary of Physical Sciences**		£1.95p
☐	**Harrap's New Pocket French and English Dictionary**		£2.50p
☐	**The Limits to Growth**		£1.50p
☐	**Pan Dictionary of Synonyms and Antonyms**		£1.95p
☐	**Pan English Dictionary**		£2.50p

Management

☐	**Introducing Marketing**	Christopher, McDonald and Wills	£1.95p
☐	**Illustrating Computers**	Colin Day and Donald Alcock	£1.95p
☐	**The Effective Executive**	} Peter Drucker	£1.75p
☐	**Management**		£2.95p
☐	**Under New Management**	Tony Eccles	£2.95p
☐	**How to Double Your Profits**	John Fenton	£2.25p
☐	**Inside Business Law**	} David Field	£2.95p
☐	**Inside Employment Law**		£2.50p
☐	**Finance and Accounts for Managers**	Desmond Goch	£1.25p
☐	**Gods of Management**	Charles Handy	£1.25p
☐	**The Black Economy**	Arnold Heertje et al.	£1.95p
☐	**Managing People at Work**	John Hunt	£2.50p
☐	**Managing With Computers**	Terry Rowan	£2.50p
☐	**Guide to Saving and Investment**	James Rowlatt	£2.50p
☐	**Reality of Management**	} Rosemary Stewart	£1.50p
☐	**Reality of Organisations**		£1.75p
☐	**The Fifth Estate: Britain's Unions in the Modern World**	Robert Taylor	£1.95p
☐	**Dictionary of Economics and Commerce**		£1.50p
☐	**Multilingual Commercial Dictionary**		£1.95p

All these books are available at your local bookshop or newsagent, or can be ordered direct from the publisher. Indicate the number of copies required and fill in the form below   6

Name_____
(Block letters please)

Address_____

_____

Send to Pan Books (CS Department), Cavaye Place, London SW10 9PG
Please enclose remittance to the value of the cover price plus:
35p for the first book plus 15p per copy for each additional book ordered
to a maximum charge of £1.25 to cover postage and packing
Applicable only in the UK

While every effort is made to keep prices low, it is sometimes
necessary to increase prices at short notice. Pan Books reserve
the right to show on covers and charge new retail prices which
may differ from those advertised in the text or elsewhere